"This book is not just for parents, grandparents and siblings, but should be read by any professional who wants to increase their understanding of just what it means to have a child on the spectrum. I was delighted with this book. It is unique, readable, engaging and tells it just as it is!" — *Maxine Aston, counselor and consultant in Asperger syndrome, Park Counseling Centre, Conventry, United Kingdom*

"*Chasing the Rabbit* is one of the most honest portrayals of raising a child on the autism spectrum that I have ever read. This book, told from the unique perspective of a father, is highly recommended for all parents and professionals, or anyone who loves someone with a disability." — *Lisa A. Phalen, IBCCES certified autism specialist*

"*Chasing the Rabbit* takes a very honest look at the joys and challenges of raising a child on the autism spectrum. Your journey has been an inspiration to me and I am definitely going to recommend this book to families I work with. It is going to help so many!!" — *Jill Pring, autism spectrum disorder consultant, Camp Discovery co-director, co-founder of POP (Pieces of the Puzzle) Camp for students with autism*

"I believe that his work should be required reading for anyone working in the field of special education!" — *Cindy Elder, Riding To The Top Therapeutic Riding Center, Windham, ME & retired special education teacher*

"*Chasing the Rabbit* is a must read for anyone who has had the opportunity to work with a child with autism. Every teacher should find the time to add this book to his or her professional library." — *Steven Benson, Ed. S., program director of autism, Cobb County Schools, Georgia*

"From your vantage point of a father, husband, and observer, a clear sense of what family life with a mixture of love, chaos, and difficult decisions presents." — *Eric Chessen, founder of Autism Fitness*

"I have read many books that have been called, 'honest,' 'candid,' but I have never seen it so clearly as in this memoir by Derek Volk." — *Tracy Murphy, mom of a son with Asperger's*

"Derek has stated that having to deal with this curveball and writing the book is part of God's plan to help others. I am here to say that it's already working its magic and that my story is proof of that." — *Eric LeClair, adult with Asperger's*

"Through adventures that will make you laugh and cry, we all learn how to chase a rabbit: with courage, resiliency, creativity, hope, and love. Beautiful, unapologetic, and engaging, Volk's powerful memoir is a must read for all parents, educators, or anyone looking for true insight into what it is like to raise a child with special needs and endless talents." — *Jennie Trocchio Kirkland, Ph.D., autism educator, consultant, DIR/Floortime provider*

"I can't put into words how much Dylan's story has helped us. This book really doesn't only apply to people with children on the spectrum. It is a fascinating read about overcoming obstacles and how you must ALWAYS have hope. Even when (as happened many times throughout the book) life seems hopeless, it is never to late to turn things around. I can honestly say that for me, this is one of the best books I've ever read. I am so very thankful Derek shared their story!" — *Jenica Gosselin, mom of a daughter with autism*

"I absolutely loved this book! I would recommend *Chasing the Rabbit* to everyone. People who have been in a similar situation will find strength knowing they are not alone. Hopefully anyone else reading this book will be more compassionate, kind and less judgemental of others!" — *Geralyn Hackett, mom of a son with a disability*

"*Chasing The Rabbit* made me laugh, made me cry, made me angry and made me think about being more compassionate and understanding with those who are psychologically challenged." — *Pastor Frank Bolella, Living Word Community Church, Dumont NJ*

"This book was one that pulled me in and touched my heart in a very personal way. I have a 9-year-old grandson recently diagnosed with autism. I hope we, as a society, can somehow come together to create awareness and support for the many people who need it. Thanks again for sharing your story and opening the door to this kind of awareness." — *Taryn Canney, grandmother of a boy with autism*

"*Chasing the Rabbit* takes us down two roads at once, all the while teaching valuable lessons about family, life, growing, and Autism Spectrum Disorders. Every touching detail is a walk both with someone who loves and someone who is physically affected by an ASD." — *Lisa Curley, MAAP Autism Services, Crown Point, Indiana*

CHASING THE RABBIT

A DAD'S LIFE RAISING A SON ON THE SPECTRUM

DEREK VOLK with DYLAN VOLK

D & A Publishing, LLC
2015

© 2015 by Derek S. Volk. All Rights Reserved.

ISBN: 978-1511585583

Published by:
D & A Publishing, LLC
11 Morin St., Biddeford, ME 04005
www.chasingtherabbit.org

Produced by:
Grace Peirce
Great Life Press
www.greatlifepress.com

Cover design: Daniel Yeager

Library of Congress Control Number: 2015937520

To Amy, the love of my life,
mother of my children,
my very best friend, my soul mate.

Thank you and God Bless.

Derek Veth

Jer. 29:11

Contents

Foreword

Dylan Volk is very likely to argue against some of what I write in this foreword. And it will probably begin with that first sentence. He won't argue because he wants to be contentious but because he will most likely see things differently than I and will make that point known to me.

We had our first meeting together on October 11, 2012 in "At the Crossroads," where I was the Clinical Director and Dylan's therapist. I wanted to acknowledge him for what I perceived to be a difficult choice—a young man choosing to fly across the country to live and work with complete strangers in a young-adult transitional program, and even more, in a predominantly white, Mormon community. For someone who then identified as closely with African-American culture as Dylan (although he himself is Caucasian), this was, in my eyes, a real stretch, and I wanted him to know that. But he would have none of it—"This wasn't a choice," he said. "This was blackmail, coercion. I had no choice. I had to come here or get kicked out. That's not a choice. Don't acknowledge me for that."

Three things about Dylan that the reader of this fascinating book should know: Dylan has a remarkable grasp of his own history. I quickly learned that if I were to bring up something from our past together, I better have a clear understanding of what actually transpired because Dylan will. He remembers words, conversations, and details and has no hesitation in making sure the person with whom he is speaking understands what he remembers.

He also has opinions. Dylan has strong opinions. One of Dylan's greatest struggles is in giving other people permission to have a different point of view. This is because he has given thought to his position and has spent time formulating and bolstering his argument like a talented violinist might fine-tune her instrument. And if you or I were to challenge that position and not agree with it, then we are challenging everything Dylan believes in. So in his world view, one of us *must* be right and the other *must* be wrong, and it is very difficult for him to cede that point. Not because he doesn't want to—but because his brain simply doesn't think that way. The last thing Dylan Volk wants to hear is "let's agree to disagree."

Dylan is brilliant. I don't know that I've worked with a young man who has the insight he demonstrates in regards to his own strengths and limitations. In one of our meetings, he pointed out to me that he was very likely to soon lose his current job. "Why?" I asked. He responded, "Because I wear on people and this is about the time when they get tired of having to deal with me. I'm great at getting jobs—I just can't keep them because people tire of me because of my Asperger's traits." He was terminated from his position about two weeks later. And within a week, he had another job.

These qualities make relationships with Dylan like a beautifully-thrown punch. You admire the creativity and raw power behind his thought process, determination, and intentions. You understand how much effort he puts into every interaction. Yet, at the same time, because of those very traits, there's a good chance someone is going to get hurt.

Chasing the Rabbit, like Dylan, is so honest and transparent that as you read, it feels that you are walking on sacred ground, a quiet participant in their intimate family moments. Amy, Derek, and Dylan's journey—continuing today—is an inspiration to any family who has struggled with their own uncertainties in how to manage chaotic and unpredictable situations, while at the same time working endlessly to make sure that each of them knows they are loved. I have long been inspired by the devotion that Amy and Derek have shown to their children, all the while managing successful careers. I am grateful that they chose to share their story. You will be, also.

Norman E. Thibault, PhD, LMFT
Washington, Utah

Introduction

The older I become the more I believe that God has a purpose for every life. That does not mean we all live in that purpose. Obviously, a lot of people miss their calling altogether, but I believe that every human being is born with the potential to fulfill a vision God has tattooed on their DNA. Sometimes that vision is obvious, as in the gift of tremendous talent or intellect. More often, however, God's plan is only clear in retrospect. It is then that we can see how perfectly the pieces of the puzzle assemble a work of art.

Back on July 1, 1989, when Derek and I vowed "to have and to hold from this day forward, for better or for worse," we knew that there were many in attendance who thought we were foolish young kids making a big mistake. Considering I was barely twenty and he not even quite twenty, the odds were not in our favor. No one suspected that the bigger challenge would be raising the beautiful baby boy we joyously welcomed into the world two years and nine days later.

The only reason Dylan was even born when he was, was because we knew Derek would have the opportunity to be almost a stay-at-home dad for the first several months of Dylan's life. His conception was a one-shot attempt at perfect timing. We really did not expect to succeed in making a baby that evening. Yet, forty-two weeks later there he was and we could not have been happier. For the most part, my long-term memory is terrible, but I vividly remember staring at him literally for hours while he slept. I had never seen anything so beautiful, nor felt a love so pure and instinctive. I am not sure there are words to describe the strength and depth of feeling a parent has for a child. When you have never known that feeling before, it is truly overwhelming.

From the very beginning, Derek was an amazing dad. I nursed all our children. The last two slept with us, but he got up to get Dylan and Mariah in the night. He would change their diapers and bring them to me, making sure they were latched on properly and I had everything I needed before going back to sleep himself. He was also in charge of bath time and fingernail clipping since I had accidentally nipped Dylan the first time I ever tried trimming his tiny nails. Especially with our first, he loved to rock and sing Bob Dylan or even Rush to the babies. He also documented their lives and took over labeling and organizing the rapidly growing collection of photos and video tapes we generated back in the days before everything was digital. To this day, he is the keeper of memories, both mentally and physically.

My husband has never spent much time worrying about what others thought of him. He moves through the world in a confident, yet mystifyingly humble way. While I worried that other parents thought I was inadequate as a mother because of our son's strange behaviors and interests, Derek excelled at embracing them. While I fretted about being mistaken for a nanny at gymboree class, he was getting reprimanded at Walmart for taking photos of vacuum cleaners for an album to give to Dylan as a Christmas gift when he was two. When Dylan loved furnaces and plumbing, Derek was comfortable taking him to "Open Houses" and pretending he had an interest in the homes so Dylan could look in the basement. Sometimes I was jealous of their time together because my time with Dylan as a stay-at-home mom tended to be more routine and task-oriented, while time with Dad was more fun. Yet, how can you possibly fault a father who is simply bonding with his son?

As things with Dylan began to get difficult, I hated to have to call Derek with bad news and especially mid-crisis. Yet, he never once complained or asked me why I couldn't handle my job as a stay-at-home mom. Although I certainly had days where I felt like a failure, it was never because of anything he said to me. Quite the opposite, he could always make me feel better and, thank God, we could usually laugh at ourselves. If I had to choose one trait that everyone needs to look for in choosing a spouse, it would be the ability to laugh together.

While Derek was writing *Chasing the Rabbit*, I refused to read it. The thought of re-living events that made for the darkest days of our family's journey generated a lot of anxiety for me, so I avoided reading the book until it was completed and he needed me to read it before sending it to the editor. I girded myself for some serious emotions! What I found instead was a book filled with plenty of trials and sadness, but also many victories and a whole lot of heart. To my great relief, I smiled and laughed more than I cried. And isn't that what we all want in life? We know we will inevitably experience our share of frustration, sorrow and anger, but what matters more is how we respond. Only love, laughter and grace have the power to counter negative emotions and give us the energy we need sometimes just to face another day.

I hope this book inspires you in some way, whether you are raising or loving a child on the spectrum or not. While it may make you cry, it is more likely to make you smile and even laugh.

Now that Dylan, at twenty-three, is an adult both numerically and maybe even developmentally (if you know anything about autism, you know what I am saying), we can see the pieces of the puzzle that God has been moving into place all along. He took a headstrong girl who was short-tempered and taught her patience and humility, while arming her for politics because she has learned to be a survivor. He took a kind-hearted and thoughtful young man who imagined a son would be just like him and taught him acceptance, as well as how to care for, protect and lead his family in all the ways that really count. And through this book, God is working to fulfill Derek's dream of being able to teach and help others.

Dylan is still a very young man. He is just beginning to unleash his own creativity and test where that can take him as an adult. He may not be where he wants to be yet and he may not be where most people would hope for a child of his age to be, but we know where he has been and are incredibly proud of who we see him becoming.

Enjoy reading about that journey.

—Amy Volk, Dylan's Mom

What is Asperger's Syndrome?

According to Wikipedia, Asperger Syndrome (AS), also known as Asperger's Syndrome, Asperger's disorder (AD) or simply Asperger's, is an autism spectrum disorder (ASD) that is characterized by significant difficulties in social interaction and nonverbal communication, alongside restricted and repetitive patterns of behavior and interests. The syndrome is named after the Austrian pediatrician Hans Asperger who, in 1944, studied and described children in his practice who lacked nonverbal communication skills, demonstrated limited empathy with their peers, and were physically clumsy. The modern conception of Asperger's Syndrome came into existence in 1981 and went through a period of popularization, becoming standardized as a diagnosis in the early 1990s. The exact cause of Asperger's is unknown. A lack of demonstrated empathy has a significant impact on aspects of communal living for persons with Asperger's Syndrome. Individuals with AS experience difficulties in basic elements of social interaction, which may include a failure to develop friendships or to seek shared enjoyments or achievements with others (for example, showing others objects of interest), a lack of social or emotional reciprocity (social "games" give-and-take mechanic), and impaired nonverbal behaviors in areas such as eye contact, facial expression, posture, and gesture.

People with AS may not be as withdrawn around others compared to those with other, more debilitating forms of autism; they approach others, even if awkwardly. For example, a person with AS may engage in a one-sided, long-winded speech about a favorite topic, while misunderstanding or not recognizing the listener's feelings or reactions, such as a wish to change the topic of talk or end the interaction. This social awkwardness has been called "active but odd," This failure to react appropriately to social interaction may appear as disregard for other people's feelings, and may come across as insensitive. However, not all individuals with AS will approach others. Some of them may even display selective mutism, speaking not at all to most people and excessively to specific people. Some may choose only to talk to people they like.

The cognitive ability of children with AS often allows them to articulate social norms in a laboratory context, where they may be able to show a theoretical understanding of other people's emotions; however, they typically have difficulty acting on this knowledge in fluid, real-life situations. People with AS may analyze and distill their observations of social interaction into rigid behavioral guidelines, and apply these rules in awkward ways, such as forced eye contact, resulting in a demeanor that appears rigid or socially naïve. Childhood desire for companionship can become numbed through a history of failed social encounters.

The Chase Begins

"Courage doesn't always roar. Sometimes courage is the quiet voice at the end of the day saying, "I will try again tomorrow."
~ Mary Anne Radmacher

My son, Dylan, is the most amazing greyhound I have ever known. No, he is not a dog, he is fully human. My son is brilliant in many ways. He has many natural gifts, along with a caring heart and a giant capacity for love. But he is challenged by Asperger's Syndrome. It is a diagnosis he lives with every day of his life. He strives to be what people with Asperger's call "neurotypical," what you might call normal. But he is not. And he can't be. The analogy I have always used is that Dylan is like a greyhound, running as fast as he can, and normal is the plastic rabbit he is chasing. No matter how fast that greyhound runs, he will never catch the rabbit. But he never tires nor gives up the chase. I know of very few people who have been knocked down as many times as Dylan has in his life. And yet somehow, sometimes with vigor and sometimes against the odds, Dylan gets back up to fight another day in a world that is often fast-paced and quite confusing to him. This is the story of my son, the greyhound. It is also the story of a dad and a mom trying to figure out how to raise a son with Asperger's Syndrome, and a family learning to cope.

I spent many years mad at my son. This is not an easy thing for a dad to admit. It is embarrassing and I am ashamed of the feelings I had toward him. I was angry with him not only because of what he did through his words and behaviors but I also held a grudge because of who he is. My son could not change the fact that he had Asperger's. He did not choose to live his life with the challenges he faces every day. It was unfair and wrong but I could not help myself. In fact, I did not even realize that I had this underlying hostility until years later when I truly learned to forgive him. I never stopped for a second loving Dylan. I always tried to do everything I could, as a dad and a husband, to do right for my family. But deep inside my heart, in a place I usually pretended did not exist, was a bitterness that was hurting my relationship with my only son. They say holding a grudge is like drinking poison hoping the other guy dies. I understand what that feels like and I have worked hard, prayed often and looked at those dark places in my heart to release myself from the anger. I have forgiven my son for what he did not have to apologize for to begin with. I have forgiven myself for feelings I had a difficult time working through. In this book you will read about my journey as a dad and a husband. I share with you, in as much honesty as I think the reader would care to know, the process of raising my son on the autism spectrum and of learning to love him, and like him for who he is, not for who I hoped he would be. Our journey is not over and I certainly do not have all the answers. I continue to grow and learn how to be the dad that Dylan needs me to be now that he is an adult. I hope my experiences and insights can help you with whatever path you are traveling down. I welcome your feedback, at www.chasingtherabbit.org.

Dylan Is Born

Dylan Seth Volk was not born by accident. He was much planned. Amy and I were twenty-one years old and in love. We had been high school sweethearts. We married after our freshman year of college, went to the University of Georgia for a couple of years and were attending the University of Maine in Orono. We had a nice little apartment in Bangor and created a home there. We had two Siberian Huskies. We were still caring for Amy's childhood cat and even had a guinea pig that went by the name Phil. Yet, even with all those animals around to take care of, there was still something missing.

Amy really wanted to have a baby. Everywhere we went she saw babies and every time she saw one, the desire to have one of her own grew. I was not so sure I was ready for that big step but I certainly didn't mind the trying part of the process.

Like I said, Dylan was planned. It was October 1990 and Amy figured out the options. We would try to conceive a child in October. If that worked it would be perfect. The baby would be born in June which would give us the summer to enjoy him and time for Amy to stay home before classes of our senior year started in September. I would take some summer classes but they would be just a couple of hours a day and the rest of the time we could be with our baby. In the fall we would ask Amy's aunt, Anna Vaillancourt, who lived just a couple of miles away, to watch the baby while we went to school.

Anna and her husband had two small children of their own. Now, plan B. If we were not able to conceive in October it must not be meant to be so Amy would resign herself to that fact and we would go to school, graduate and work for a few years before starting a family. She thought maybe we would do some traveling and see the world while I established myself with a career somewhere.

I'll never forget the night of October 4, 1990. My brother, who was living in New York City, had gone to see *The Cosby Show* filmed and it was airing that night. I had to lie and tell him we saw the show but the truth is that we missed it. It was on that night that Dylan was conceived. After our special evening we went to Anna's because it was Amy's grandfather's birthday. We went over and celebrated with Grampy Blake and the family. In our hearts we both felt we had just made a baby.

It did not take long to suspect Amy was pregnant. I came home from classes just a couple of weeks later to find my wife fast asleep on the couch. I had been with Amy as much as humanly possible for six years by that time and I had never seen her take a mid-day nap. In fact, she thought nappers were lazy and could not imagine how anyone could just fall asleep in the day with all the lights on. We knew she was either sick or pregnant. She suggested we head over to the university clinic to get tested. Amy gave the nurse a urine sample and we anxiously waited for the results. The nurse walked in very stone faced. She sat us down and said, "I have to tell you, you are pregnant." We both started giggling. The nurse, who suspected that as young college students we would be in terror at the news, looked extremely confused. Amy and I just kept on giggling. Afterwards we were sure the nurse thought, "Oh, yeah, these two are mature enough to have a baby." The fact of the matter is that were just too thrilled to speak.

We decided it was best to keep it a secret until the end of the first trimester. Amy's mother had several miscarriages prior to having Amy so we didn't want to tell everyone and then have to deal with the emotion of a miscarriage with the world. We were also not so sure how our parents would react. So, the only ones we told were Anna and our best friend at the time, Robert Menezes. Anna and Rob were both very excited for us and we knew they would be supportive. A few weeks later Amy's father, David, was visiting our apartment on his way back from closing up his lake cottage for the winter when he saw the delivery truck arrive. We had bought a washer/dryer because Amy wanted to try cloth diapers when the baby arrived and going to the apartment complex laundry room all winter, dragging a baby and clothes across the snowy parking lot, didn't seem like a good idea. Amy's father left that day, went home to Windham and told Amy's mother, "Janet, Amy is pregnant." He knew Amy well and the washer/dryer didn't make sense for a couple living alone.

At ten weeks we went to the OBGYN for her first sonogram. We were hoping to see a heartbeat. Once we saw that heartbeat we were going to tell everyone our big secret. Dylan's heart was beating. There was a live baby inside Amy and he appeared completely healthy. We were good to go tell the world.

We drove home to Portland that weekend and right to my parents, Ken and Diane, in the North Deering area of Portland where I grew up. We didn't make it out of the first room of the house when we said, "We have something to tell you." We nervously pulled out the sonogram picture and showed it to my parents. They were still supporting us financially in many ways so we weren't sure how they would feel. They were ecstatic! In fact, they did not even seem surprised. My mother turned to my father and said, "I told you!" Apparently Amy, who was always very little and not a big eater, had told my mother, "When I get pregnant I'll eat better because I'll have to." When we had come down a couple of weeks earlier for Thanksgiving my mother noticed that Amy seemed to be "eating for two" and took plenty of second helpings. She had known Amy for six years and never saw her eat like that. She was convinced Amy must be pregnant.

We then drove up to Windham where Amy's parents still lived in her childhood home. When we told them the news, David immediately said to Janet, "I told you." We were shocked that he said he knew. He then told us that the washer/dryer was the giveaway.

Everything went great with her pregnancy. There were no glitches until it was time to actually give birth. Dylan just did not want to come out. He was due on June 27 but like every first time parent we were hoping he would arrive earlier. We went in for a midwife appointment at the beginning of June and she said, based on what she saw and felt, we would "definitely have this baby in June." My father, owner of a corrugated box factory in Biddeford, Maine, put together a company pool to guess the date and time of delivery. The dates went from June 15 to July 7. The first date was June 9, Father's Day. That came and went. Then there was full moon on June 26. No baby. The due date came and went, no baby. Okay, it was the last day of June. The doctor said we would have the baby in June. June 30 arrived and went. Every night we were going for long walks in the hopes of kicking her into labor. July 1, our anniversary came and went but Amy was still pregnant. July 4 came and went. Finally the midwife said if the baby didn't come by July 10, she would induce her. At least we had a date. We saw a sonogram at week twenty and there was no question it was a boy. We had the nursery ready to go and I had already bought him his first little tennis racket.

On July 10 we got up at 6:00am and went to the hospital to have a baby. They started by using some gels and other mild forms of inducement but nothing seemed to work. At 10:00 they decided to break her water. We had been told, and read, that once your water breaks things can start to happen very fast. We called my parents, who had just left Portland on route to Bangor for the birth, to let them know the doctor had broken Amy's water so they might want to hurry. I think Mario Andretti would have had a hard time keeping up with my father. They were in Bangor in record time. However, nothing seemed to be happening. She was having contractions but they were mild and mostly seemed to be hurting her back. Little did she know that was just the beginning of her long day of back pain. It turns out that Dylan was in there kind of upside down so his head was pushing hard against Amy's back.

By around 3:00, she was in a lot of pain and the labor wasn't progressing. At 5:00 the doctors gave her a sedative to relax her in the hopes of helping the contractions kick in better. The problem was that her back was in so much pain she could hardly feel the contractions. They had her hooked up to an IV with Pitocin, a drug used to help labor occur. We later learned that Dr. Eric Hollander of Mount Sinai Medical Center in New York presented a theory at a 1996 annual meeting of the American Psychiatric Association that linked autism with Pitocin-induced labors. He put forward the idea that Pitocin interferes with the newborn's oxytocin system that results in the social disabilities of autism. We will never know if the Pitocin affected Dylan.

At 7:00 medical staff came in and told me that the Pitocin level was as high as they could go so if she didn't start better and more active contractions soon they would begin preparing a room for a C-section. Amy had beautiful visions of her first experience with childbirth and this was not proceeding anywhere close to her plans. She had a midwife hired to oversee the delivery but at this point she was doing a lot of consulting with the doctors at the hospital. Amy wanted to deliver naturally and had no intentions of taking any drugs, pain medication, and certainly not delivery by C-section. I had been sitting there for hours watching my wife in terrible pain and hardly speaking or moving. I also sat there watching the heart monitor and the Pitocin drip machine. First it was set at 30-something, then 44, then 52, and maybe another number in between but at 7:00 when the doctor said it was "maxed out" the number read 72. It was about 8:00 when the nurse came in and moved the number to 84.

I remember thinking; didn't they just recently tell me that she was getting as much Pitocin as they could give her? Why did they just increase it? But I was twenty-one years old and I wanted that baby to come out so I didn't question the authority of the nurse, midwife or the doctor when they jacked up the Pitocin drip 12 points beyond what they told me was the maximum. It did appear to be working. Her contractions started to become stronger and at about 9:30pm they told Amy it was time to start pushing. Wow, I had never seen anything like that in my life. Amy pushed for over 100 minutes with strength and stamina I can pretty much admit freely that I do not possess. If that had been me on the table I would been saying, somewhere around 3:00 that afternoon, "Okay, where is the epidural and heavy medication?" Amy was determined she was delivering this baby naturally and there was nothing that was going to stop her. At 11:12pm on July 10, 1991, Dylan Seth Volk entered the world. This was the baby we had been dreaming of and he was perfect. Well, almost. His head, because of the labor he had been through coming out the wrong way, was bent, warped and quite crooked. We knew babies were often born with cone heads but Dylan's head was not only coned, it was also way off to the side of his skull. We had never seen anything like it before. Amy's aunt Anna was there when the baby was born as was her mother, Janet. Anna went out to tell Amy's dad and my parents that they were grandparents and also to warn and reassure them about Dylan's head and that it would look fine in a couple of days. Regardless of his crazy looking head, he was perfect in all of our eyes.

The First Months

Just as they said, a few days later Dylan's head was back to normal. Years later, as we struggle through everything we have gone through, I have often wondered if something happened to his brain in the those late hours of Amy's labor. I realize that there is no research on the topic of brain damage from back labor. I have seen books and newspaper articles and countless magazine stories about the impacts of immunizations and the possible connection with autism. What I go back to on a regular basis in my mind is how different Dylan's autism is from so many other kids on the spectrum. Yes, in many ways he presents like other kids with Asperger's. But there are so many ways he is an unusual case. We try not to dwell on the cause of his disability. I will note here that I may be calling it a disability and that could offend some politically correct readers who do not like that word. Sorry. That is what it is. Even Dylan would be quick to admit that, as I will discuss when I get to our visit to Northeastern University when he is sixteen. He is disabled, period. He is less able to perform normal life functions and live peacefully and successfully in society than the average person. That makes him disabled. He is not differently abled and I will not use that term as it demeans the struggles he goes through every day of his life. I have never read any of the books and have only scanned the stories about immunizations. I do not like reading them because there is no way to know what happened to Dylan or why he is the way he is. And even if I did know, I cannot change it. Therefore, I find those books frustrating. What I will always wonder is how a baby can have his brains so smashed and twisted and distorted with no effect. People that night told us that babies' brains are built to go through the child birth process and everything is fine. If that is the case why does everyone freak out every time a little kid holds a baby because they are so nervous they will touch that soft spot on his scalp too hard? "Be gentle!" they all say to the little kid and point out the softness of his head as if the kid touches it the poor baby will immediately die of brain damage. And yet, my son comes out looking like Dan Aykroyd and Jane Curtin's son from a 1976 *Saturday Night Live* skit, but it had no impact whatsoever on his brain development? I can never prove it and it does not matter, just like the immunizations do not matter. But you will never convince me that Dylan's head shape at birth had no affect on the reason he has spent a life struggling with his case of Asperger's.

Dylan was a good baby. He was the first grandchild on both sides. All the grandparents came to visit him in Bangor or met him when we came home to Portland a month after his birth. Everything seemed perfect, except for that ride to Portland. We put Dylan in the car and he immediately started crying. He cried and cried and screamed and screamed. We didn't even make it much outside of Bangor when we stopped at a local truck stop. We were already getting very frustrated at our lack of knowledge in how to comfort our baby. We yelled at the dogs and shoved them into the back of our Volvo. Amy sat in the back seat and tried to comfort Dylan. Years later, with our other children she would learn the impressive skill of nursing in a moving car while the baby remains in the car seat. But in 1991, she had not mastered that unusual technique, so Dylan cried and cried and cried again, and then cried some more. It was raining. It was dark. Traffic was moving slowly. At one point, Amy yelled at me because the person in front of us was going too slowly. She suggested I flash my high beams so they would get out of the passing lane so we could get this crying baby to Portland faster. I flashed my high beams, which led to the flashing blue lights of the police car behind me, who pulled me over and told me that he didn't like my antics and there was no hurry for me to get anywhere during a rainstorm. I apologized and told him we were just frustrated because our baby had been crying for almost two hours. He said that the most important thing is to get our baby safely where we were going so relax and drive safely. Luckily, he didn't give me a ticket for my antics.

We were less than ten minutes from my parents' house in North Deering on the north end of Portland when Dylan finally fell asleep. We had many car rides like this. He just did not like being confined to a car seat and would often cry. It was really the only thing that we could point to prior to age two that made him seem different from any other baby.

I was in my senior year of college and I arranged with a professor to do an independent study about Dylan. I studied, for the first six months of his life, Dylan's communication. I researched baby communications at great lengths. I would read book after book about baby communication skills and then I would match them up to what Dylan was doing for his first six months. I did a number of experiments with him testing his communication on video and added that as part of my study on Dylan. When it was finished, I had a fifty-page report about Dylan's communication for the first six months of his life. And all of those communication markers were right on track. There was absolutely no indication for those first six months that he would someday have a neurological disorder that was directly tied to his ability to communicate. All the tests that I did on him, the little experiments, he performed perfectly on target. I was excited to write about each new communication skill that he gained throughout those six months.

Moving to Portland

My original plan after college graduation was to move to Modesto, California, to work at the box plant of a friend of my father's. He wanted me to get some experience outside the family business and then return in a few years to begin the process of running Volk Packaging Corporation. Our family business, started in 1967 by my grandfather and my father, is the only Maine owned and operated corrugated box manufacturer. We have a 141,000 square foot facility in Biddeford, Maine, with eighty-five employees. My long-term goal was to run the family business but my father felt a few years in California would be beneficial. I did not have a problem with that plan and looked forward to the experience. However, after we graduated from college, we moved back to Portland. I think the fact that Dylan came along changed his opinion about my leaving the state. Years later when I would talk to him about it, he would tell me that part of the decision in not encouraging me to work in Modesto, California, was the concern that I would never come back to join the family business. In hindsight, he was probably right. Both Amy and I really enjoy warm weather. If we had gone to Modesto, I'm fairly certain we never would have moved back to Maine.

At the end of December 1991, we packed up our apartment and moved to Portland. Amy was a stay-at-home mom. I had a job at the family business. I started out working in the shipping department as part of a process to learn the whole company. I had worked through high school and college in the plant, so in order to learn the business, I started in the shipping department, moved into the design department, and then into customer service. Every day I would come home and Amy would tell me about all the things Dylan had done that day. I was very jealous because for the first six months I had seen all those things and now all of a sudden I wasn't seeing them anymore. However, I loved hearing about them and staying up with Amy and Dylan until ten at night trying to get him to do all the cute things he had done during the day. We would read to him, play with him, tickle him, and simply spend time with him.

We lived in that house for a couple of years, until Mariah was born in April of 1994. We knew we had outgrown our little house. I have some great memories. In fact, every time I drive up Forest Avenue past that street to this day, I remember nothing but good memories spending time with Dylan. Saturday mornings I used to put him in a backpack to let Amy sleep in a little and we would walk up to the neighborhood convenience store. I would get a newspaper and buy Dylan what he called a "boo-berry muttin." And he loved his "boo-berry muttins" and I loved taking him up there to get them. We would hang out for a while and then walk back down and spend time with Amy on those Saturday mornings.

Dylan and Amy, 1992

"Something's Not Quite Right with Dylan."

People often ask me, "When did you know or when did you suspect that Dylan was a little different?" Well, when I knew and when Amy knew were two very different times. In 1993, when Dylan was about two, Amy was a stay home mom and we lived in a neighborhood in Portland with many working mothers. Some of the moms had child care issues on certain days of the week so Amy thought it would be a good way to get to know some of the kids in the neighborhood, help the neighbors out, as well as make a little extra money. One day, when I came home from work, she had a couple of the little boys over. They were just about Dylan's age, one a little older and one a little younger. The two boys were playing together but Dylan was not participating in their fun. I asked Amy how things were going. She just looked at me and said, "Something's not quite right with Dylan."

"What do you mean?" I asked.

"I don't know what, but something isn't right with him," she said.

Now of course, my immediate response was what I would think any parent would immediately respond with, "Oh no, he's fine. He's just really smart." Dylan was a very unique little boy. He used to love to play with vacuum cleaners, sometimes for hours. In fact, every Saturday in the winter, we would take him out for breakfast in Portland and after breakfast, we would take him over to South Portland where he would play with vacuum cleaners at Service Merchandise, a department store no longer in existence. However, at the time, it was a very popular store and they had a display of 10 or 15 different types of vacuum cleaners. The display was on top of a 12' by 12' stage about six inches off the ground and all around it were outlets which allowed the customer to test out the vacuum cleaners. This was all the entertainment Dylan would need for the day. Often times, Amy would bring a book, I would bring a *Sports Illustrated* and we would sit as Dylan would go from vacuum cleaner to vacuum cleaner, playing with them, inspecting them, telling us all about them. We would put our books down and he would tell us the pros and cons of each type of vacuum cleaner. This was unusual behavior for a two year old but we thought it was adorable.

He was also fascinated by plumbing. He used to like to look into the back of the toilet as it was flushed to watch the water go up and down. One of his favorite things to do was to visit open houses and go inside the house as if we were a prospective buyer. After wandering around a little we would venture down into the basement to look at the furnace. He loved furnaces. In fact, when he was three years old, he was a furnace for Halloween. If he got really lucky, while at the open house the furnace would start up and then the excitement would really hit. Dylan was unique to say the least.

Amy paused for a moment as tears welled up in her eyes. She said to me, "No Derek. There's something not right with him. He doesn't interact with the other kids. They play together, talk to each other. He just keeps to himself the whole time. He doesn't have any interest in what they're doing."

That was the first time Amy realized something was wrong. Dylan was different. But what did we do about it? It was 1993. At that time, Asperger Syndrome (also called Asperger's) was not even an official diagnosis. We could have taken him anywhere in the country and they would not have told us he had Asperger's. We didn't do anything. We were young parents with a beautiful little boy. We'd figure it out when the time was necessary.

But then other things began to clue us in to the possibility that Dylan may be wired a little differently. He spoke at a typical age—dada, doggy, and mama—your basic words. He got to about eight or nine words and then he stopped for quite a while. He did not seem to be expanding his word vocabulary at all. We were concerned but not panicked. He had hit the other milestones just fine. He was adorable, fun to be with, and a relatively easy little boy to deal with so we weren't panicked.

Just before his second birthday, Dylan pulled a book out of his bookshelf, looked up at me and said, "How about this book?" The little boy who had barely added a word to his vocabulary for months was suddenly speaking in complete and grammatically correct sentences. We were shocked to say the least when "How about this book?" turned into the vocabulary of a five-year-old within a couple of weeks. He was saying words we didn't even know he had ever heard, and was using them correctly, speaking perfectly, clearly, and grammatically correct to us and to everybody else. People often commented on his vocabulary and how he talked like a five-year-old.

Even though his vocabulary was impressive, it didn't ring any alarms to us whatsoever. We didn't know any better. Nobody told us that was common for kids with Asperger's because no one thought anything about Asperger's in 1993 or 1994. We just enjoyed our son, marveled at his growing vocabulary and his ability to communicate with us. We loved and bragged about the fact that Dylan could memorize an entire story book, word for word. We enjoyed all the time that we spent with him, fixating on his, what are now known in the world of Asperger's as "special interests." We didn't call them special interests at the time. We just called them "what Dylan likes to do." When he was three years old and wanted to be a furnace for Halloween, we obliged. I brought a box home from work. I went to a customer in Massachusetts that made piping equipment and asked for some samples of small pipes of various sizes.

"Why would you want that?" my customer asked.

"Well," I responded, "as it turns out, my son wants to be a furnace for Halloween. I want to help him make that costume and furnaces have pipes." They thought that was the cutest thing ever and were happy to help me out.

Then I called the company that serviced our furnace. I said, "I know this is going to sound very unusual to you but I was wondering if you could send me some stickers that talk about turning off the emergency switch and the energy and have the company phone number?" They wanted to know why I was interested in their stickers and once again, I explained that my son wanted to be a furnace for Halloween. As the pipe company did, they got a chuckle out of it. They were happy to send me a collection of stickers. Between the piping, the box, the furnace stickers, some aluminum foil, and some black paint for his face, we had ourselves the cutest little furnace in the neighborhood. As we went from house to house that Halloween, everyone was curious as to what Dylan was dressed up as. He became more and more agitated as the evening went on that people did not realize he was a furnace. But everyone who saw him and found out what he was dressed as couldn't help but smile at the little furnace asking for candy that Halloween night.

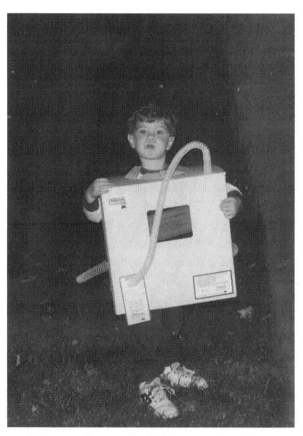

Dylan as a furnace for Halloween at age three

2

Growing Family, Struggling Child

New Baby, New House and First "Diagnosis"

Dylan was two years old, happy and healthy, and at this point there was no obvious sign that anything was wrong. Like so many parents with a two-year-old, Amy and I started talking and thinking about expanding our family. At one point we talked about having four kids, but we really were just taking it one at a time. In 1993, we started planning to have another baby.

In the fall of 1994, Dylan was three years old and ready to start nursery school. We had a new baby, Mariah, born in April and a new house shortly after that. We stayed in Portland but moved from the Riverton area back to the part of Portland called North Deering, where I grew up. Our goal was to get into a house in a neighborhood called Pineloch Woods but, at this time, we could not afford any of those homes. We purchased a three bedroom house on Sturdivant Drive, about a mile from my parent's house. It was a good sized colonial and plenty of house for us. We saw it from the beginning as a transition house and figured we'd stay there for a couple of years before pursuing a new house or a home in Pineloch Woods. We definitely wanted to get out of the starter home because we wanted baby Mariah, or as Dylan would affectionately call her, "Yidew Ma-Wiyah" to have her own room.

We signed Dylan up for a local pre-school, which was based out of a nearby church. Dylan was fine going to school. He was a very social little boy and was not shy. He didn't have a problem with us dropping him off at school. He especially liked hanging out with the janitor, who would talk to Dylan about the different pipes underneath the water faucet and in the bathroom. Everyone at the school found that very entertaining. We actually toilet trained him by offering to let him look under the toilet cover if he went on the toilet.

Dylan, with Mariah watching, being rewarded for his toilet training success

When it came time for his very first teacher conference, we went in without a lot of expectation that there was going to be much to talk about other than your typical things they would say at a three-year-olds teacher conference. When the teacher told us that she and the other teachers felt that Dylan had ADHD, we were shocked and quite upset. It wasn't so much because she told us he might have ADHD but it was the first time that someone told us that there was something wrong with our son and that he needed to be medicated. She explained to us that we should put him on Ritalin. The thought of putting our son on a brain altering drug at three years old knocked us for a loop and we refused to consider it. She told us that Dylan was very impulsive. She did not see his behavior as malicious but simply as an inability to control his impulsiveness. This especially manifested itself when they were either at the "sand table" or the "water table." There were stations for kids to play at around this nursery school. One of them was a little table that was full of sand and you could move the sand through different toys and ride little trucks around the sand, lifting things up. His teacher said that Dylan would often be at the sand table playing fine, either by himself or with another child, and then with no warning, he would grab some sand and fling it at his classmate. She told us he would do the same thing at the water table. Without any explanation, he would just randomly splash another child getting them all wet and then be surprised when they were upset. The teacher felt these behaviors could be controlled with Ritalin.

We went home and the next day Amy went out to the bookstore and bought a book about ADHD so we could see if this was something our son suffered from and how we as parents could better deal with it. As we read the book, there were things within the pages that we felt were descriptive of Dylan. He was impulsive. We had seen that. However, there were a lot of chapters in the book where we would read page after page and think to ourselves, "This doesn't seem anything like our child." We were hesitant to follow his teacher's instructions and have him put on Ritalin.

Yet, at our next parent-teacher conference, she once again encouraged us to medicate Dylan, and once again, we resisted. We just didn't feel we were ready to start down a path that seemed impossible to get off once we were on it, the path of mind-altering medications.

Inability to Multitask

We started noticing things that Dylan could do and things that Dylan could not do and wondered what was normal and what was not normal for a four-year-old boy. We did not have much of a baseline of comparison. We got information from books and from what Amy remembered from her days babysitting as a teenager, but most of those experiences were limited and very rarely did the books talk about the issues and concerns we were facing.

One concern we had with Dylan had to do with multitasking. It was not necessarily what an adult might think of as multitasking, which is often described as doing several tasks at the same time. Multitasking, in its true form, is very rare. In most cases, people think they're multitasking, but they're actually accomplishing one task effectively and one task ineffectively. What I'm talking about here was not something that we felt was a rare skill. It was a deficit that Dylan seemed to have when it came to following directions after being assigned several tasks.

For example, it might be time for Dylan to go to bed, and we had some cleaning up to do downstairs. We would give Dylan a common series of requests by a parent to a four- or five-year-old, "Go upstairs, get in your jammies, pick out some stories, and brush your teeth." Ten minutes or so later, one of us would go upstairs, expecting to see Dylan on our bed or his bed with three or four books, in his pajamas, ready for us to read to him, and instead we would go upstairs to find Dylan standing in his room just staring at the wall or playing. We would say, "Dylan what are you doing? We told you that you needed to get in your jammies, brush your teeth, and pick out some stories."

He wouldn't make excuses and he wouldn't say, "I couldn't remember what to do" or "I couldn't do all those things." He would just say, "Oh…" as if he completely forgot what the assignments were.

We learned later that it is very common for kids and adults with Asperger's Syndrome, to be challenged when assigned several tasks as a series. If we were to give him a single task, "Go get your jammies on," and then once he'd done that, tell him to brush his teeth, etc., he would oblige without argument and be cooperative. However, given the assignment of three tasks all in one sentence, it was so overwhelming that he just shut down. He was four years old; we were years away from a diagnosis. So in 1995, on those days we would walk up the stairs and see Dylan just staring with no idea what to do, we would respond in similar fashion. We would just stare because we had no idea what to do about our son who seemed to have an inability to follow instructions.

"Empty Folders in his Brain Files"

Dylan would throw terrible temper tantrums and be inconsolable and uncontrollable for what seemed like hours. These were probably not as long as they felt. Yet, it was certainly longer than the typical five-year-old meltdown. Years later we attended a seminar in Bangor, Maine where author Tony Atwood visualized what this looked like in the brain of a child with Asperger's. I thought he provided a great analogy. The way he described it is that our brains are like a computer screen and within that computer screen are folders on the desktop of our brain. In each one of those folders, there's a title that describes a situation in which we might find ourselves. When we find ourselves in one of those situations, our internal mouse double-clicks on one of those folders and it opens up documents that give us choices for how to handle those situations. For example, a five-year-old's desktop may have folders that say things like, "Did not get the dessert I wanted" or "Overtired" or "Jealous of a friend's toy." When a normal five-year-old gets in one of those situations, their "brain mouse" would double-click on, for instance, the folder about the friend's toy, and it would open up to a number of documents that might say, "Share one of my toys" or "Grab the toy away from him" or "Distract my friends, so I can take the toy." And if you double-clicked on one of those, it would give descriptions on how to handle that situation. The problem with a child with Asperger's is that when he or she double-clicks that folder, there are either a very limited number of documents to choose from or even worse than that, when they double-click the document, it's simply empty. Those empty documents lead to outbursts and behaviors that don't make sense, behaviors that lead parents to wonder what they have done wrong. We asked ourselves how our child could behave so erratically. Those empty documents make other people wonder what poor parenting occurred to allow a child to behave like Dylan did.

I can't tell you how many times in the last twenty-three years, we've had people look at us with contempt or confusion because Dylan was behaving in a way that their child never would. Those people may be other parents, teachers, and waitresses. We often talked about having a business card to carry around with us that on the front said: "I apologize for my son's behavior. He has a form of autism called Asperger's Syndrome." On the back it would have a brief description of what Asperger's is and why he might behave in a manner that looked like the result of extremely poor parenting.

However, when he was five, we didn't know he had Asperger's. We didn't know what was wrong. We just knew that other kids didn't act like that and that other parents seemed to be able to control their children's behavior better than we could control Dylan's. We often felt contempt and confusion from other parents when looking at us. We assumed we were doing something wrong. In our hearts we knew that there was something different about Dylan. We hoped and prayed that eventually somebody would be able to help us; somebody would be able to tell us what the explanation was for why Dylan would react the way he did in various situations. At this point in our lives, we either blamed ourselves or worse, we blamed Dylan. I would often yell at him, "Why are you acting like this?" or "Why don't you just calm down?" Of course, he couldn't answer any of those questions because he was just a little boy with empty folders.

Our "Monster"

The next summer we enrolled Dylan at Middle Day Camp. He would get to the bus each day with my eighteen-year-old cousin, Danielle, who was a counselor. Dylan would head to Sebago Lake for a day of fun in the sun doing activities and playing games. He had just turned four and was signed up to go a couple of days a week. We thought there might be some issues with him and the camp, but we never expected the call that we received in mid-July just a couple of weeks after he had started.

I was sitting at work when the phone rang. On the other end was one of the head counselors of the camp. She had called to tell me that I needed to come pick up Dylan and that he couldn't stay at camp anymore. When I asked what the problem was, her exact words to me were, "Your son is a monster."

Now this was the person who was the head of the camp, who sees hundreds of kids every day each summer and has been trained to work with children of all ages. I will never forget that moment because it was the first time that somebody attacked Dylan for what he could not control—behaviors that were as frustrating to him as they were to anybody else. He was an adorable four-year-old boy. He was the furthest thing from a monster, especially to a father hearing those words. I was not sure if I should cry or reach through the phone and punch her in the face. I wanted to do both.

I immediately hung up the phone, called Amy, and we headed up to Windham to get Dylan. When we got there, he was sitting very quietly in the main office of the camp and didn't seem to have any idea why we were there or what was wrong. When we asked what had been the problem to cause that phone call, she just said that he was too difficult for them to deal with, that he had been making very impulsive decisions and was disrupting the rest of the kids with what she called "rude interruptions." Now, I'm not an expert on children and I certainly wasn't back in 1995 when I had two little kids. But I was under the impression that "rude interruptions" at age four was a pretty common occurrence. I could not understand what the issue was that would result in my son being called a monster by the camp director. That day was the impetus to get us thinking that we needed to address whatever it was that Dylan was struggling with, figure out how to work with the issues, and how to best help him change his behavior.

First, we called our pediatrician, Dr. Tony, and told her we needed to meet with her to discuss Dylan. Although she is very smart and caring she had no answers for us. As we were later to experience time and time again, the professionals that we counted on to help us with our son did not have any answers that were really helpful at all. In fact, oftentimes they were harmful. In many cases, it was not malicious. Dr. Tony cared; she did not give us a lack of assistance because she wasn't interested in helping us with the challenges of working with Dylan. Asperger's would have been a very unlikely diagnosis in 1995. It was not even recognized by the American Psychiatric Association

(DSM-IV) until the previous year. She just did not know what the resources were in the greater Portland area for a child like Dylan. As time went on there was counselor after counselor, expert after expert, that gave us either no good advice, no advice at all, or absolutely horrible advice in dealing with our son.

The First P.E.T.

When we enrolled Dylan in kindergarten we had to have a P.E.T. (Pupil Evaluation Team) meeting with the school to plan where he would be placed for kindergarten. The way the school worked at that time was that, for kids who had summer or fall birthdays, it would be a two-year kindergarten program. During the meeting, we explained to them our concerns. We discussed how Dylan had difficulty forming peer relationships, used inappropriate means of making peer connections, had a lot to say, and had difficulty making eye contact and taking turns. We also explained how abrupt transitions were challenging for him. It still boggles my mind to this day how, with all of those characteristics, none of the professionals made the connection that Asperger's Syndrome may be what was causing the problem. There was so little knowledge of autism and Asperger's at the time.

Deciding to Have Lilly

In the summer of 1997, we were visiting my parents at their cottage on Sebago Lake. It sits nestled in a cove off an area of the lake called Jordan Bay. It's very quiet and the water is always calm in the cove. It was a particularly hot day for Maine. The kids had been swimming a lot, and they had gone inside to get a snack with my parents, whom they call Nana and Papa. Amy and I stayed down in the water, swimming around and talking.

With two little kids, ages six and three, it was rare that Amy and I had quiet time to talk, so it was nice. Amy laid on an inflated inner-tube and I held on and moved it around while we talked in the water. I don't remember what kicked off the conversation about having another baby, but Amy brought up the idea of having a third child. We had talked when we were teenagers about having four kids, and then life happened. Dylan started having problems, became more and more challenging, and we really hadn't had a conversation in a while about how many kids we were going to have.

When Amy brought up having another baby, my immediate response was, "I kinda thought we were done. We have a boy and a girl—everything seems to be going fine. Dylan is enough of a challenge to keep us busy. I didn't think we were probably going to have any more kids." The look on Amy's face was a mixture of shock and disappointment. It never even occurred to her that we would stop at two. She just wondered whether we would have three, or four, or maybe even five. Amy loved being a mom, and she was really good at it, so why would I possibly only want two kids? It was not that I only wanted two kids, it was more that I hadn't really thought about having another one. I just was making the assumption that we had all we needed.

Amy looked me in the eye without hesitation and told me, in no uncertain terms, that she had no intention of stopping after two kids. I honestly don't remember much of the rest of the conversation but I could see how important having more children was to her. If she wanted more kids and she was determined that that's what direction our family was headed, I really didn't feel the need or have the heart to argue with her. Amy was the most important person in my life and if this was what she wanted, we would make it work.

A few months later Lilly was conceived. On August 26, 1998, on a stormy night with lightning cracking and thunder booming all over southern Maine, we went to the hospital and gave birth to a beautiful baby girl we named Lillian Robin Volk. Her middle name, Robin, was given in honor of Dylan and his love of birds.

Dylan was very fond of his new baby sister. He was always a very loving brother to Mariah and now he had a new baby sister to show his love to. It was very sweet to see Dylan with Lilly. Those times reminded us that despite his large meltdowns and camp directors calling him a monster, Dylan was a sweet little boy with a loving heart. Throughout the years we would take notice that as difficult or angry as Dylan got with us he was never aggressive toward his sisters. Lilly, to this day, has special memories of Dylan getting up early on Saturday mornings, even to the point of setting his alarm, so he could make her Mickey Mouse shaped pancakes. We thanked God often that Dylan was such a thoughtful and caring big brother and praised him for it.

Dylan and Lilly with his special Mickey Mouse pancake

3

Special Brilliance, Diagnoses and Confusion

The Year of the Birds

First grade may have been the best year we ever had with Dylan once he entered school. It ended up being kind of sad looking back and seeing how it all went downhill after first grade because it was a very successful year for him. He had a terrific teacher who seemed to really understand him. Delia Murphy was her name. She was kind, understanding, patient, and even better, she let Dylan be Dylan and used his special interests to help educate him.

In first grade, Dylan was really into birds. In fact, he was *obsessed* with them. He knew everything about birds, had read everything he could about birds, and he couldn't get enough information. We had countless bird books all over the house all the time. He would spend hours looking through these books. For a long time, we just thought he was looking at the pictures when all of a sudden, we realized he could read. He started telling us information that he couldn't get unless he were reading the books. He taught himself to read through these bird books.

We didn't think a whole lot about it. We just thought it was cute, unusual, and kind of special so we encouraged it as much as possible. We would take him to Smiling Hill Farm in Westbrook on weekends. But Dylan wasn't really interested in the farm. At the base of it, there was a little pond where there were ducks and geese and the occasional Canadian goose. And that's where we would hang out. Dylan would spend hours just looking at all the birds, drawing pictures, asking questions, looking at the bird books and telling us about each of the birds in great detail. He would collect feathers. We had a huge piece of corrugated that I brought home from work that he would tape feathers to and mark what type of bird they came from.

One day we went to the Cumberland Fair. Of course most kids go to the fair to go on the rides, play games, and maybe have some cotton candy or a candy apple but not Dylan. We went from building to building looking at each bird, comparing them to his bird book where he would read us information about the bird; often quizzing us about the bird we were looking at. We would look around to make sure there was no one official nearby, and then we would reach our hand into whatever bird cage we were standing in front of and pull out a feather. We always hoped to find one in the wood-chips or sawdust at the bottom of the cage and we usually were successful. Every once in a while, we had to kind of tug at the bird a little to get at feather. There was not a single bird cage that we did not walk by at the fair without getting a feather. And then we would make a note of what that feather was so that when we got home we could mark them all on his board.

When we went down to Florida to visit Amy's sister, we went to a big lake in the center of town and we walked around the entire lake to spot every bird that was there and chased them down to get a feather for Dylan's collection. We even had some rare feathers on Dylan's collection board—some hawks' and even a bald eagle's feather that someone had given him because they knew how much he loved birds. We later found out that it was illegal to be in possession of a bald eagle feather but we didn't know that and we probably wouldn't have cared. We were doing everything we could to encourage Dylan's obsession with birds, what we later learned was called his "special interest" for people with Asperger's.

People with Asperger's are often fascinated with one topic to the point where it is almost impossible for them to talk about anything else. Their knowledge of the topic is borderline genius but it makes it difficult to talk with the person with Asperger's. We would often have to redirect Dylan in conversations because no matter what we were talking about he would somehow bring the conversation back to birds. We would try to explain to him that we were having a conversation and it was not about birds. In what we would learn later was very typical Asperger's behavior, he could not understand why anyone would want to have a conversation that did not involve bird facts. We would experience déjà vu many times throughout his life again and again trying to help him understand that everyone does not always want to talk about what he wants to talk about.

Mrs. Murphy was a great teacher. She even allowed Dylan to present to the class what he knew about birds. He had been presenting about birds at home for quite a while, oftentimes on Saturday mornings. He would get the family together to play "school" with Amy, Mariah, Lilly (who was just a baby), and me. We always used to joke that Lilly was the principal of Dylan's school, even though she was in a car seat. Dylan would stand at the front of the "class" with a whiteboard and quiz all of us about birds. He knew the length of every bird, their migratory patterns, and the size of their eggs, what they ate, and the sounds they made. He had a bird clock that would make a noise every hour of whatever bird was at that hour. There was very little he didn't know about birds and he wanted everyone else to know as much as he did so he would ask us questions and give us quizzes.

He used to call himself "Mr. Plygon" (I'm not really sure where that name came from). Amy and I would often get silly in the class and try to lighten the mood or flirt with each other while Dylan was teaching, but he would have none of it. He was very serious. And Mariah, who was only a little over four years old at the time, would take it as seriously as Dylan. She would sit very quietly in class and try to answer all of Dylan's bird questions as best she could. She looked up to her big brother and didn't see anything wrong with what he was doing or anything strange about it at all because it was the only thing she knew.

When Mrs. Murphy asked Dylan if he would teach his first grade class about birds, he jumped at the chance. We spent several hours at home trying to figure out what Dylan would talk about in his one-hour availability in class. He was going to put a little quiz together so the kids could try to learn and take something away from his presentation. However it was a challenge for us to try to figure out how, in only an hour, Dylan could say all the things he wanted to say and teach his class all the things he wanted to teach them about birds.

When the day came for Dylan to present to his class, he was so excited. He was like a kid on Christmas morning. I took the day off to go into the class in order to video his presentation. He got up at the front of the classroom as if he did it every day, as if he were a professional teacher, and proceeded to teach his classmates everything he could in an hour, but the one hour stretched to an hour and ten minutes, and then an hour and twenty minutes, and then an hour and thirty minutes, and finally at just about an hour and forty minutes, Mrs. Murphy had to tell Dylan that the class was over and it was time for him to wrap up his presentation. The funniest thing about it was that Amy and I just thought it was great. It never occurred to us in a million years that this could be part of some neurological disorder that would affect him the rest of his life. We just thought we had a really smart kid who happened to like birds a little more than a typical child would. We took great pleasure in watching him present. It was an hour and a half we will never forget. Dylan really shined and felt like a million dollars at the front of that class. We knew that day that although Dylan may have had many challenges and he was not going to be easy to raise, he had some gifts that made him exceptional. The question we asked ourselves was, "how do we help him make the most of those unusual gifts?"

Dylan teaches his first grade class about birds

The Spirited Child, Is That a Real Thing?

It was during first grade, as well as things were going at school, that we really started seeing more and more of what we later called, "meltdowns." Now I know other kids have meltdowns, but Dylan's were epic compared to most kids. When he was in meltdown he was inconsolable, much as he was when he was a baby in his car seat. It didn't matter what we said or did. When he got upset or frustrated there was almost no way to calm him down. None of our discipline would do it and we couldn't just walk away because he followed us everywhere. This is something that we dealt with right up through high school. Therapists would tell us to just walk away but that was impossible. He wouldn't let us; he was relentless and he was that way even in kindergarten.

So we knew there was an underlying issue. We just had no idea what it was. Someone recommended that we get counseling for him. They gave us the name of a woman in Portland. Dylan would go in and sit with her once a week and draw bird pictures and she would ask him about them. He would spend hours drawing these pictures in great detail over and over again, and he was very good at it and happy doing it. But after months of seeing Dylan and sitting with him, the psychotherapist told us that he had "Spirited Child Syndrome." I tried to find a definition but could not find anything formal because I do not believe it is even a legitimate diagnosis. It is a "catch all" for a kid that no one knows what to do with.

I found this definition on WiseGeek.org:

> A spirited child may be also called a challenging child, high needs child, or difficult child. Spirited child is often more politically correct, especially over the term "difficult," which has negative connotations. The spirited child is truly a challenge to parents, because even parents with older children may find themselves stumped by spirited child behavior and reactions. Frequently, one can see a young child, even an infant, who resists efforts and comforting, and cries often, even after all needs have been addressed and the infant is being held.

In 1998 Amy and I had no idea what Spirited Child Syndrome was and didn't have Google to help us out. It almost sounded like a good thing, a spirited child. How could that be a bad thing? "My child has lots of spirit! YAY!!" But it just didn't make sense that Dylan's crashes and meltdowns were because he had so much spirit. The diagnosis seemed too simple but we didn't know any better. This counselor was the first real expert that we saw who put a name to anything we were experiencing with Dylan, so we ran with it and bought a book about Spirited Child Syndrome.

We began Dylan's path down what we would later call, "The Diagnosis of the Month Club." What we soon learned is that this particular highly regarded therapist had a specialty in Spirited Child Syndrome so it was no coincidence when she said that is what our child had. For many years of Dylan's early life we had different therapists each telling us that Dylan's diagnosis was whatever their specialty happened to be. Spirited Child was the first of those "official" diagnoses.

Dylan's first grade year was when we started to notice some other odd behaviors. For the very first time, we saw facial and vocal tics. His vocal tics were both visual and auditory.

Dylan's vocal tic was called *ecolalia*. This tic would cause him to say a word or a sentence and then, only with his lips but with no sound, repeat the last couple of words of the sentence or maybe just the one word that he said. So for example, if he said, "I'm not happy with this dinner," he would mouth the words, "happy with this dinner" or "this dinner." If you have ever seen the TV show, *The Middle*, it is what the youngest child, Brick, does in every episode but Dylan did it with no sound. When we asked him about it, he had no idea why he was doing it. In fact, he didn't even know he was doing it. And Spirited Child Syndrome, which he was "diagnosed with," had no explanation for this or for the blinking that emerged toward the end of first grade.

Another really positive experience of Dylan's life in first grade was that he had friends. Friends in first grade are often "the boy who lives next to you" or "the girl that lives two doors down" and you're friends because it's convenient. But the year Dylan was in first grade, we were building a house in Scarborough, Maine, and living in Portland in my parents' house after they moved down to Florida for the winter and there were no little kids in the neighborhood. So the two boys Dylan became friends with were friends with him because they actually liked him and he liked them. That was the first time that Dylan had a couple of friends that he could hang out and play with. However, as the school year went on, for whatever reason that we never really found out, they stopped calling him, they stopped inviting him for playdates, and that was a pattern that would follow him for years. He would make a friend and then slowly that friend would disconnect from him.

What struck us most about his experience with the Portland psychotherapist was that here was an expert in child psychology and sitting in front of her was a young boy with an incredible special interest, clear social awkwardness and a failure to connect with other kids his age, and yet for the entire time she was seeing Dylan, she never mentioned or even brought up the possibility that he might have Asperger's Syndrome. Amy and I, to this day don't understand that. It was still a relatively new diagnosis in 1996-1997. Maybe she didn't even know about Asperger's and what a typical child with it might look like. But we went to her hoping and trusting she would have the latest information and we never heard a word about Asperger's. Instead she suggested very strongly that we have Dylan begin taking Ritalin. We finally gave in and Dylan began taking his first medication intended to influence his behaviors.

Chiropractic "Help"

When we realized our current therapist was not going to get us the answers that we needed to help Dylan, we looked for other options. Somebody mentioned that kids with ADHD would benefit from chiropractic care, so we went to a local chiropractor. At our first visit, after barely meeting Dylan, they assured us with complete confidence that through a lengthy series of chiropractic treatments, they would be able to help Dylan with whatever it was that he had. And so, as he did with all the people we dragged him to over the years, Dylan went to appointment after appointment without a complaint. He let people poke and prod him and adjust his neck. It made no impact on his behavior. This was just one of many alternative treatments that we would seek for Dylan over the years. We stuck with it for a couple of months before pulling the plug on this expensive and time consuming experiment which yielded nothing more than an increasingly sore neck. Dylan never complained about his neck until after they started messing with it.

The Little White Pills

In May of 1997 we took him to Falmouth, Maine, to see a homeopathic doctor. He convinced us that he had a magic bullet which had the ability to make a significant impact on Dylan's behavior and social issues. Once again we believed him because we were so desperate to find some answers for our son. Every day, morning and night, Dylan took mustard seed sized white pills that this Falmouth doctor convinced us would change Dylan's behavior. As you might guess, it had no impact at all. In fact, after months of trying different kinds of pills, all of which looked exactly the same, and testing out different options of what time to take them during the day, we went to an appointment with this doctor. During the appointment, Dylan had a meltdown, and in the grand scheme of Dylan's meltdowns, it was a pretty minor one. He got upset, a little disrespectful, rude, and his voice elevated. However, for Dylan, it was a relatively minor incident. The homeopathic doctor looked at us with this overwhelmed look on his face and said in a shocked tone, "Is he ever like this at home?"

The doctor was not nearly as shocked as we were. This was a man who had seven or eight kids, apparently very well-behaved kids of his own. We were blown away by his response to Dylan's relatively minor explosion in his office. Amy and I looked at each other, looked at him, and said, "Are you kidding me? This is nothing." At that point, the doctor literally threw his arms up in the air and gave up working with Dylan. We had spent months giving Dylan tiny little white pills and trusting this doctor at his word that he was very capable of helping us with Dylan's behavior. What on earth had he been treating this whole time? Did he not believe us when we told him Dylan was explosive? Apparently his definition of an explosive child was dramatically different from what we had been experiencing. We were left with empty promises and disappointment in another professional who claimed he could help us. We still did not have the answer to Amy's comment from several years earlier, "Something's not right with Dylan." We wondered, "What was it and would anyone ever help us?"

Next Special Interest: Star Wars

Toward the second half of Dylan's first grade year, he continued to have his interest in birds but it began to wane a little when Star Wars came out with their twentieth anniversary re-release, entitled *Episode IV: The Original Star Wars*. I took Dylan to see it in the theater and from the moment he saw it, he was captivated. He loved the story and almost immediately started having an additional "special interest." Once again, we accommodated this interest as much as possible. We bought all the movies and Dylan would watch them over and over again. We also went out and bought the books for him and he would read them over and over again. And like the other special interests he had in the past, we just thought it was really interesting that he could be so focused on one topic.

Dylan and Sports

Dylan never really liked sports. In fact, he had very little interest in sports. I have always loved sports so, for a long time, it was not an easy thing for me to accept. When Dylan was little I signed him up for football, soccer, tennis, golf, and karate. None of those sports worked out very well and Dylan quickly gave up on them. Baseball, however, was a sport with which Dylan experienced some success both on and off the field. It also allowed me to coach him in the sport which has always been a great love of mine. Dylan played three years for Scarborough Little League and, more than his success on the field which even included a minor league all-star team selection, he made some real friends while being a part of a team. This was something

Dylan had not experienced before and something he would not enjoy again after he completed Little League. For those eight weeks during those three springs, Dylan was just another kid playing baseball. The best reward for his time playing baseball resulted in having the ability to invite four friends from the team to Sebago Lake for his tenth birthday. I still smile every time I see the pictures from that birthday party. Dylan could not have been happier. His friendships with Eben Bradley, Pat Damicis, Adam Saltz and David Ornstein would later fade but if you brought those boys together again today I am sure they would laugh and reminisce about their days playing Little League baseball. For Amy and me those were special times. It meant so much to Dylan, and to us, to have kids who genuinely liked him and actually called him to play. It was rare and we remember those boys fondly.

Dylan also had success skiing—both waterskiing and snow skiing. As with baseball, they both presented me with an opportunity to bond with Dylan. I started snow skiing with Dylan when he was eight years old. It is not unusual for people in Maine to take up skiing as a way to get through the long winters, but for me it was a chance to spend time with Dylan. It also gave Amy a break. She was a stay-at-home mom and, therefore, the primary care giver for Dylan. She appreciated my taking Dylan skiing for the entire day. For me, it was not about the skiing. Spending a day driving almost two hours to the slopes with Dylan while listening to Kasey Kasem's Top 40 countdown, riding on the chair lifts alone with my son, and navigating the trails was more important than the skiing itself. We even went on a couple of overnight trips to the White Mountains of New Hampshire. I have not been skiing again since the last time we skied together.

It was on the water where Dylan really excelled. I started waterskiing at age seven and still enjoy few things more than cutting across the water of a beautiful Maine lake. Dylan first waterskied at age seven and by age nine was skiing on one ski. It was not uncommon for Dylan to ski for twenty or even thirty minutes! One day Dylan waterskied on the ocean, using one ski, from Pine Point in Scarborough to the mouth of the Saco River in Biddeford. That is 13.5 miles and it took him forty-five minutes. When I finally shut off the engine because I was worried about the number of lobster traps in the water, Dylan was upset with me because he wasn't done yet.

We will never forget the first time our son skied on one ski. We were on Crescent Lake visiting my Uncle Doug and Aunt Gail. Dylan wanted to take a ski run across the lake. After about ten minutes he was faced with some large waves. He made it through the waves, but when we looked up, he was missing a ski. To our shock and amazement, he continued waterskiing. He just slipped his open foot in the back of the remaining ski and, in an instant, Dylan had become a slalom water-skier. Shortly after that, he would begin getting up on one ski. He still is an impressive water-skier today.

Derek and Dylan while skiing in Maine

This Month's Diagnosis is . . . Tourette's

During this same period of time, we started noticing a lot of outbursts that were harder and harder to manage. Dylan was generally happy in first grade but when he became upset it was very difficult to settle him down. We also started to notice some peculiar behaviors. For example, his facial tics became more and more prevalent. We were not really sure what that was all about, but somebody told us it might be Tourette Syndrome. We did not know much about it but we knew it caused facial and vocal tics. Dylan had started making a guttural sound in the back of his throat earlier in life and we had not thought much about it at the time, thinking it was just an annoying noise he would make for whatever reason. The tics were getting more visual and obvious. We realized there was definitely something going on. His eye tics, which had been just an occasional occurrence, were becoming so frequent that he was having trouble focusing in school. It was also so noticeable that kids were starting to make fun of him. I think this was the first time Dylan had experienced any kind of feeling of being different from other kids. He never had noticed or cared before that he was different from others. Teachers would actually even be insensitive enough to tell him to stop it, as if he was doing any of these facial movements just to annoy them. His eyes would twitch, his chin would jut out, his neck would stretch, and he would turn his head and twist it in a jerky and almost physically painful looking motion. Sometimes he did not even notice he was doing it.

I'll never forget sitting in *Star Wars* and watching while he enjoyed the movie as his chin moved in and out and his head bounced up and down. And he sat there watching the movie as if none of it was happening. It was very upsetting. I went home and told Amy how hard it was to not tell him to stop or to just hold his head still for him.

One of the stranger moments for this time for me was when I went out on the road with one of my sales reps who had a facial tic. His eyes would twitch a lot. It was something everyone noticed but no one really talked about. We were driving around Massachusetts visiting his customers, and there was a moment of silence when I felt I could fill it in with a question I was dying to ask him. He knew about Dylan and some of the challenges we had had with him but he did not know anything about Dylan's facial tics. As we were driving along, I wondered to myself, "Is this something I could bring up? Could I ask him about his eye twitch?" It was awkward and uncomfortable. This sales rep had been working for me for a number of years and his wife worked at the company as well. She had actually worked directly with me when I was a sales rep, so I felt I knew them pretty well and had a solid enough relationship to talk to them about a personal issue.

So when that moment of silence came in the car, I turned to him and I said, "Jeff, do you mind if I ask you a very personal question?"

He said, "No, that's fine."

I said, "Dylan has been having a lot of facial tics lately. His chin juts out, he makes noises, and his eyes twitch. Some people are telling me it might be Tourette Syndrome and I was just wondering if anyone has ever diagnosed your eye twitch as a form of mild Tourette Syndrome." No one that I knew of had ever talked to him about his eye twitch because it was something you just didn't talk about as polite adults. However, given the situation with Dylan and the feeling of frustration that we were never getting any answers,

I broached the topic, expecting to hear that he either had or had not been diagnosed with Tourette's and how he had dealt with this eye twitch.

He turned to me and said, in all shock and awe, "I have an eye twitch?!"

At first I thought he was kidding, just pulling my leg, but he knew how serious this topic was so I quickly realized he wasn't kidding. If there were a shoe big enough to put in my mouth, I think I had just done it. I looked at him and awkwardly said, "Well...uh...yeah."

Immediately he jerked his head up in his rearview mirror and started looking at himself, "Since when do I have an eye twitch?"

I was speechless. Here I thought I was going to get some answers, but instead I just sent one of my employees to a place that he apparently didn't know existed—the possibility that maybe *he* had Tourette Syndrome. So I said, "Do you really not know that your eyes twitch a lot?"

He looked at me and said, "I have no idea what you're talking about."

At that point, I felt I had no choice but to minimize how his eyes twitched and change the subject as quickly as possible. I said, "Well it only happens on occasion, maybe when you're tired. Don't worry about it, it's no big deal." And then I immediately changed the topic to some business issue and that was the end of my research about Tourette Syndrome that day.

We had no idea what was causing Dylan's outbursts or his facial tics. We made some inquiries and brought him to a psychotherapist who specialized in Tourette Syndrome. After meeting with both Dylan and us, she concluded, not surprisingly, that Dylan had it. She also warned us what we had in front of us because of Dylan's Tourette Syndrome. She described a very unhappy childhood lay ahead for Dylan, explaining that he'd go to school and have to hold in the tics all day long and then when he got to his room after school, he would explode in tics for hours. She talked about the tension and stress he would feel from holding the tics back and discussed the outbursts and behavioral issues that would occur because of the frustration, and of course she talked about the social aspects of being so visibly different from other kids. It was a sobering and terrifying meeting.

On the way home, we stopped at the book store and bought a book about Tourette Syndrome. It was very difficult to hear all those predictions regarding Dylan's childhood but it also did not match the little that I knew about the neurological disorder. When I was in high school, there was a guy on my golf team who had Tourette Syndrome. Most of his tics were facial but once in a while; he would make a guttural noise. However, he was able to control it while on the golf course and was actually a very good golfer. I don't remember Tony, my golf teammate, being a particularly unhappy person. In fact, I would say, if anything, he was the opposite, always smiling and very friendly. He did not seem to be a social outcast or tormented in any way.

As we read the book about Tourette Syndrome and learned more about it, we had the same reaction we had with many other diagnoses. Our thoughts were, "Yeah, that sort of sounds like Dylan but not *really*." There were too many characteristics of people with Tourette Syndrome that did not match our child at all. Despite her diagnosis, we were not convinced. The diagnosis did not explain the big picture of Dylan's life and behaviors. We had also seen that the tics came and went. He had some, then he had others, but none of them seemed to stick. In most of the book, it talked about how the tics of people with Tourette Syndrome are consistent and ongoing, and we had read in other papers and articles about transitory tics—tics that came and went—especially with kids that had issues of one kind or another. Long story short, we did not see that therapist for very long because we just simply were not convinced that this was the crux of what made Dylan such a challenging child.

The Brain Doctor . . . Also Useless

Dylan continued to do well in first grade. His life at school and at home was as peaceful as it had been in several years. His special interest in birds was very easy for us to encourage and feed to keep him happy. He was focused on his special interest and his brain was being nourished by that special interest. The outbursts were still challenging but he was usually happy. If he was happy, our family was happy. We continued to wonder what it was that was not right with Dylan. Just because we were in a good phase it did not mean it would last. It did not change our goal of truly finding out what made Dylan different. We received a recommendation to get a neurologist's opinion. There was only one pediatric neurologist in greater Portland. Our options were quite limited unless we wanted to venture down to Boston.

We heard excellent things about Doctor Brazelle, so we called to make an appointment. Since he was the only pediatric neurologist in the area the wait was about five months. We figured we would probably wait about that long to see someone in Boston as well, so we made the appointment and patiently waited for our visit. In March of Dylan's first grade year we finally arrived at our appointment with the doctor. We were very excited with the anticipation that he might have answers. We went in to see him and after waiting almost half an hour in his waiting room, they finally took us to another room, where we waited some more. At last Doctor Brazelle came out to see us. He did not have much of a bedside manner. In fact we found him quite rude and almost disrespectful. He asked us three or four questions but appeared thoroughly uninterested in our answers. Then, in what may have been the silliest doctor visit we ever had he told Dylan to walk up and down the hallway of his office while he observed. I'm not a pediatric neurologist or psychologist but I couldn't for the life of me understand how he was going to tell us why Dylan has outbursts by asking us four questions and then having him walk up and down the hallway. He asked us a couple more questions and the visit was basically over. We were very disappointed. He had no answers and as best as we could tell had no interest in exploring what made Dylan the child that gave us such challenges. We left with our heads down, frustrated once again with a professional who had zero answers.

Watch my Eyes, the SORRY!® Experiment

There were many times in Dylan's youth when we knew something seemed off but we could never figure out exactly what it was that caused his different behavior or reaction to events. An example of this was when I was playing the board game, SORRY!, with Dylan. He loved the game and, if there is any skill to a board game, he was actually quite good at it. He knew when to use strategies like putting someone in Start even though putting another player in Start might appear better because they were closer to your Home area or using the 11 card to switch with someone setting them back even though moving 11 might appear a better move. If you have ever played SORRY! You know what I am talking about. He did not just pick a card and unthinkingly move ahead the recommended spaces. One thing I noticed, and to be honest, was annoying when I played board games with Dylan was that I had to remind him constantly that it was his turn. He was often distracted or would just look at the board after my turn, not making the connection that if my turn was completed it was now his turn to pick a card.

We knew that Dylan seemed to struggle with non-verbal language but we had no idea why. One day, while playing SORRY!, I decided I was not going to tell him it was his turn. Instead I simply went ahead with my turn and then, without words, stared him in the eyes and then looked at the board. I did this over and over again hoping that looking at him and then looking at the cards would alert him that it was his turn to pick a card. However, what

I discovered but couldn't explain was that over and over, every time I did this experiment, Dylan would just stare at me without any indication that my actions were alerting him to take his turn. Eventually I would give up and say, "Dylan, it's your turn." His lack of ability to decipher this quite simple non-verbal cue fascinated me. I told Amy about it but she, too, did not know what it was that caused this disconnect in his brain. We knew one thing, it wasn't because he was a "Spirited Child," had Tourette's or needed to see a chiropractor. There had to be a reason and we prayed that eventually someone would give us some answers.

— 4 —

Correct Diagnosis But Little Help

The Asperger's Diagnosis

Dylan entered second grade in Scarborough, Maine, in the fall of 1999. We had moved to our new home over the summer. It turned out to be not only one of the most challenging, but also one of the most pivotal years for us on our path with Dylan. We were very optimistic heading into the year because first grade had been so successful. We met with the school and told them some of the challenges they would face dealing with Dylan. Unfortunately the teacher that Dylan had in second grade was a woman who was just a couple of years away from retirement and also a couple of years beyond when she should have retired. She had no patience with any of the kids, especially with Dylan. In fact, Dylan would tell us stories of her walking around when the kids were in a circle and she would kick the kids' feet if their feet reached into the circle too far, and then Dylan would laugh and she would get mad. Dylan often found conflict like that funny and he had a hard time holding back laughter, especially during conflicts between people or in uncomfortable situations.

One thing we also discovered is that all the boys in our neighborhood were in this teacher's class. The best that we could later figure out was that the school knew they had a teacher that shouldn't be teaching anymore so all the new kids got stuck with her because the parents who had lived in Scarborough for a while knew she was awful.

As the year went on, it didn't take us very long to realize that, although we didn't have a name for what was wrong with Dylan, we knew that he was different. We knew that he had issues and there was some diagnosis that we would eventually find that would make sense. We just couldn't name it. However, his second grade teacher simply thought he was a bad kid, and she was not very subtle in her feelings toward him.

Interestingly enough, there was a student teacher in the classroom that year, a young lady attending school at the University of Southern Maine in Portland studying to be a teacher who, shortly into the year, discovered a little boy who was very different from the other boys. Dylan was now into cars and she asked if she could focus her final paper about her experience in that classroom about Dylan. That story later became a paper called "Joe and His Cars." She also, despite her schooling, never connected the dots or maybe never even knew that Asperger's was a possibility for Dylan.

School in second grade was not going well. We knew we had to get to the bottom of what was going on with Dylan, but we didn't know what to do because every time we turned around, someone was diagnosing him with something different. What we noticed over and over and over was that what they specialized in is what they diagnosed. The therapist that specialized in Spirited Child diagnosed him as a Spirited Child. The psychotherapist that specialized in Tourette Syndrome diagnosed him with Tourette Syndrome. The therapist that specialized in Obsessive Compulsive Disorder (OCD) inevitably diagnosed him with OCD.

In September of Dylan's second grade year, we received a letter in the mail from my brother Judd who lives in New York. Judd was reading an article in the *New York Times* about a fifteen-year-old African-American boy from the Bronx who had a new diagnosis called Asperger's Syndrome. They described it as a high-functioning form of autism and admitted that they didn't know much about it or how many people might be affected by it. However, they said it seemed to be more predominant in boys than girls, as autism is, and it was defined by social awkwardness and extreme special interests.

The boy in the story sounded remarkably like Dylan. The sticky note that my brother attached to this small story said, "Doesn't this sound like Dylan? Maybe you should check this out." What particularly struck my brother was the fact that this fifteen-year-old boy, when he was two or three years old, was fascinated to the point of being obsessed with vacuum cleaners. You can't say that about a whole lot of toddlers. The connection between this boy and Dylan was hard to miss. And yet we had gone to therapist after therapist who had missed Asperger's Syndrome as a potential diagnosis. Now at fifteen, the boy could take any two streets in New York City and tell how to get from one to the other by subway. There were no two streets in the five boroughs that he could not tell you the exact subway pattern that you would have to take to get from one street to the other. He had the entire subway system memorized. This is the kind of obsessive thinking that Judd had seen in Dylan with birds. Between the connection with the vacuum cleaners and the amazing ability to absorb information about one topic, it seemed like this may be something we should investigate.

Amy and I looked up Asperger's Syndrome and tried to get some information about it online. The internet was still pre-Google so it was not easy to find out about this disorder. We read that in 1944 a man named Hans Asperger, an Austrian psychiatrist first described this form of autism in a group of highly intelligent, verbally weak boys who were not engaged in their schoolwork but were extremely and intensely interested in one or two topics like trains, dinosaurs, or astronomy. He dubbed them the "little professors." Dr. Asperger challenged the commonly held belief that all children with autism were either cognitively disabled or mentally ill. Almost forty years later Dr. Asperger's research was still not translated from German to any other language. It was buried in scientific journals. In 1981, a woman named Dr. Lorna Wing, a British psychiatrist with an autistic daughter, discovered Dr. Asperger's study and had it translated to English. Her report, "Asperger's Syndrome: A Clinical Account" was published later that year. Prior to this publication the only one who had heard of Asperger's was Hans Asperger himself. It was Dr. Wing, along with fellow British psychologist Dr. Judith Gould, who created the now widely held idea that autism is a spectrum, not a set list of characteristics and behaviors. Reading about Asperger's Syndrome blew our minds and we were determined to find out if this was the source of Dylan's personality and struggles.

Amy and I brought this up to the OCD therapist whom Dylan was seeing at the time and she quickly brushed it off. I have no idea if she even knew much or anything about Asperger's Syndrome, but she acted like she did and basically told us that it was definitely not what he had. She said it was the OCD (which was her specialty) that Dylan was most impacted by. After going through so many therapists who couldn't help us, we had come to the point where we just didn't believe her. The days of taking a "professional" at their word had passed for us. This would, in the long run, become a very good thing. Too many people count on the "experts" to help them with their child when sadly, what we have found, is that few "experts" could help us with Dylan. That pattern continued right through his high school years.

Amy and I then had to figure how to determine if Dylan had Asperger's Syndrome. The first thing we did was the same thing we did with every previous diagnosis we received. We went out and bought a book. The book we bought was written by Tony Atwood, who was and still is the world's premier expert and *actual* expert on Asperger's Syndrome. The book was called, *Asperger Syndrome: A Guide for Parents and Professionals.*

As we read this book, we were torn between great relief and great sadness. The relief was that we felt we had finally discovered what was causing so many of Dylan's behaviors and the sadness was that, from all reports, there was no cure, very few treatments, and very few people who knew much about it. Based on our experience in the greater Portland area, we had little to no hope we were going to be able to find somebody who could help us.

As we continued through the book, we were shocked by how many times we could have replaced the words "the child" with "Dylan," and the sentence would have made perfect sense to us. Page after page, chapter after chapter, almost everything in the book spoke to us about Dylan. There were things about Asperger's Syndrome that we were learning that didn't fit Dylan and that's why they call it a spectrum. Every person diagnosed with it falls somewhere along a spectrum. Now it was up to us and whoever we could find to help to figure out where on that spectrum Dylan was and what we could do about it.

Our first step was to find someone who could give us that diagnosis that we were almost sure was the legitimate one. Amy had heard that they do testing at Maine Medical Center and what she said was, "That's probably the best place to go because they don't have a therapy program for Asperger's but they might be able to diagnose him." What that meant to us was that there was no "agenda." In our experience, the "agenda" was what had been holding us back all those years. The fact that every "expert" that saw Dylan diagnosed him with whatever their specialty was seemed too much of a coincidence for us to ignore and something we had to try to find a way past.

Dr. Ellen Popenoe, a neuropsychologist at McGeachey Hall at Maine Medical Center in Portland who did this kind of diagnosis, was recommended to us. We immediately called Dr. Popenoe for an appointment. Of course, appointments were not readily available and we had to wait three months before we could get in. It was scheduled for early December.

The visit with Dr. Popenoe would consist of an interview with Amy and me that would last a couple of hours and two days of testing with Dylan. We sat down with Dr. Popenoe and she started talking to us and asking us questions about Dylan. We went in with the hope that we would come out with an Asperger's diagnosis, but we were very clear with her that the reason we were there was not to get the diagnosis we wanted, but to get an un-biased, non-agenda driven diagnosis from a professional.

As with every discussion that we have had about Dylan that lasted for more than a few minutes, there were times that were very serious, almost somber. However, there were also times where we would laugh and take great joy in talking about how special and unique he was. But this meeting was mostly to talk about the challenges that we had with Dylan, his difficulty making friends, his social awkwardness, his "special-interests," and of course, his extreme outbursts and temper tantrums that would sometimes go on for hours and control the entire mood of our home. From the time Dylan was very little, he was the barometer for our family's mood and that would be the case right up until he moved to Utah at age twenty-one. If Dylan was having a good day, there was a high chance Amy was having a good day and our family would have a good day. But if Dylan was having a bad day, there was almost no way anybody else could have a good day. Sometimes we would even ask him, "If you're having a bad day, why do you have to bring everybody else down with you?" But of course, there was nothing he could do about it.

As we talked with the neuropsychologist, we had to try to keep the conversation within the timeframe she had available. We often find this difficult when the topic at hand is Dylan. Even today, when somebody asks "How's Dylan?" or "What's going on with Dylan?" it's almost impossible to answer that question in the timeframe they had in mind when they asked me. There's never a simple answer with Dylan, and truly answering the question "What's going on with Dylan?" is never brief.

After we finished the conversation with Dr. Popenoe, we went home and talked more about the possibility that Dylan had Asperger's Syndrome. It was a topic we couldn't stop talking about when Amy and I were alone.

The next day we brought Dylan in for his meeting with her. One of the things she told us, in preparation for the testing for Dylan, was to expect him to possibly be very irritable or tense and almost definitely exhausted at the end of each of the two days because she would be putting him through a battery of tests that would push him to answer questions and to perform tasks, quite often timed. But what she didn't know about Dylan was that he actually loves these kinds of tests and would continue to love them right up through high school. Each time Dylan took a neurological evaluation test, and he would take many of them over the years, he enjoyed it. Dylan has always been very interested in learning more about how his brain works. He has had tremendous insight from the time he was very young on why he would say and do things if you could ask him at the right time. If you tried to ask him why he was having a temper tantrum during the temper tantrum, of course you would get nowhere. But, if the timing was right and you could explore how he saw his brain working, his insights were often amazing.

Dylan went through these tests like a champ and Dr. Popenoe was surprised how much he seemed to enjoy them. He was also happy to have a couple of days off from school and away from the teacher who quite obviously didn't care if he was around or not and probably preferred that he wasn't. A couple of weeks went by before Dr. Popenoe finally called us to tell us that she had the results and asked us to make an appointment to meet with her.

We were nervous in anticipation for what she was going to say about our son, but the prospect of finally finding out Dylan's diagnosis was so exciting, we booked an appointment as soon as we could.

Dr. Popenoe gave us a twelve-page, very detailed report on her research and findings regarding the diagnosis. She discussed the results of the various tests he took, including the Children's Memory Scale, NEPSY: A Developmental Neuropsychological Assessment, the Wechsler Intelligence Scale for Children-III, the Wechsler Individual Achievement Test, and several other tests, interviews, and questionnaires that evaluated Dylan in extreme detail. Amy and I listened intently but all we could focus on was whether or not she was going to give us the diagnosis we so desperately needed.

Finally, she explained her conclusion based on the results of the study:

> Dylan Volk is an eight-year-old boy who has a history of difficulties with attention and impulsivity as well as some motor and speech delays, accompanied by what are now good expressive and receptive language skills. Social relationships are extremely impaired; he has no peer relationships and is quite isolated. He is also impulsive, has very poor tolerance for frustration and poor ability to adapt to change. He has always had odd and intense preoccupations; when younger it was vacuum cleaners and now is Top 40 songs. He never engaged in imaginary play. The results of this evaluation indicate that Dylan has extremely variable abilities, ranging from the superior to extremely low range. Verbal intellectual abilities are in the superior range, while nonverbal intellectual abilities range from extremely low to average. Visual special processing and visual motor integration skills are low to high average, depending on the complexity of the stimuli. Of serious concern, however, is that Dylan demonstrates severe weakness in nonverbal reasoning abilities, with these abilities in the borderline to extremely low range. This is in sharp contrast to his superior verbal abilities.
>
> The results of this evaluation indicate Dylan is experiencing

a developmentally based neurocognitive disorder that affects nonverbal abilities, sensory processing, and fine motor control. Dylan's pattern of strengths and weaknesses is most consistent with a pattern of learning problems often described as a nonverbal learning disorder. This pattern, along with his severely impaired interpersonal relationships, lack of imaginary play, and his stereotyped and restricted patterns of interests and activities, indicates that Dylan is also experiencing Asperger's Disorder, a form of Pervasive Developmental Disability.

As a result of these strengths and weaknesses, Dylan is likely to have difficulty grasping new and complex language and concepts. He will tend to make very literal and functional interpretations of new material and will have difficulty grasping underlying structure and developing strategies. He will also have difficulty with organization, grasping the big picture, and the overall theme of new material. Dylan's interpersonal difficulties are likely influenced by his difficulties with picking up and responding to the visual and nonverbal aspects of communication.

We finally had a firm diagnosis, a diagnosis that made sense, a diagnosis that had power: autism. We were strangely excited about having a diagnosis that would help Dylan in the school system because at the time, we thought it actually would. And then we had our meeting at Pleasant Hill School, the elementary school Dylan was attending. We sat down with the principal, his teacher, and the special education director, and we presented the evidence that Dylan had Asperger's Syndrome, a form of autism. It gave us some power with the schools that we had not had before. Prior to this, they would just put him down with some random, nondescript disability that did not really provide him with any real services. Now, with autism, we could hopefully get some of the services he needed.

We were disappointed but not shocked when his nearly-retired second grade teacher literally rolled her eyes and seemed completely uninterested in the discussion we were having about Dylan being on the autism spectrum. She showed no tact or respect at all in regards to the diagnosis, and basically told us that she thought it was inaccurate. Fortunately, there was nothing she could do because we had a diagnosis from a professional and in the public schools that meant something to them.

Now the question was, what do we do with it? We talked about putting

Dylan in special education classes, but at the time we did not feel like that was necessary, partly because we didn't really even understand what special education classes were. In our minds, like in the minds of many people, the vision of a special education child is one of a child who is slow, maybe with a physical disability as well, and clearly not like the other kids.

Although we knew Dylan was not like the other kids, we were resistant to putting him in a special education class. And so we began many years of special education technicians. These are people that are trained, or supposed to be trained, to work with kids with special needs. We would learn later the hard way, as we always did, that oftentimes the person that was assigned to a special education child had no particular training whatsoever. They were simply a body that was willing to get paid little as an ed-tech to do very challenging work.

Next Special Interest: CARS

Dylan's interest in birds disappeared almost as quickly as it arrived. For a little while he was a very unhappy kid. We always said the worst time for Dylan is when he's between special interests, when one special interest fades and he hasn't figured out what the next one will be. He didn't know what to do with himself and we didn't know what to do with him. He was bored with his life and didn't like it.

One thing I was frustrated to learn about Asperger's is that you cannot force or even tilt an Asperger's child towards a special interest. The interest has to come from within. And that interest often becomes their identity. Dylan once told us, when he was losing interest in birds, that it made him depressed to not have a special interest. He said, "When I was into birds I was 'Dylan, the kid who loves birds' but then I became just Dylan." Many kids with Asperger's have a special interest in baseball. I'm a huge baseball fan. I have always loved baseball. Baseball is the ultimate sport for people with Asperger's. There are a hundred years of statistics and data. There are hundreds of players every year coming in and out of major league baseball to learn about and track. I devised a plan to read Dylan a book about baseball's hundred greatest players with the hopes that he might find all the statistics intriguing enough to make baseball his new special interest. Every night as I put him to bed I read a book published by the *Sporting News* that listed in order, according to them, the hundred greatest players in history. We started at number 100 and worked our way down. Every night rereading the names of the ones we had

already covered I thought was the kind of thing I knew he had the potential
to grasp. A couple of weeks later when I saw Dylan looking at the book all by
himself I was beside myself with excitement. "I did it!" I thought, "I did it."
Special interest "Operation Baseball" was a success. Dylan is going to become
obsessed with baseball. I went over to talk to Dylan and said, "Hey buddy,
what are you reading about?" He started telling me how different players had
been born in the same year or on the same day. Instead of memorizing their
batting average, on base percentage, home runs or strikeouts he was memorizing their birthdays. He had no interest in the stats. Dylan couldn't care
less about Walter Johnson's wins or Ty Cobb's batting average. He wasn't
interested in how many games Cal Ripkin Jr. played without missing one and
he didn't give two hoots about Joe DiMaggio's hitting streak. But he could
tell you the year in which almost all 100 had been born and died. While I was
tremendously impressed that he had the ability to memorize all the birthday
and death days, I was disappointed that my plan was unsuccessful.

Not long after the baseball attempt, Dylan started talking about cars.
He started asking questions about different cars and looking in the Sunday
paper about all the cars that were for sale. Within a matter of a few weeks, cars
were all Dylan wanted to talk, read, and think about. In much the same way
as the bird phase, we found the addiction to cars not only interesting because
we learned so much as well, but it was pretty easy to feed and keep interesting.
The knowledge level Dylan reached about cars was similar to his knowledge
level about birds. It was amazing. I don't say this lightly when I say his ability
to retain information about all the different cars on the market was nothing
short of brilliance. He knew all the features of all the cars. It got to the point
where he could tell you at night what make a car coming toward us was, and
in most cases he was right. It was almost like a Vegas act. "Hey for fifty dollars
I bet you my son can identify the make and model of the car coming down
the street in the dark." We spent our Saturdays during Dylan's second grade
year visiting car dealerships. When he spent time with his grandparents they
would do the same. He sat in the cars and asked questions of the sales rep and
he brought home stacks and stacks of flyers. He sat and read through all of
them, studying as if studying for an exam. When we were at the dealership
it was inevitable that someone would ask him, "So, do you want to sell cars
when you go grow up?" Dylan would always look at them and say, "No,
I'm going to own the dealership." His dream of being an ornithologist was
replaced with the dream of owning a car dealership where he could spend his
days talking about cars.

I remember in February of Dylan's second grade year, I had a good customer in Gorham called the Foreside Company. The buyer that I worked with was named John Pitcher and we became quite friendly as I serviced the account for several years. I got Celtics tickets and invited John to the game. I told him Dylan would come along and asked him to find a fourth. He decided to take his brother Joel. Our plan was to meet at Volk Packaging in Biddeford before driving down to Boston. Dylan and I arrived first and waited for John and Joel. A few minutes later they pulled up in a large Ford pick-up truck. They got out of the car, grabbed some belongings and jumped into my car. John sat in the front and Joel sat in the back with Dylan. Dylan turned to Joel and said, "Is that your truck?" Joel, beaming like a peacock, puffed out his chest and said, "Yeah it is! I just got it." Dylan cocked his head and said, "Big mistake." I immediately dropped my head in embarrassment. Joel said, "What do you mean 'big mistake'?" Dylan then went on to inform Joel of all the reasons why the Toyota Tacoma was a superior vehicle to the Ford F-150 and what a big mistake he had made purchasing his new car. Unfortunately, Dylan had all the information and data in his head. As embarrassing as it was, it was pretty hard to argue with. Joel just laughed with good nature and said, "Aw man, I bought the wrong truck!" We all had a good laugh and continued to Boston to enjoy the Celtics game.

On Dylan's ninth birthday we asked him how he wanted to celebrate. Did he want to have a party? This was always very awkward because Dylan rarely had enough friends or even good acquaintances to fill a birthday party. On his ninth birthday, still obsessed with cars, he told us he didn't want to have a birthday party. He wanted to spend his birthday at a car dealership. I had recently become involved in a new organization in Portland based out of the University of Southern Maine called the Institute for Family-Owned Business. Through this organization, I met Adam Lee, the owner of the vast Lee Auto Mall in Portland and Auburn areas. I called Adam and asked if he would be willing to host Dylan for a day. I explained to him that Dylan had Asperger's and was really into cars. Adam was extremely gracious and said he would be happy to have Dylan spend some time with him on his birthday.

We arrived at Lee Auto Mall in Westbrook around 9:00am. Dylan was so excited. It was like Christmas morning for most kids. We pulled into the parking lot near the offices and walked in. I introduced Dylan to Adam. Dylan said, "Is that your 1997 BMW?

Adam said, "Yes, it is. How did you know it was a '97 and not a '96 or '98?"

Dylan then went into great detail with Adam about the shape and tinting of the headlights on the '97 versus the other models as well as the angles of the frame that made it different. Adam was blown away. He walked Dylan over to a desk with an older gentleman sitting in a chair. He said, "Dylan, this is Jim, my used cars manager. Jim, this is your replacement."

Dylan got quite a kick out of that comment and was probably wondering when he would be able to start. The rest of the day was spent going from car to car sitting in them, looking through the inside (mostly the dashboard, or IP as he called it, the instrument panel, as that was his favorite part of the car) and test driving as many as Adam was willing to let us take out. It was probably the best birthday Dylan has ever had and it is a day I will never forget. I only see Adam Lee about once a year but I never hesitate to thank him again for that very special day.

DYLAN'S TAKE: *I'm really glad I found an interest in cars because the interest in birds, while educational, was not a very cool special interest. Being into cars was fun because it is pretty normal for guys to like cars. The special interest in birds didn't stick with me at all. I had pretty much forgotten everything I knew about birds a year or so after the interest faded. However, I still to this day am very knowledgeable about cars. It is more at a healthy level of interest than an obsession like it was back then. I'm glad I went through this phase and that it kind of always stuck with me. I don't tend to like very many "guy things." I find watching sports so pointless I can't even have a conversation with another guy about football teams (or whatever a typical example would be) but I can still pick up a* Motor-Trend *magazine and talk about the coolest new cars of 2015. So, even if I'm looking at the latest in pickup trucks while watching* Sex and the City *re-runs and petting my cat, it's kind of a saving grace for me and my manliness.*

Anxiety Behaviors

Dylan started third grade about the same way he finished second grade—it was rocky. He was in a new school that was a combination of three elementary schools in our town, so it was a very large school compared to Pleasant Hill. Wentworth Intermediate was grades three through five with about 300 kids per grade. These are all the same kids he would eventually graduate with, as they would continue on through Wentworth, the middle school, and then the high school.

His class was in the multi-age program. We decided that a multi-age program would be best for him because it was too difficult every year to re-explain how Dylan worked to new teachers. Our hope was to find a good fit for him for those three years critical to his education. We were very nervous that the wrong fit for three years could be a disaster for Dylan and for us, both at school and at home. We were happy very early on, after meeting his teacher, Christine Woodward, because she not only had the patience for Dylan but she was willing to be flexible to help him succeed in school. He was also assigned an ed-tech, an older woman named Nancy Gage. She also was very kind and patient with Dylan, and actually seemed to like him, which was very important, as we would discover year after year. A teacher that didn't like Dylan was never going to work because Dylan knew when people didn't like him and reacted accordingly.

In late September, we sat down for his annual special education review, which always occurred a few weeks after school started. There were a number of people in the room as there always were when we had a meeting for Dylan. Amy would remark a few years later after one of these meetings how she was overwhelmed by how many people it took just to get Dylan through a day of school, and that would be the case from second grade right through his senior year.

We sat down at the meeting with the principal, his teacher, his ed-tech, the occupational therapist, the counselor who ran the social skills group, the school nurse, the social worker, and the school administrative special education director. All of those people were taking time out of their day for one child. Ms. Woodward, his teacher, and Mrs. Gage, his ed-tech, opened up the conversation. They said that academically Dylan was doing okay. He was struggling in math but was ahead of his grade for his reading ability, reading somewhere around the fourth grade level and decoding well, but his comprehension was not as high. His math skills were there but he had a hard time focusing on math and would often act up or be silly or just inattentive during work time.

It was the summer before third grade that Dylan first started picking at his skin. This would later become an on-going problem that would create scabs and scars all over his body and continued to be a challenge for him into his twenties. We first noticed it with mosquito bites in the summer. He would get mosquito bites and they would never heal because he would pick and pick until they bled. They would scab and he would pick at them, thus becoming an on-going cycle. As Dylan headed into his first year at Wentworth, without anyone knowing him, this was one of the first impressions they had—a boy covered with open wounds and scabs. He often picked at them so much in fact that his socks would turn red or he would have blood dripping down his leg. It was not only unsightly but unhealthy as well, and rather disturbing. It was similar to a form of cutting that often is related to people with mental issues and it was also therapeutic in a strange sort of way for him. When he got anxious or nervous or overwhelmed, it gave him something to do to distract his brain. His teachers were reporting that during math he picked at his skin to the point where he would get his math work all bloody and no one would even want to touch it to give him a grade.

Amy noticed one day that he had a strange bald spot on the back of his scalp. Dylan had started pulling chunks of hair right out of his head when he was anxious. We were overwhelmed with how to handle these strange anxiety behaviors and were getting very little help from any professionals.

The good news was that his teachers reported that there was no reason they could see that Dylan couldn't do the work. He had the cognitive ability to accomplish the schoolwork of a third grader. However, his behavioral issues were so distracting to him that the work rarely got done on time or at all. We asked them what they were doing to help him overcome these issues that were hindering his academic advancement. Then we went on to the occupational therapist.

Dylan was working with the same occupational therapist at the beginning of third grade that he was working with at the end of second grade. She was a young woman in her early twenties, no more than a year or two out of school. We noticed a trend later with occupational therapists that they were quite often under twenty-five years old. I'm not sure what happens to them after they spend a couple of years in the school system, but they always seem to disappear. The woman that was the occupational therapist for Dylan in second and third grade was very kind and patient with him, but she pushed Dylan to do things that he was not comfortable with and to talk about things that he wasn't comfortable talking about (his anxiety, his picking at his skin). Most of the things that she wanted him to do were physical. Dylan never liked physical activities, and so he called her "the criminal."

She would make him lift things, put weights on his back and walk around with them, weight-bearing therapies they felt would help his behavioral issues. We would continue to hear right through middle school that these kinds of activities would be helpful for Dylan. We never saw any sign that they were. I would sit in these meetings and think, "How is doing wheelbarrow exercises around a room going to help change his behavior?"

It really didn't make any sense to me, but I just figured at the time that they're the professionals so they must know what they're talking about. I'm just an overwhelmed dad trying to get his kid through the school day while maintaining a job and raising two other kids, so I never questioned it verbally. But I certainly did with Amy, and she felt the same way.

We then heard from the social skills teacher, Tori Vaillancourt. Her task was to gather a bunch of kids together who all apparently had poor social skills and to help them try to learn from each other and from her how they could improve their social skills. Dylan would attend these kinds of classes for several more years until he finally refused to go to any more social skills groups. He went to them at school and we also had set him up with private groups. Dylan was usually a star in these settings because he did not fit the profile of most kids with social skills issues. Many of the kids in the group, although not yet diagnosed on the autism spectrum, would most likely be diagnosed at some point later. Asperger's was still a very rare diagnosis in the year 2000, at least in Maine. Some of the kids in the group were just exceedingly shy, the kinds of kids that would hide behind a couch when company would come. Dylan was anything but that child, so when he got in a room full of very shy kids or recluse kids, he often looked like a rock star in comparison. He would be very engaging and seemed to have all the right answers. The problem was that it was all a mirage. He had no actual ability to use the skills that he talked about in these classes in real life situations, so he would attend social skills groups for the next several years receiving almost no tangible benefits and remain incapable of connecting with his peers.

As expected, Mrs. Vaillancourt reported that Dylan had "wonderful insights" and then she talked about how he would have a comment about every topic that was brought up, sometimes to the point of talking too much in the group. Dylan was too social for a social skills group and yet had no social skills. She also reported that Dylan was exceedingly honest. We would see that later in many of these kinds of environment. Dylan has always desperately wanted to change his behavior and his life situation and was never shy when talking about his deficits. When Mrs. Vaillancourt found that Dylan was being too vocal or getting silly during the group, she would send him to a quiet spot in the room, basically put him in a corner, where he could decompress and get himself together.

The final presenter during the meeting was the school nurse. She reported many of the same behavioral issues, even in her brief visits with Dylan, about being silly and not being able to settle himself down. Her biggest concern was the picking of his skin. She was very concerned that all these open sores would eventually get infected and would cause Dylan some bigger problems than just some bloody school assignments. Another disturbing behavior that teachers were seeing and caused the nurse great concern was Dylan's recent behavior of spitting on his hand and then rubbing it on his face. When he would get anxious, he would get hot and sweaty, and when he would get hot and sweaty, his reaction was to spit on his hand and then rub it on his face, often causing his face to get filthy from his dirty hands and grossing everybody out. It made his schoolwork sloppy with saliva. It would get on the desk and on the pencils and really alienated other kids. This was strictly tied to his anxiety and they felt it needed to be handled medically. We would later talk to his psychiatrist about it as well.

When the meeting was over, they decided that Dylan would need thirty minutes a week of occupational therapy, fifteen minutes a week of consult with the occupational therapist, thirty to sixty minutes a week of social work consult, the social skills group twice a week, thirty minutes a week of special education consult, ed-tech thirty-five hours a week and health consult up to fifty minutes per week. All of those were required to get Dylan through school. What we learned years later was that as important as many of these things were or seemed to be, they were all interruptions and distractions to Dylan's education. This is why, years later, when he graduated high school, we would look back and see that his behavioral issues were so consuming that they took the place of his actual education.

Don't Pat the Dog!

Dylan's fourth grade year was a rocky one as he really began to feel the impacts of his social inadequacies. Despite the fact that he had a caring teacher and attentive ed-tech, Dylan's anxiety was extremely high heading into fourth grade. He was overwhelmed with school and the workload of a fourth grader. He was still mainstreamed for all his classes so he was trying to keep up both socially and academically while being pulled out of class frequently for all his services. The teachers also reported that he was becoming more and more argumentative and he seemed to be losing the ability to focus that they saw in third grade. It was not surprising to us that Dylan was becoming more argumentative. The more comfortable he was with someone the more he felt he could argue with them to get what he wanted. In third grade he was still getting to know his teachers. Now that he was in the second year of a three-year multi-age program he was becoming much more comfortable and, as we expected, more argumentative. To deal with his anxiety, it was recommended that we take another look at his medications. We were still uncomfortable with Dylan being on medication, but we were starting to feel like there was no other option as professional after professional told us that he needed to be medicated. It was very difficult to find a local child psychiatrist. Someone recommended a new local psychiatrist so we made an appointment.

We went in to see the psychiatrist and almost immediately had a sense that it was not going to be a good fit. She had a dog in her office and Dylan went up to pat it. The dog growled and she grabbed it by the collar and pulled it back, trying to get it to lie on its bed. She then told us that the dog did not like children. We had no idea how to respond to that with Dylan because his lack of impulse control and his affection for dogs made it very difficult, if not impossible, for him to resist reaching out to pat the dog and yet, this child psychiatrist, who deals with young children with social and emotional difficulties on a daily basis, brought a dog to work every day that didn't like children. It made absolutely no sense to us, and almost immediately, she lost all credibility.

We stuck with her for a while because we had no other choice. We were told that she knew about Asperger's, and at the time very few professionals knew much about it. However, her knowledge was very superficial and didn't appear to be much deeper than what she had read in magazine articles or medical publications. She certainly had never come across anyone like Dylan, a child who didn't fit the typical Asperger's profile of being shy and reclusive. She recommended some meds to us, but we didn't see much of a difference in Dylan's behavior so we started looking for a different psychiatrist.

The Medication Merry-Go-Round

When Dylan was three years old his teachers told us he needed to be on Ritalin. They saw impulsive behavior and assumed he must have Attention Deficit Hyperactivity Disorder (ADHD) so Ritalin would be the quick fix. I am not sure his two pre-school teachers had any idea there was such a thing as Asperger's Syndrome, but in 1994 almost no one knew of Asperger's. Their logic was that he is a boy, he is impulsive and sometimes hyper, and it must be ADHD. We resisted and refused to put our three-year-old on a mind-altering drug based on the advice of a pre-school teacher. We were able to push away the idea of giving any medications to Dylan until the winter of his first grade year when he was suffering from tics. They were bothering him and making him feel very different from the other kids so we gave in. His first medication, at age seven, was Clonidine. Although it is primarily used to treat high blood pressure, Clonidine had shown some effective results for people with tics.

The doctor felt it would not only help with his tics but also some of his explosive behavior. What we later learned was that it is also a powerful sedative. Dylan had become addicted to it in order to fall asleep, and by fall of that year he could not get to sleep without his Clonidine. He would often wake up in the middle of the night to go to the bathroom and, without the Clonidine in his system anymore, he'd be up for the day. By 2:00 the next afternoon he was falling asleep at his school desk. We started weaning him and by Christmas he was back to his normal sleep pattern. The following spring (age eight) we finally gave in and allowed a trial of Ritalin. After two months we saw no difference in his behavior so we took him off that drug as well. The med parade would continue with no great, long lasting results for any of them. He was on Prozac (age nine), Tenex (nine and a half), Adderall (eleven), back on Clonidine (eleven), Strattera (eleven and a half), Seroquel (eleven and a half) and Zoloft (eleven and a half).

Dylan began seeing a doctor named Dr. Key. Dr. Casey Key was a child psychiatrist located in Biddeford, only a mile or so from my office. In 2003, at age eleven and three-quarters, Dylan had been on or was on so many different medications Dr. Key was having a difficult time, as were we, figuring out which ones were working. At age twelve we took him off all medications so we could re-establish a baseline. A few weeks later Dylan started taking Lexapro. We saw some positive effects of this med but it was making him gain a lot of weight. He was now headed toward middle school and any benefits it was having for him were offset by the anxiety it was causing because he was gaining so much weight. In July he stopped the Lexapro and started taking Adderall again. He was also taking Seroquel at night or when he was extremely anxious.

Dr. Key told Dylan he needed to increase the Seroquel to three times per day. This meant Dylan would have to go to the nurse at school to take his mid-day dosage. Dylan was vehemently opposed to this idea. Dr. Key pushed back telling Dylan is was the next necessary step for him. Dylan told Dr. Key and us that there was no way he was going to the nurse's office during the school day. It is hard enough for him to be seen in the special education room all day so there was no negotiation about visiting the nurse because everyone would know he was taking medication. We explained to Dylan that there are a lot of kids that have to visit the nurse during the day so he should not feel uncomfortable. Dylan's response was one I will never forget. He looked right at Amy and said, "Let me ask you a question. Would you have a problem taking a poop right now in front of Dr. Key? I bet you would. So, would you feel any more comfortable if I told you that lots of people were taking a poop in front of Dr. Key?" That was the end of that discussion. We all agreed that Dylan did not have to take a mid-day medication.

He later went on to more Adderall, Topamax (age twelve and a half), Depakote (twelve and a half), Risperdal (twelve and a half), more Depakote (especially when he was out of control), Buspirone (thirteen and a half) which he felt made him extremely "spacey." At age fourteen he tried Abilify but said it made him jittery and also seemed to cause quick weight gain. At fourteen and a half he was put on Focalin to help with his anger issues but it created terrible tics so we stopped that med in less than a month. At age sixteen we left Dr. Key and began seeing a psychiatric nurse practitioner named Ronnie Noiles. We had lost confidence in Dr. Key and felt it was time for a fresh look at Dylan's medication needs. He was put back on Strattera and at seventeen was taken off Depakote because of concerns with his immune deficiency. Tests were done that showed Dylan's white blood cell count had dropped to dangerously low levels. At seventeen and a half we noticed that his tongue was hanging out of his mouth so he was taken off Abilify which was causing that side effect.

This potential side effect and no good answers led us to the decision to leave Ms. Noiles. We took Dylan to see Dr. Joseph Bowdon who was located in our hometown of Scarborough. Dylan was now eighteen years old so he was able to make his own medical decisions. Dr. Bowden put him on Amitriptyline and put him back on Adderall. He also later added Intuniv. Dylan graduated from high school and went to Florida to join New Directions for Young Adults. There he started with Dr. Michael Presley who, over the course of a few months, put him on Strattera, Luvox, Zolpidem, Adipex and Vyvanse.

We eventually lost track of what he was taking for medications until his brush with insanity in 2011. If I had to do it all over again I would never go more than twelve months without checking with another doctor to see what they would suggest. Most of these medications have no long term studies about their impact on the developing brain of a child. If there was ever an example of why they call it "practicing medicine" it would be what we experienced watching doctors try to medicate Dylan into a different person.

"Seriously, That's All You've Got?"

Things continued to spiral downhill in fifth grade. We were not sure what was going on in school. We would often find when Dylan would start to feel comfortable with somebody, he would push the envelope. We had a strong suspicion that was exactly what was happening in December of his fifth grade year. His ed-tech and his teacher had been working with Dylan for almost three years now, and he was very comfortable with them. For most kids, if a child started feeling comfortable with a teacher and making an emotional bond with that teacher, the child would feel more obligated to behave and get along. But Dylan always seemed to do the opposite. He was very argumentative and difficult at home as well. We were finding ourselves in constant battles with him about everything and as he moved into fifth grade, he started getting bigger, stronger, and more defiant, making it very difficult for Amy, who was the front line of most of his hostility.

We were once again looking for somebody that could help us. There had to be somebody out there who could give us some strategies for effectively dealing with Dylan, his outbursts and his tantrums. It was about this time that Dylan would get even angrier, especially at me, when I used the word tantrum. I would call them "temper tantrums" and he would get extremely irate with me. There was a certain part of me that fed that tantrum by calling them temper tantrums. I was so angry with him for what he was doing to our home life, and I knew how much he hated me calling his outbursts temper tantrums, that I would knowingly and verbally refer to them as such in a somewhat twisted attempt to demean him by using a word that is generally tied to two-year-olds. I think that's probably exactly why he didn't like the term; he knew that it was generally used when referring to a crying fit by a toddler. It offended him to be described in that fashion, and that's exactly why I did it. Looking back, it was probably immature of me and it certainly didn't help the situation, but I couldn't help myself.

My bitterness toward the destruction that he was causing in our family made me want to hurt him and since we had decided before he was even born that we would never physically strike our children, no matter what they did, this was my way of striking out at him and making him hurt for how he was hurting our family. I can't say I look back proudly at that admission, but I can do so with honesty that that's why I did it. I don't recall Amy ever using that term with Dylan, so I can understand, intellectually, what I was really trying to accomplish. When he was having one of his extreme outbursts, there was nothing in the term "temper tantrum" and using it out loud to him that helped diminish or extinguish the circumstances that we were facing.

We started asking around again for the umpteenth time since Dylan was born, trying to find somebody who had some kind of knowledge about Asperger's who might be willing to meet with us. We were at the point where we almost felt like there was nothing we could do to change Dylan, and so we needed someone to help us learn how to work with him as much as we needed someone to help with his behavior. A friend of ours referred us to a man who was both a counselor and psychiatrist in downtown Portland. We were told he had a vast experience with kids on the spectrum and would be very helpful to us. We called and made an appointment to see him as soon as we could.

On our first visit, we sat down privately with Dr. Bookman. He asked us a lot of questions and gave us several questionnaires to fill out and bring back. He wanted some detail about the different times of day Dylan had his outbursts, what caused them, how we react, and how Dylan reacts to how we react. They were sort of like journals of his meltdowns. Dylan came in and the three of us sat with Dr. Bookman. Whenever we would sit with Dylan in a counseling session, it never lasted peacefully for more than five or ten minutes before we were in the middle of some kind of argument because we would say something that he felt was untrue or he would say something that would not match the actual circumstance. Dylan had a really hard time with our opinions on his behavior and often had a much distorted view about how his behavior impacted Amy and me as well as the family dynamic as a whole. This circumstance was no different at Dr. Bookman's office. Within a few minutes, we were at battle in an argument about arguments. It was rather ironic.

We left the session, brought the questionnaires home, and started filling them out. We brought them in to Dr. Bookman each time we would meet with him. He would meet with Amy and me followed by a private session with Dylan and then we would sit down all together. The majority of the time was spent with just Amy and me. Dr. Bookman wanted to help us better manage Dylan's behavior, and the best way to do that was to change the way we approached our challenges with him instead of trying to change him directly. If we could change the way we dealt with him, he would ultimately change himself. This continued for six or seven weeks, going in every week and meeting for an hour, sometimes even a little longer.

In our seventh week sitting down with Dr. Bookman, Amy and I were getting very frustrated because we were doing all the talking and we did not really feel like he had provided us with any help at all. We continued week after week in almost constant conflict with Dylan. If we said the sun was out, he'd say it was cloudy. If we said it was cold, he'd say it was hot. *Everything* was an argument. And you could never just have an argument with Dylan; he had to *win* the argument. In fact, it was about this time of his life when he made the comment, "You're not arguing if you're right. You're the one who's doing the arguing. I'm not arguing because I'm just stating fact." That's the way Dylan saw the world. He was right and everybody else was arguing with him about what he knew to be fact, no matter what the situation or the circumstances around him. It was impossible to end an argument with him and just agree to disagree. The argument would not end until we saw "the facts," which was always whatever his opinion was.

When we went to see Dr. Bookman on the seventh week. He told us that he appreciated all the information we had given him and that he would like to talk to us about how to move forward working with Dylan.

"Finally!" we thought, "He's finally going to give us something we could use to make our home life a little more peaceful."

He then proceeded to talk for almost twenty minutes about creating a sticker chart. A sticker chart! We had just spent almost two months pouring our heart out and begging this so-called "expert" to help us with our fifth-grade son who was having daily meltdowns that often turned into hours of yelling and screaming, and his answer was a sticker chart. I was blown away. I looked at him and said, "That's what you have for us…a sticker chart? For our eleven-year-old-son? A sticker chart? Are you kidding me?"

Dr. Bookman was taken aback by my confrontational reaction, but I was so devastated that yet another "expert" was letting us down. We could have picked up a *Parents* magazine or typed in *parenting 101* on a search engine to come up with a sticker chart. When our son was having a meltdown, you could walk up to him with a running chainsaw in your hand, hold it up to his shoulder, and say, "I am going to cut your arm off right now if you don't settle down," and Dylan would not be capable of settling down. This guy actually thought that putting a bunch of stickers on a piece of paper and posting it on the refrigerator was actually going to change Dylan's behavior. I asked him, "Do you have any other suggestions?"

Dr. Bookman said, "No I really think this will work."

"You have no other suggestions? This is all you have for us….a sticker chart?" He just kept reiterating over and over again that this was a very effective form of parenting.

We left that appointment almost distraught that we were going to have to find somebody else and start all over again seeking help. That's all Dr. Bookman had. One issue of *Parenting* magazine could have saved us a lot of time and money. There we were in the middle of the winter, sitting in our car in downtown Portland, wondering who we would turn to next in our efforts to figure out how to parent this very difficult child.

Dr. Kermit—Another Expert Disappoints Us

Our next idea, since we were running into road block after road block in Portland, was to go to Boston. We decided to call a local autism organization. Through that organization we were able to get an appointment to have a meeting with Doctor Chandler Kermit. Dr. Kermit was a well-respected author who had written many papers and a couple of books about Asperger's. We thought this might be the best approach to take next. If getting us help meant driving to Boston once a week, we were determined to do that. Anything was on the table at this point in an effort to make some positive gains in how we dealt with Dylan. In the spring of that year, when Dylan was eleven, we drove to Boston with Dylan to have a two-hour meeting. We were not sure how we were going to explain everything we were going through and get feedback in only two hours. Since people that we were talking to were experts we thought it would not be that hard to talk to them because we would not tell them anything they hadn't heard already. Dylan was not happy about going on this road trip. He didn't want to be pulled from school for another day to see a doctor whom he also worried would not help us. It was hard to argue with his logic after what we had already gone through, with knowing how little help we were going to have in the future. Amy and I sat down on the couch in his office. Dylan was off to the side in a chair. Two of Dr. Kermit's assistants heard our story and took feverish notes with a plan to pass the information onto Dr. Kermit, who came in to sit with us. It reminded me of being in a dentist's office where you meet with the hygienist who does the background work on whether you need more help. Then the dentist comes in for the last five minutes, goes through what the hygienist found and tells you the next steps. The hour went by very quickly as we told story after story of Dylan's outbursts.

About halfway through the meeting, they asked Dylan to go into the lobby to wait for us so that they could ask us some questions without his commentary. We never went into a meeting with the three of us where Amy and I could talk openly about our experiences, without Dylan challenging our recollection of events. In some cases Dylan would flat out say we were lying, and the circumstances we were describing had never even happened. He was always very convincing during these times. It was almost as if he didn't remember what had happened or had somehow convinced himself that it hadn't. They recognized that we could not talk freely and asked Dylan to leave the room. He was not very happy about leaving because he knew there would be no one there to challenge whatever we said. Amy and I continued to tell the doctors what we were going through and they asked questions. After an hour we took a break and joined Dylan in the lobby while waiting for our time with Dr. Kermit. We were glad they booked a two hour meeting and it appeared we were going to have the second hour with Dr. Kermit. He came out and asked all three of us to come into his office. We suggested that maybe we meet with him privately first but he felt that it would be best for us to meet all together. If we wanted to talk privately, we could ask Dylan to excuse himself.

We met for a couple of hours alone with Dr. Kermit and also with Dylan included. At the end of the session he didn't have any suggestions for us that were not straight from his book. Dylan was not like other kids. What works with most kids has rarely worked with him. It was not the help we were looking for so our search for help continued.

Wow, Thanks for Nothing

When we realized that our plans to utilize Dr. Kermit's plan were a bust we started asking around again if anyone knew someone in greater Portland who could help us. After several phone calls, our next road took us to a child therapist in Portland. We had heard of her but were under the impression that she dealt more with kids younger than Dylan. After being assured by a friend that she was the go-to person in greater Portland if you had a child with Asperger's, we called and within a few weeks we had our first appointment. She took a different approach from those with whom we had worked with in the past. She met primarily with Dylan and then we were brought in the last five or six minutes to recap what they talked about. Her approach was to help Dylan manage his behavior not helping us manage Dylan. We were fine with that as long as it worked. At this point we would have probably agreed to a witch doctor if they could convince us that our home life would be peaceful. After the first meeting she told us that Dylan talked to her about the reasons why he didn't need to be in there and how difficult it was to see doctor after doctor when not one could help him. The next couple of meetings she met primarily with Dylan. On the third meeting we hit a road block. Actually, it was more of a brick wall at 100 miles per hour. When the fifty minutes ended she sent Dylan into her waiting room, and Amy and I entered her office. She sat in silence for what seemed like an eternity. She then looked at us, up in the air with her eyes, exhaled a big sigh and said, "Wow, yeah, wow!" Amy and I did not know how to respond to "Wow, yeah, wow." What did that mean? Where was she going with this? She said again, "Wow, I don't think I can help you."

"What?" we said shocked. "What do you mean you can't help us?"

All she said was, "Wow he's a handful. I don't think I can help you." With that our sessions with Portland's Asperger's expert concluded. We were heading into another summer, a summer that we had to keep Dylan occupied and entertained, with no help from the Asperger's expert who could only say "Wow."

Possibly the Worst Parenting Advice Ever

It was a long summer and that fall was challenging as well. Nothing had changed with Dylan's behavior and we had not gained any new skills or tactics to handle him. If there was any hope that the New Year was going to be a better one, that optimism faded quickly in January. One evening, Dylan had a complete meltdown. He was yelling and screaming and inconsolable. We didn't know what to do. It was also the first sign that he really felt like his life was spiraling away as he was talking about killing himself, which he had never done before. When your first child is in fifth grade and he starts talking about taking his own life, it's really hard to describe how lost you feel.

When Amy was pregnant and when Dylan was a baby, we read everything we could about parenting. We subscribed to a couple of parents' magazines, and we bought all the books we could find that we thought could help us be the best parents we could be with the most current knowledge from the best experts. But here we were, about ten years later, completely clueless regarding what to do about our son. We tried holding him down because that is what our most recent counselor advised.

We were recommended to go visit a counselor by the name of John Leesburg. He was a very matter-of-fact and no-nonsense kind of guy. He talked openly about the fact that he had been in prison, although he never described what brought him to that point in his life, and now he was advising us on how to handle Dylan. His basic theory for almost all of Dylan's behavior can be summarized in two words: poor parenting. He told us that we had been too lenient with Dylan, that we had let him get away with too much, and that we let him control every situation. Every time we left his office, we felt more and more ashamed and dejected about our parenting skills. We spent almost the entire session focusing on what *we* should be doing better and what we were going to do the next time Dylan had a meltdown.

Mr. Leesburg told me in particular, as the father and the strongest adult in the house, that I needed to physically take control of these situations before we let Dylan take control of them. Anything less than complete submission by Dylan meant I had, once again, failed as a father.

One night a couple of weeks into our sessions with Mr. Leesburg, we were faced with Dylan in full meltdown mode. Convinced at this point that I had been a complete failure as an authoritative parent, I took control and did what Mr. Leesburg told me to do. I grabbed Dylan off his bed and, as if using a move from professional wrestling, I pinned him face first into his carpet. This was the advice I had been given by an "expert," and since nothing we had ever done had helped and I now believed I was as much of the problem as Dylan, I did what I was told. Dylan's face was smashed into the carpet with all of my weight on top of him. This threw him right over the edge. He went from meltdown to complete collapse. He was having a breakdown and my aggressive move only made things worse. Dylan was foaming at the mouth, screaming, red-faced, and thrashing around on the floor, but I held on tight. I held him into the ground waiting for him to settle down.

As I look back on it now and as I looked back on it even later that evening, I wonder what the hell I was thinking. How could I possibly think, knowing Dylan as well as I did, that pushing his face into the carpet (and those are the literal words that Mr. Leesburg told me, "push his face into the carpet until he calms down"). How on earth was that going to calm down an eleven-year-old boy with Asperger's Syndrome?

I finally could not take any more of his screaming and I was afraid that I might be hurting him, so I pulled him up off the floor and held him tight, trying to control him but avoiding the carpet advice. This was no more effective and Dylan sprung free from me, grabbed a glass of water that was sitting on his nightstand, and hurled it across the room, smashing a picture frame. Glass flew everywhere, and Amy and I realized for the first time, that we were simply in way over our head and we needed more help than any counselor could give us. So we called the police and told them that we needed an ambulance; someone needed to take our son to the hospital. We maintained the situation for another seven or eight minutes until a police car and an ambulance arrived. It was about eight o'clock at night and any fear or concern about what the neighbors would think was far from our minds. We just needed somebody to help our son, and we knew that we couldn't do it.

Between the time we called the police and the time they arrived, Dylan had somewhat settled down although we knew that he was potentially just a moment away from being right back where he was before. The police came up to his room and talked to Dylan and he tried to explain to them why he was so upset, but at this point I'm not sure he even knew or remembered what started this whole thing. He followed the police downstairs and there was the ambulance driver and assistant. They also talked to Dylan to see if he could explain what could be done to help him settle down. He yelled at the ambulance drivers to leave, that he didn't need them, and that was when they got a glimpse of what we were dealing with. We told Dylan that he needed help, that we couldn't help him, and he had to go with the ambulance until we could figure out what was going to be the best way to help him.

The surreal part during this whole experience was what Mariah was doing. As the police and the EMTs wandered around our house while our son was having a complete mental breakdown, Mariah, who was only nine years old, sat at the kitchen table very calmly playing with four-year-old Lilly, trying to distract her from everything that was going on around her. As I looked around the room to witness the whole scene around me, I was taken aback by Mariah's ability to calmly distract Lilly in a moment of complete chaos, and I was so thankful that she was able to do that.

It wasn't long after that night that Dylan had another meltdown but not as bad, on an afternoon after school. Mariah was home and had a friend over playing in the basement, but there was no way they could avoid hearing everything that was going on. When everything finally calmed down later that night, Amy, while she was tucking Mariah into bed, asked her if she got embarrassed when Dylan acted like that in front of her friends. Amazingly, she said no. Amy said, "It's okay if that embarrasses you. That would be normal."

Mariah said, "No, it really doesn't."

Amy said, "How could that be? What do you tell your friends?"

"I just tell them that his brain works differently than ours."

Mariah was mature beyond her years. Just a couple of years later Mariah looked up to Amy with her big brownish green eyes and said, "Mommy, I

am going to have to take care of Dylan someday aren't I?' Amy did not know
what to say. She was not even a teenager, yet she was already thinking that the
burden of caring for her brother would fall on her shoulders when we were
gone. How would that thought even come into the mind of a kid? It was
because she saw something in her brother that concerned her. She saw that
he was not capable of handling himself and maybe never would be. And she
knew, as his sister, she could not leave him to his own devices. The bond of
family responsibility was thick even at her young age.

Amy said, "Honey, we hope not. We are doing everything we can to
make sure Dylan is able to take care of himself someday."

Mariah never brought it up again but we know it must have crossed her
mind again over the years as it has crossed ours many times.

The night ended as many nights had in the past. We went to the hospital emergency room. Several doctors and nurses came in and out of the
room to ask us questions we had either heard already or had nothing at all to
do with the situation that brought us there. Eventually, Dylan calmed down
and got tired enough for them to feel like they had actually accomplished
something. They then recommended we talk to our pediatrician and sent us
home just as lost and confused about how to handle Dylan as we were when
we had called 911 a few hours earlier. Thankfully, enough time had passed to
settle Dylan down so when we returned home, he went to bed.

— 5 —

Middle School Mayhem

Serena Joins the Family

We were plugging away in our lives with three busy children. Amy and I had talked in the past about having a fourth child. Something inside of both of us felt we were not complete as a family, but a fourth child made no sense at all. Dylan was extremely difficult and consumed a huge amount of our daily time and energy. The idea of a fourth child was just illogical and probably not wise. However, we were both feeling this sense that our family was missing someone. We would say things like, "Having another baby, with Dylan like he is, is crazy. How would we handle a baby right now?"

One day, in that repeated discussion, I said, "We need to remember something, if we have a baby we may have a few tough years but, God willing, we will have that person as a blessing in our lives for the next sixty years. Are we going to sacrifice sixty years of loving another child for a few rough ones at the beginning?" Amy thought about that but we never actually agreed, and verbally said, "Okay, let's have another baby."

It was not long after that discussion that we rolled the dice and Amy became pregnant.

It was really funny how Amy told me she was pregnant. She said, "I'm pregnant, we're going to Europe."

I laughed and said, "What?!"

She said, "I am pregnant and I want to visit Europe. If we don't do it now, we will have a baby and we won't be able to go for at least five years. And then, when we can go, we'll have to find someone to watch four kids instead of three, including teenagers. And, our parents will be five years older so that'll be even harder for them. We should go to Europe while I am pregnant."

I was so excited that we had another baby coming, and I am always happy to be away from the kids and work to be alone with Amy, that I agreed immediately. We started planning our trip to Italy and thinking about life with four kids.

It was about this time when I was given some very good advice. I was told I had to mourn the son I thought I would have before I could truly love the son that God gave me. As I waited for our son or daughter to arrive I began to start this process. It did not happen overnight. It took years to work through it and sometimes, even today, I find moments where I long for that son. That is a hard emotion to admit because I love my son very much and have learned to like him as well. But it certainly was not a quick process. Giving up that image of my son as the captain of the baseball team and prom king took time. If you are a dad struggling with those images, I recommend you begin the mourning as soon as you can because your son needs you to love him for who he is, not who you hoped he would be.

Everyone we told about the pregnancy assumed that I wanted a boy. They knew that Dylan was a challenge and did not share my love of sports so people assumed I wanted a boy that I could play baseball, football and watch ballgames with. But, strangely, that was the furthest thing from the reality of my wishes. I was actually very nervous about the possibility of having a boy. I was very afraid that I would have the exact kind of son everyone thought I desired. My fear came from how that son would impact Dylan. If I had a son that loved sports it would be almost inevitable that I would favor him. It would be human nature. How would Dylan feel knowing that I finally had the son he couldn't be? What would that do to him to see me bonding so strongly with another boy twelve years his junior? It broke my heart to think about so I prayed to God to give us our third daughter.

God answered my prayers. At 2:06pm on January 6, 2004 Serena was born. Our family was complete.

Dylan with newborn sister, Serena

The Katie Beckett Battle

Several of the experts and school officials told us we needed to take care of ourselves and our family. They told us there were services that could provide respite care for us and there were state-run social services that could benefit Dylan. When we inquired about these programs, however, we discovered that none of them would take our money. They would not take a check or even cash from us. The only way we could utilize the services available was through a program called Katie Beckett. We applied. We were rejected.

When Dylan was a baby his grandfather, Ken Volk, and great-grandfather, Benjamin Volk, set up an account for him and put some money in it. Every year for the first few years of his life they added to it until it became a nice amount of money. It was set up as an UGMA (Uniform Gift to Minors Act) account. This meant that, technically, the money was Dylan's. When the state saw this money in his name they rejected us for Katie Beckett Medicaid services. The crazy thing is that we did not even want or need Katie Beckett.

We had the financial means to pay for the services we wanted but the service providers would only bill through Medicaid. We contacted the people at the Maine Department of Health and Human Services and explained to them the situation with Dylan's money. The person we spoke to suggested we apply again and write up an explanation of Dylan's money. We re-applied. We were rejected again.

We called our financial advisor requesting he create a trust that we could transfer the money into so it was no longer in Dylan's name but under a trust. This would make the money untouchable until Dylan was at least twenty-one and hopefully allow us the services of Katie Beckett. He created a trust. We applied a third time. We were rejected again.

I went in person to speak with someone at DHHS. I asked him why we were rejected when the money was clearly no longer in Dylan's name. He said they know the money went somewhere and were concerned we would have access to it again after we were approved. He suggested we apply once again and write a letter explaining where the money went including a legal copy of the trust document. We applied for the fourth time to Katie Beckett. We were finally approved!

After all that work and repeated attempts to gain Katie Beckett status we had a difficult time finding anyone willing to do respite care with Dylan. The DHS worker they assigned to our case tried to be helpful but was not. In the end, there were very few services that would change our lives as we knew it at that time. We were on our own to get through this difficult time.

Middle School Begins

We were anxious all summer about what the middle school's plans were for Dylan because they had not lined him up with an ed-tech before the school year ended. Amy had called the school several times over the summer to ask if they had made any progress hiring an ed-tech for him. They had not but told her not to worry about it. That was easy for them to say. We knew the wrong ed-tech could make the beginning of middle school a disaster. Finally, a few days before the school year was to start we were told they had hired someone for Dylan. They were quite pleased with themselves because the person they had hired to work with Dylan was a cool young guy that Dylan would like— he was the high school baseball coach. We were immediately concerned.

As a rule Dylan did not connect well with jocks. We expressed our concern but they assured us it would be a good fit. A few days later we attended the school's beginning of the year open house. We met Mr. Baseball. He was a nice guy and seemed to have a good disposition but then panic set in. He knew absolutely nothing about Asperger's Syndrome. And when I say he knew nothing I mean he barely even knew how to pronounce it! He had no idea what it was, how it impacted Dylan or what effect it had on his schooling and social life. Lilly was four and probably had a better handle on how to help Dylan through the day. We were shocked and upset and rather pissed off. It was our belief, and still is today, that the school had hired him as the baseball coach and needed to find a spot to employ him. Dylan was just a filler for their employment needs. Amy stopped by the school the next day with a copy of Tony Atwood's book about Asperger's and begged Mr. Baseball to read it, quickly.

Sixth grade began so rocky that we started to think there must be other options. There had to be another way we could educate Dylan in an environment more conducive to his ability. Amy and I were both very frustrated with how the school was handling his inability to stay focused in class. His teacher and ed-tech seemed quite overwhelmed by his almost constant arguing and challenging of authority. It was about this time that we really started to see Dylan feel as if he was entitled to certain treatment that was a standard he felt he deserved, regardless of how he behaved. He would talk about people not respecting him and we would explain to him that you earn people's respect. People don't just give you respect. Rather, it is something that is earned and it is something that can be lost easily by bad behavior. We would find ourselves having this same discussion with him right through high school and even beyond.

There were not a lot of options for kids with special needs in southern Maine, but there was a private school not far from our house. It was a private school for kids with learning disabilities. There was no question that Dylan had a learning disability. The big question was could they handle his behavioral issues. We made an appointment to speak with the people at the school. We sat down with the principal of the school and the lead administrator. Their school was basically a very small, old building and their offices were in a double-wide trailer. The office was quite cluttered. There were papers everywhere and there seemed to be no organization or attention to cleanliness but I didn't think much of that at the time. I just thought that they must be really busy without time to clean up their office.

My office is always neat and organized. A cluttered office drives me crazy. Some people say that a cluttered office shows that you're working hard so if you walk into my office you might think that I'm on vacation, but it's just the way I am. I like everything to be in order, so it struck me that her office was such a mess with papers and junk. What I didn't realize was that that same sense of disorder would end up being Dylan's downfall at the school.

We spent over an hour with the principal and the administrator. We went into great detail about Dylan's outbursts, his lack of ability to stay focused, his inability or unwillingness to accept direction, criticism, and instruction, even from authority figures. Amy and I almost went out of our way to scare them away from Dylan. We were going to pull him from the public middle school and place him in a private school at our expense. Whether we were going to say anything or keep our thoughts to ourselves, the underlying message to the middle school was going to be, "You failed our son, you can't handle him, so we're going to take him somewhere else." It would be pretty hard for that message to not be conveyed whether we wanted it to be or not.

The staff assured us that they would be able to handle Dylan. They assured us that they had students on the autism spectrum before and they felt confident that Dylan would fit into their curriculum and their program. They told us about success stories of kids who had been struggling in the public school and were not struggling at their school but they, just like everybody else that has ever dealt with Dylan, underestimated his issues. It didn't take long for them to realize it.

Amy and I went to the public school, sat down with the principal and the head of special services for the town, and told them that we had made a decision to pull Dylan from the public school and send him to private school. We asked for a copy of his records to be transferred as he would be starting the following Monday at his new school. They tried to convince us that this was unnecessary, asked us what they could do to help Dylan stay in the public school, but neither the principal nor the special education director seemed to go out of their way to convince us that Dylan should stay there. He had only been there a month and yet we could almost see the sense of relief they had knowing Dylan was leaving.

We left the meeting at the middle school very unsure whether we had made the right decision. Usually Amy and I, after talking and working out all the options, would feel confident that, based on the information that we had at that time and place, we were making the right decision. We would look back years later and think of other ways we could have handled things or other decisions we could have made, but hindsight is really 20/20. We never made any decision about Dylan hastily. We *always* talked and talked until we felt that we were heading in the right direction. Very rarely was there anyone that we could talk to about the choices we made regarding Dylan. We almost never had a counselor in whom we had any confidence, and even those closest to us—our parents, our friends and siblings—didn't understand what we were really dealing with. They tried to understand, but unless one lives it they cannot fully understand.

The following Monday, we drove Dylan to his new school. He was relatively cooperative as he knew that this might be a better fit for him. He was extremely overwhelmed and unhappy at the middle school. A small school with more one-on-one attention might be just what he needed, and despite his almost constant arguing, he did want to be successful.

The first couple of days at the new school seemed to go fine. There were no major issues. They put a plan together for what his daily schedule would look like, and he seemed to be transitioning well with the new school. The only issue he told us he was having was with the lunch room. The school was very crowded, and they did not have a special place for lunch or enough staff to clean in between the groups of kids that came in for lunch. Many of the kids at the school had special needs that were lower functioning than Dylan, so the tables tended to get quite messy at mealtime. A clean table for Dylan to eat at was a major issue for him. It was part of his OCD. He could not eat at a table with leftover food on it. It wasn't that he didn't want to; it was that it made him so uncomfortable that he not only couldn't eat but he couldn't even sit at a table where someone else had left pieces of their food. It made him physically and mentally uncomfortable. Every day, Dylan would insist that they clean the tables, not just wipe them with a paper towel, but completely wash them down fully before he would sit down and eat. We heard directly from Dylan that this was a problem, but we didn't realize how big a problem it was until the following Monday. Dylan had been at the school for six days, and the administrator called to inform us that it would be his last day at the school.

"What?" we said, extremely alarmed and taken aback, "What are you talking about? How can it be his last day at the school?"

They told us that they had been trying to deal with his OCD issues, but it was too difficult. He was just too challenging. We asked them again, "What are you talking about? We told you all about his OCD. We went into great depth about these kinds of things and his difficulty handling certain situations, and you said you were fine with all of it, that you could manage him. And now, after you've told us this and after we went to the public school and basically told them that they had failed and we were taking Dylan somewhere else on our own dime, now you're telling us that you can't handle him? That's unacceptable! You have to let him stay longer!"

The school refused to even consider it. It was a done deal, the decision had been made. Dylan was out. We had to call the middle school and tell them that he would be back. We were devastated and completely humiliated. Now we would have to go back to the school with our tail between our legs, knowing that they would have to take Dylan back because it's a public school, but also knowing that we had lost our ability to prove to them what a horrible job they had done educating Dylan. Even a school specifically designed for kids with special needs could not handle our son.

Dylan went back to the public school and it went better than expected. The school year was actually going pretty well for Dylan.

Fortunately their terrible choice in an ed-tech was offset by a terrific fit as his primary teacher. Mrs. Cooper was kind, soft spoken, understanding and extraordinarily patient. She really seemed to "get" Dylan. This could not be said for some of his other teachers in sixth grade. Mr. Michaels, his science teacher, seemed to have no patience for Dylan. He was a big sports enthusiast who, to Dylan, was just another jock who didn't like him from the start. At one point, during a P.E.T. meeting he said, with great frustration, "Dylan is very rude. He will often ask a question about something we talked about fifteen or twenty minutes earlier."

I said, "Have you even read his Neuropsychology tests? He scored in the one percentile for process speed. So when he asks you a question about something you discussed twenty minutes earlier he is not being rude at all. His brain is just finally processing the information that you were discussing twenty minutes ago." He heard me but I don't believe he was listening.

I think he was one of those teachers that just thought Dylan was a pain in the ass and nothing more. But Mrs. Cooper was a blessing. She was terrific at setting up both learning and behavioral systems that worked really well for Dylan. We incorporated them into his Individual Education Program. An IEP is designed to help a child with special needs and define for the teachers exactly what his program will look like on a day-to-day basis. For the first time since Mrs. Murphy's first grade class, Dylan was actually enjoying school. Our son was telling us that he liked school. We could not have been more thrilled.

Something totally unexpected occurred in February of 2004. Dr. Key put Dylan on a new medication called Risperdal. We're not sure whether it was outside factors or the Risperdal, and we'll probably never know, but Dylan was different. He was much less argumentative. We went a couple of weeks without seeing any meltdowns, and for the first time in a long time, he was enjoyable to be around on a regular basis. We thought it was a miracle drug. We compared it to the reaction of Robert DeNiro in the movie, *Awakenings*, when Robin Williams gave a ward of mental patients a drug that turned them from zombies back to the people they had been earlier in their lives. Unfortunately for us, much like the movie, it would be a short-lived reprieve. But we enjoyed every minute of it and tried not to overanalyze what was going differently for Dylan.

One thing that we could point to was Mrs. Cooper. She had really started to figure him out, was working well with him, and was anticipating meltdowns and disrupting the pattern. She allowed him to go to the library or the small room off of the principal's office as soon as she saw his anxiety rising. This had been written in his IEP, and she was using it brilliantly to make life easier for her and for Dylan. We were shocked one day when Dylan came home and told Amy that he really liked school. He had not said that he had liked school this much since first grade. This was music to our ears, and we thanked God that maybe the right combination of meds and school staff had finally aligned for Dylan. Maybe we had finally turned a corner. And then March came in like a lion.

Dylan's teacher went out on an early maternity leave, and the school brought in a permanent sub for his class. We had a meeting and talked with the sub about Dylan. The administrators met with her to discuss him, as well as with Mrs. Cooper before she left on her leave.

What we didn't know was that the school, particularly the principal, got involved in Dylan's day-to-day program and either changed or simply chose to ignore what was written in his IEP. Dylan started acting up again at home. Things started falling apart quickly, and we couldn't figure out what was going on. One day when Dylan was having a meltdown at home, we screamed at him, "What is the matter with you?! Why are you all of a sudden acting like this when everything has been going so well? Isn't your life easier when you just get along with everybody and do what you're supposed to?!"

Dylan immediately started crying, "I just want things to go back to the way they were before Mrs. Cooper left on maternity leave. Why can't they go back to the rules that she was using?"

We said, "What do you mean…the rules that she was using? What are you talking about?"

"They've changed all the rules on me. It's too stressful. I can't handle all these new rules. I can't meet these expectations."

"What expectations?" we said, "They can't change anything without having a formal meeting and changing your IEP."

"Well they did!" he screamed as he continued to cry, "They changed everything! I just want things to go back to the way they were. I was doing so well. It was a good system. Why did they have to change everything!?" We insisted that Dylan was either making all this up or exaggerating because we couldn't imagine that they would make wholesale changes to his program without a meeting or even the courtesy of a phone call or an email to us.

The next day I went into the school to talk to the principal, Mrs. Little. Amy was unavailable because of a previous commitment, but we felt it could not wait until we both were free to come in. I always preferred to have Amy with me for meetings like this, but in this case, I would have to talk to the school on my own. What happened at that meeting brought me to an acidic combination of fury, sadness, and shock. They had in fact changed how they were treating Dylan, how they were handling his anxiety at school. They changed his IEP without as much as a word to his parents or our hired consultant. Dylan had always been getting two warnings per class before he was asked to step out. It gave him time to gather himself with a couple of warnings, and it was working out well as he was staying in the class more and more leading up to March. What we found out was that they had changed the warnings to two per day. He went from getting two warnings per class period to two warnings total in an entire day.

I said to Mrs. Little, "Dylan is telling us that he can no longer go into the library or the room next to your office when he's bordering on a meltdown or feeling a high sense of anxiety or stress."

She said, "That's correct. It was not working out."

"Not working out? What does that mean?"

"It's better if he goes into the next classroom," she said.

I told her that Dylan, who was already at a high stress level, found it even more stressful to walk into a classroom where another twenty-five of his peers would see his distressed state. To walk to the back of the room as they all stared at him and asked him why he was there was not helping him to settle down. This was a nightmare for him—the worst scenario he could imagine.

When I told Mrs. Little how horrifying it was for him to walk into a classroom of his peers in the middle of a lesson, after already being so stressed out, and sit in the back of the room as everyone stared at him, her response to me was, "He could do it if he wanted to."

I was mortified that she would say such a thing. I said, "How can you say something like that? Do you think that just because my son's disability isn't visible, it makes it any less of a disability? Would you even think in your wildest dreams of telling a twelve-year-old boy in a wheelchair that he could walk up the front steps of the school if he wanted to? That's an outrageous statement. You owe me an apology."

She refused to apologize or even retract her statement. And she refused to change his IEP.

IEP Changes and the Result is Spring Harbor

It was only a couple of weeks later when we received a call we never thought we would get. The middle school called us to inform us that Dylan was beyond their ability to handle. They told us we needed to come get him. He was no longer welcome at the public school. We thought, "Can they do that? Can they just kick our kid out of school with no place to go?" Apparently they could because they did in early April 2004. I went to the school to pick Dylan up. Amy was at home with Serena who was just a baby so it seemed like a better plan for me to go pick up Dylan. I went in to the school feeling unsure about what I was heading into. I was concerned Dylan had become violent or some behavior had appeared that we had yet to face. That was not the case. Dylan was just an emotional disaster. It had been building for weeks and on that day it finally erupted. He simply could not get through another school day.

I picked him up at school and called Paul Garcia, the counselor we had been working with, for suggestions. He recommended that I drive Dylan to Maine Medical Center in the hopes we could get him admitted to Spring Harbor, the local psychiatric hospital. He felt Dylan needed serious observation that was beyond anything he could do alone on a weekly basis. I called Amy and told her of the plan. She bundled Serena up and met us at the Emergency Room. Dylan had calmed down a little but was still extremely agitated and was talking about ending his life because he could not go on at the school and in life. It was heartbreaking and terrifying to hear a sixth grader talk of ending his life with such deep emotion. These were not casual attention getting threats. He genuinely felt that his life had no purpose and no possibility of improving.

Doctor after doctor visited Dylan over the next several hours. They asked him questions and they drove me crazy with questions about his birth and what he was like as a baby. I became more and more frustrated as I just could not understand the relevance of a line of questioning regarding his life as a newborn. Paul also came to the hospital and was instrumental in helping convince the doctors that Dylan needed more than a settling down and a ride *home*.

* * *

After several hours in the hospital, Paul had felt he had done everything he could do so he left. We waited. We had several people working behind the scenes to try to get Dylan into Spring Harbor, and we finally got the word around 9:00 that night that they had a bed for him in the teenage wing. We drove over to Spring Harbor in complete and utter silence. Dylan didn't know what he was facing with the rest of the night's events, and he stopped protesting. At some level I think he knew he needed more help than we or a counselor coming in once a week could give him. He knew he was out of control and he wasn't any more happy about it than we were. We arrived at Spring Harbor and went in the front door where we were greeted, as they knew we were coming. They brought us into a room to fill out some paper-work, just your basic insurance information. At that point, Dylan started to get scared and asked us not to leave him there. We told him the decision had been made; this is what we had to do, and he started crying, "Please don't leave me here. I promise I'll do better, I promise I'll behave." But we had heard that many times before when he had felt desperate about a situation, and we knew, as much as he wanted to honor that promise, it was beyond his control.

The staff told us that he would be in the teenage wing, which meant he be would be with kids from thirteen to eighteen years old. As soon as we walked to that area, Dylan really broke down and started begging us not to leave him there. This was our little boy; the boy we dreamed of; the boy we named when we were sixteen; the boy that we spent three years doting over, dedicating every spare moment we had before Mariah was born, sometimes just staring at his face for hours on end; the boy we videoed so much that you can actually pick a random day in his first year and be able to see what he was doing through our home videos; the boy I used to put in a backpack and walk up on Saturday mornings to get a paper and "boo-berry muttin." In that moment at Spring Harbor, it took every ounce of energy and self-discipline not to grab him and hug him and say, "Okay honey, come home with us, it'll be okay" because it never seemed to be alright, and lately it just seemed to be all wrong.

They put Dylan in the room and told us it was time for us to leave as he cried and cried. They told us it wasn't going to get any better if we stayed longer, we needed to leave. And somehow, we turned around and walked away but not before giving him a hug and kiss, telling him we loved him, and that we would do anything we could to help him. But we left. Walking from that room to the exit, out into the parking lot was the longest and most excruciating four minutes of my life. Amy had come in another car, so we hugged each other and went to our cars to head home. I sat down in my car, closed the door and burst into tears, sobbing like I never had before.

After a few minutes, I picked up the phone to call my parents. I was almost thirty-five years old, but at that moment all I wanted to do was talk to my mom and dad. I knew they would be supportive of our decision to leave Dylan, and they would offer to do anything to help us. I needed to hear that, but when they picked up the phone, I couldn't even talk. I started crying all over again and couldn't even get the words out to tell them that we left him at a mental hospital. Those words, mental hospital, or mental institution have such a horrible connotation for so many people: images of movies they have seen where crazy people are locked away, thoughts of Jack Nicholson and Nurse Ratched.

Spring Harbor is not like that at all. It's a clean, warm, caring environment. The nurses and doctors were all very understanding of the difficulty we were going through that night, but saying the words "We left Dylan at Spring Harbor" was so hard. I couldn't get them out without sobbing. My parents were understanding and supportive, as I expected they would be. They told me we did the right thing, we did the best we could and that they all loved Dylan, and just wanted what was best for him. While I knew that to be true, and I could tell myself that, or Amy and I could tell each other, there was something stronger about those words coming from Mom and Dad.

When you go into Spring Harbor you have to sign in, leave all electronics at the front desk, and only certain people are permitted to visit the patients. Amy and I wrote his grandparents on the list. My parents decided to fly home to help us with the girls and see Dylan. We also added our priest from the Episcopal Church we were attending in hopes that he would come to visit Dylan in his time of need. Unfortunately, for the ten days Dylan was at Spring Harbor, our priest never came to visit him. This was extremely upsetting to us because we knew this was a time for Dylan to hear that, despite everything that was going on, the trials he was faced with, God loved him. Jesus still loved him. He needed to hear it from someone other than his parents and grandparents. There was a lot happening at the church while Dylan was at Spring Harbor but that was no excuse. We felt abandoned by our priest but we let it go because of the situation at the church.

In the meantime Amy and I met with the doctors, nurses and counselors while they tried to figure out what was going on with Dylan. They gave him neurological examinations and then presented us with their findings. They set up a very strict red-yellow-green system for everything they did so he knew where he stood and whether he was making progress, as required for release. Overnight they had moved him from the teen wing to the youth wing, and we were relieved. Although he was almost a teenager, he had a very young face and was quite naïve and innocent. The teen wing was very intimidating for him.

Dylan did well at Spring Harbor, staying in the green on the behavior chart most of the time. He didn't like being there because he was mostly confined to a small room with just a cot. He was not even allowed to go to the bathroom without asking, even though he had his own bathroom. Dylan had to ring a buzzer in order for them to open the door. There were things in the bathroom that apparently could be used for suicide—shower curtains, water, etc., so no one was allowed in the bathroom without a staff member knowing when they were going in and coming out.

One of the big dilemmas we were facing while Dylan was at Spring Harbor was that we had already booked a Disney cruise for the following week using our Disney timeshare points. The trip was a little over a week away and not refundable without major penalties. In addition to the cost of canceling our Disney trip and flights was the underlying motivation for the trip. It was a vacation we really needed but how could we take a vacation without Dylan?

We talked to the counselors at Spring Harbor for their advice. What should we do? What would they recommend? We were actually surprised at their response. I think that they could see a family possibly at the breaking point. They encouraged us to take the cruise and Dylan would be fine. He needed a reason to leave the hospital and probably wouldn't have one at the time we would be going on the cruise. They told us that we could use that time as a couple and as a family even though we felt like we weren't a family if Dylan wasn't there. We didn't feel right leaving him in the hospital to go on a

Disney cruise. We expressed this concern with the counselor and the doctors and they were insistent that we should go.

The next question was what we were going to do with Dylan's ticket. We already had Dylan's plane and cruise ticket. We planned on six of us for the trip. Amy suggested that we take her mother because she had never been on a cruise before. That would allow us to have some time to ourselves with a built-in babysitter. I was fine with that idea as I have always gotten along well with my mother-in-law. The kids enjoy her company and she would be helpful, especially with Serena being only four months old. Having Janet on the trip would allow us both to go in the swimming pool and participate in the fun activities on the cruise with Lilly and Mariah that we would not be able to do if one of us had to hold a baby. Amy called the airlines and Walt Disney World, and for a relatively small fee, the tickets were changed and the plans were set.

Now we just had to tell Dylan he was not going to come with us on our cruise. We asked the counselor to join us in case his reaction led to a meltdown. But it did not. Dylan knew, without saying, that he was in no shape to go on a Disney cruise. We had been nervous about taking him on the cruise to begin with because of the commotion and noise inherent with being stuck on a boat with 500 other kids and their parents. He may have been nervous as well since he put up no fight about missing the trip. We found ourselves surprisingly disappointed that Dylan didn't want to go on the cruise with us or that he didn't put up more of a fight about being part of our family trip. It just felt a little disappointing that he was so easily willing to give up spending time with us, but he was as burnt out as we were and there was something relaxing and peaceful about Spring Harbor. He knew the rules. Everything was black and white for him and very structured, so it was an easy environment to live in.

We had a wonderful time on our vacation. We were relaxed and we knew that Dylan was safe and in good hands. In only a few days we knew we would be back to reality and probably bringing him home but we were hopeful that we were on a new path going forward.

We returned in mid-April from our Disney cruise and went right in the next morning to meet with the staff at Spring Harbor. They felt Dylan was finally ready to be discharged, but we were quite anxious, as really nothing had changed. They did not make any recommendations to change his meds; they didn't give us any new great ideas on how to manage his behavior; they didn't even have a solid recommendation for a counselor we could work with who was up to the task. So in a sense, all we got from Spring Harbor was a two-week respite and a wakeup call to the school that what they were doing was not working.

It had just been a few weeks ago that they told us things were going fine, that they had changed Dylan's program, and it was going okay. They told us all was well while, at the same time, Dylan was telling us all was wrong. We had taken the school's word that Dylan was making it out to be worse than it was and we didn't force them to go back to the previous IEP instructions. We were still naïve enough to believe that the school knew what they were doing. However, while Dylan was at Spring Harbor, we had a private conversation with a middle school staff member. This conversation was in person and very much unofficial and off the record. She told us things had not been going well for Dylan at the school for quite a while. She told us that Dylan was accurate when he described how much things changed after his teacher went on maternity leave. She also told us that the principal had no patience for Dylan, did not really like him, and was not convinced that he even had a disability. Then she told us something that shocked us because it was so unexpected. Everything she had told us before we already suspected: we knew the principal didn't like Dylan, we knew from her comment about him "doing it if he wanted to" that she didn't believe in his true disability, and we now believed Dylan's assessment of the changes after Mrs. Cooper left. But what this teacher told us in confidentiality was that things were so bad with Dylan at the Middle School that there were teachers actually threatening to quit their job if something wasn't done about him. When you think about how much teachers value their seniority in a school system with the financial benefits and the security of those jobs and then you think about how someone would actually be willing to quit their job because your son is so difficult to educate, it really struck a nerve as to just what we were dealing with.

Years later, as Dylan would go from program to program, and program director after program director would tell us how he was "one of the most difficult students they have had," it got easier to hear those sentiments. After a while, when professionals were overwhelmed by Dylan, we didn't feel so bad; we didn't feel so inadequate as parents and caregivers. But at that point in Dylan's life, knowing this inside information, we knew there was no way Dylan would be able to go back to the public school and the search for other options began.

Home Without a School—The School Search Begins

Dylan was now released from Spring Harbor and had been sent home. They had an action plan for us, but we were not terribly confident that anything was going to change. We had to figure out where he was going to go to school for at least the rest of the year and possibly the beginning of seventh grade. A public school was not an option. My parents had been very concerned about us and wanted to help in some way, knowing now we were going to have Dylan home for at least a short time while we navigated through the school options. They generously offered to have him stay in Florida with them for a week so we could begin looking at schools and assess school choices without having to deal with him at the same time. We thought he would probably be better behaved with his grandparents in Florida getting all their attention than he would be at home where we not only had a baby but we had two girls playing softball. And, on top of that, we had to start driving around southern Maine visiting alternative schools. We didn't waste any time getting Dylan on a flight and sending him down to Florida.

Amy had been doing some initial research based on the possibility that Dylan would not be able to go back to a public school. The local private school, the most logical first choice was not an option, as he had already been kicked out of there earlier in the school year. We narrowed it down to four possibilities for Dylan's academic life. The first candidate, but likely not the most conducive for Dylan's challenges, would be Wayneflete in Portland. It is a private school that extends right through high school. It's very expensive and well-known as the academic choice of the more wealthy in the area. It has a terrific reputation. We were not sure whether Wayneflete would be able to handle all of Dylan's behavior challenges or whether the Scarborough school district, who we were expecting to pay for this out of district placement, would be willing to send him there. We had made the decision that if we toured the school after visiting our options and it was the best choice, we would pay the difference between what the school district was willing to pay and the tuition cost. As it turned out, it was not a good fit for Dylan.

After having no success at Wayneflete we looked at options for Dylan's schooling that were more therapeutic in nature. The next school we went to was in a town about forty-five minutes away. This was a school for kids with serious disabilities. It was very small; I don't think there were even thirty-five students in the school and it was very therapeutic in nature. We knew Dylan would be absolutely mortified at the possibility of attending this school. He would not want to be spending his day with kids that were so far from where he felt he was on the neurological disability spectrum.

However, the school had its advantages. Number one was the fact they would accept him so that made it a very viable option. The biggest hurdle to choosing this school was the distance. Not only would it mean Dylan would have to leave home very early every morning and get home late due to the forty-five-minute ride, but the school district would have to pay for his transportation for the fifty-mile ride from Scarborough. It was really hard to picture Dylan at this school. It tied back in to the concept of mourning the son we thought we would have and watching the kids at this school knowing that our son was really not that far from where they were. We still had difficulty seeing him in that vein and the word disability was still a hard word to say for us. It was even harder for him to accept because he was neurologically capable of understanding what normal is and what he is. It is something that would frustrate him for many years and yet it was real.

It was difficult taking another day off from work to address the needs of my son. I was coming to grips with the reality that I had a son with a disability. That fact required more time away from the office than I would prefer. I am very lucky to be my own boss and in a financial position that allowed Amy to not have a full-time job. She worked out of the house running a personal stationery business called "Personally Yours" that had been my mother's for twenty-five years. It brought in some additional income for us and the schedule was completely flexible, based on meetings Amy set up with customers.

It must be an even more difficult challenge for families with two working parents. The amount of time I had taken off from work that spring between Dylan's breakdowns and my medical issues had been significant. There were some days where I would be sitting at work and the phone would ring, and it would say Derek and Amy Volk on it with our home phone number. I would see the caller ID and immediately start throwing papers in my brief case in anticipation that I would be going home shortly to handle a crisis. Sometimes when I picked up that phone, all I heard were screaming voices—Dylan's meltdown or Amy yelling at me to get home. Dylan would often grab the phone out of her hand and hang it up before she got the chance to get even those words out.

I would grab whatever I had been working on, hurl it into my briefcase, and run out the door. It was a twenty-two-minute ride from my office to my home and could be done quicker if need be. Sometimes on that ride home, I would get a call from Dylan screaming at me not to come home, telling me that it was unnecessary and everything was fine. Yet the tone in his voice and the decibels that were coming through the phone told me a very different story.

I would say, "Dylan I'm on my way home" and sometimes I would even threaten him saying things like, "And you're not going to be happy when I get there" or "You better have damn calmed down by the time I walk through that door." I'd say anything I could to scare him into taking responsibility for the situation and getting himself under control. Sometimes it worked. I would get home and he would have gone to his room, or turned the TV on, or simply left the house, and he would tell me, "I told you that you didn't have to come home." But the threat of my coming home may have been just enough to stop his meltdown. However, all too often I would pull into the driveway and in the spring, summer, and fall when windows might be open, I would literally hear the fighting going on between Dylan and Amy the minute I opened the car door. You would think that that would concern me as a respected businessman in the community. One might think that I would be upset and embarrassed about the almost certainty that the neighbors would hear that screaming as well and would wonder what was going on in that house, "Why can't the Volks control their kid? Are they doing something to him that makes him act like that? What kind of parents would scream at their child like that?"

Parents of neurologically normal children, parents of children that are easy to love and easy to like, parents of young children who have never faced a twelve-year-old in major meltdown mode cannot imagine, cannot fathom, cannot comprehend the emotions endured when dealing day after day with a confrontational, argumentative, explosive special needs child. They read parents' magazines, and as one of the moms up the street told Amy once, "It's so frustrating that Nate is so popular. Kids are calling him to play all the time and he has a hard time balancing all his friends." How does a parent like that rationalize a child like Dylan? How could they appreciate and empathize with what we were going through? They can be caring. They can be thoughtful. They can be understanding. They can even be loving but they can't understand what would make a mom or a dad scream at the top of their lungs at a twelve-year-old child. Yet for us, it happened on a regular basis, and as much as we wished it didn't and as regretful as we were when we laid down in bed at night and recapped the day with each other or in our own heads, we knew it would probably happen again, sooner rather than later and more often than we could have ever imagined on July 10, 1991 when we first met Dylan.

The overwhelming opinion of the people we talked to was that the school in Auburn, although it may have the services Dylan needed, was too far away. We presented it to the middle school, but the logistics of getting him forty-five minutes away every day would not only be inconvenient, but costly. Our next visit was to a school in Gray, Maine, at the former Pineland Center. In the late seventies when President Jimmy Carter made a movement to close down mental hospitals in favor of small, privately owned group homes, it led to the eventual closing of the Pineland Center. However, the infrastructure of the building was still intact in Gray, making it the perfect location for micro businesses and a private school.

The Collaborative School was one of the businesses that started up at the former mental hospital. It was a school for kids closer to Dylan on the development spectrum than those seen in Auburn. Some of the kids at the school were on the autism spectrum and some had other mental disabilities, but a few were just challenged for whatever reason by the public school and would be more successful at a private school. Another thing that we liked about the Collaborative School in Gray was how clean it was. The other school had linoleum floors that looked like they should have been replaced several years earlier.

It was spring in Maine, which means a lot of rain and mud. Mainers call it "mud season." We go from summer to fall to winter to "mud season." So when a school has linoleum floors, it is very hard to keep the dirt out and invisible. We knew this would be a difficult issue for Dylan in Auburn, as he is uncomfortable in dirty environments. We also liked what they had to say and their approach to educating challenging students. We thought they were up to the task of educating Dylan. Similar to the other school, it was a thirty-five- to forty-minute ride from our home.

We then visited a school called Sweetser, which was located in Saco. The school would have been convenient because Saco is the town directly south of Scarborough. We were impressed with the program they had but did not feel as if it would be the best fit for Dylan. It was certainly an option and we did not rule it out. We liked that they also had a small farm. Dylan always loved animals so that kind of hands-on learning would have been both enjoyable and educational for him.

The last school we looked at was the Spurwink School located in the next town of South Portland. Before we even saw it we knew that this school would have a significant advantage over the others when we were making the decision, simply by the geography. We could pull out of our driveway, take three rights, drive four miles or so, take a left and we were there. Even if the school were not ideal, we knew that it would be the choice of the public school administrators. We sat down with the head of the school and explained to him as best we could everything about Dylan. Much to our surprise, he did not seem shocked or concerned about anything that we said. We had met with people before and felt confident that they could handle Dylan but they had failed greatly. So while we appreciated his confidence, we took it with a grain of salt.

We toured the school. It was an old and rather rundown, stereotypical brick building. It had been there a long time and it showed. One of the things we liked about the school was that it was large enough that they could put Dylan in a classroom with other kids who were relatively high functioning. None of these kids were high functioning by the definition most people would think of, but on the autistic scale, they were considered to be at the higher end of the spectrum.

A few days later we had a meeting at the middle school. All the usual suspects were there, including our advisor, Lou McIntosh, who made sure the decisions were made for the right reasons instead of the money. It was Lou's job to look out for Dylan—not for us, not for the school, and certainly not for the teachers. From the time he came to our first meeting it was clear that he only had Dylan's best interest at heart, and for that, we really appreciated his attendance at the meetings.

To no one's surprise the public school was pushing hard for Spurwink. They were concerned about finding someone to drive thirty-five to forty-five minutes on a daily basis for a year, let alone two years. There was no plan in place for when Dylan would come back to the public school and, in fact at this point, there were not even any guidelines set in place, no mile markers to tell him whether he was on the right track to get back to the public school. However, we didn't mind because we weren't sure whether he was even capable of going back to a public school. Private school might turn into the new norm for Dylan and the good ones did not come cheaply.

As the discussion continued, the administrators at the public school tried to push us towards Spurwink. They finally convinced us with one key advantage for the transition back. "If Dylan wanted to come back to the public school at some point between now and eighth grade," they said, "it would be very difficult if it was a forty-five-minute ride between schools. If he was at Spurwink, he would have a better chance of re-entering the public school, even on a part time basis."

We went home to talk to Dylan and ask him what his thoughts were regarding going to a different school, and he cried, telling us that his goal was to get back to the public school to graduate with his friends. It never seemed to matter to Dylan whether school was going well or not; whether he had friends or not; whether the school caused him stress or not, he always wanted to be part of a crowd. He always wanted that one true friend that rarely comes along. Some people have a friend once in every stage of their life, a true friend in elementary school, middle school, high school and college, and oftentimes that true friend as an adult is a spouse. Dylan had never had a true friend; he was rarely even noticed, but he wanted to get back to the public school as a regular student. Due to this goal, we all agreed that starting in the "summer camp," which was really summer school, Dylan would become a full-time student at Spurwink Roosevelt School in South Portland, Maine.

Mother's Day Meltdown

I don't know what happened on Mother's Day 2004, but I know it was a disaster. It seemed like days that were designed to bring attention and focus on someone else were particularly challenging for Dylan. It eventually got to the point where even we downplayed the girls' birthdays because of the fear that it might set Dylan off. On this Mother's Day, something set him off. It was nothing in particular or significant but it turned into something very big and bad. Dylan had one of his biggest meltdowns to date on the afternoon of Mother's Day 2004.

He became so out of control that I grabbed him and physically forced him into my car and drove him to the Sweetser crisis unit on St. John Street in Portland. The ten-minute ride from Scarborough to Portland was interrupted as we were pulling onto the ramp of Route 295 North when Dylan pulled Serena's car seat out of its seatbelt and hurled it at my head while I was driving. It struck me in the back of the head as I was navigating a rather sharp angle onramp. When I felt the pain of a car seat to my head, I lost it. I swerved over to the side of the road, and tore Dylan out of the car. There was a large hill as the ramp goes from a lower road to the height of Route 295. As I pulled him out from the car I whipped him around with all the strength I had and he went tumbling down. As angry as I had been just a moment earlier, I was struck by what I was capable of as I watched him roll down the hill. I ran down and grabbed him and asked him if he was okay. Instead of a moment that we might reconnect emotionally, he shoved me hard and stormed up the hill. My moment of sympathy went away as he ran for the car. I was afraid for what he might do. Was he going to get in the car and lock the door? Was he going to get in the car and try to drive it? Was he going to damage the vehicle by vandalizing it in some way out of anger? I ran up after him to make sure that he didn't do something to damage my car or, more importantly, himself. I told him to get in the car but he refused and started walking away. Luckily I was still bigger and much stronger than he was. So, I chased him again, grabbed him and forced him back into the car in hopes that I could make it the next five or six more minutes to the exit where I would bring him into the crisis unit run by an organization called Sweetser.

Amy called and told them we were coming so at least they were prepared when I knocked on their door. We arrived at the small building in the middle of a roundabout in an industrial area of Portland. From the front door you could see Casco Bay. From another angle you looked directly at a large chicken processing plant.

I had never been in this building before but since Volk Packaging sold boxes to the chicken processor I had been by it hundreds of times. Inside the small building was a living room set up with a couple of couches and a television. There was a small office and five or six bedrooms. They did not have a lot of room to house kids in crisis. Luckily for us they had room that night. I basically told them I was not leaving this building with my son; they would have to help him because he wasn't coming with me. They were very understanding and told me that they would keep Dylan there at least for the night and we would meet with them in the morning to discuss what the next steps would be and how long he would stay. I filled out some paperwork and I left.

I was shocked as I sat in my car, less than a month from the time that I walked away from him at Spring Harbor, less than a month from when I sat in my car crying to the point where my shoulders were shaking and I could barely speak. This time I left him without a tear. I knew we needed more help. I knew he was out of control. There had to be somebody we had not talked to or met with or counted on who could help us. Before I left, I gave them Amy's name and our parents' names and again the name of our priest in hopes that since the drama of the church treasurer's death had ended he would find the time to visit Dylan. The ride from Cape Elizabeth to the Sweetser building was an easy one. It was right across from the Casco Bay Bridge. There would be no excuses this time if he did not come see Dylan, but he didn't. It was this lack of interest in our lives that led us to leave that church. God, however, always works for good. He directed us to the Church of the Holy Spirit.

At CHS, a Charismatic Episcopal Church, we found a wonderful family of believers who genuinely cared about us. The pastor, Father Jim King and his wife, Deborah, went out of their way to welcome us and offered to do whatever was necessary to make Dylan feel comfortable and welcome. It was such a breath of fresh air and exactly what we needed to keep our faith from a devastating blow. At CHS we finally found a church and a group of people who loved us for who we were. They didn't judge us or look down on Dylan. It was such a stark difference to the treatment we received from our previous church. A couple of months after we started at the church Dylan lost his beloved cat, Marlee. Father Jim didn't just call Dylan to express his sympathy. He came to our house and spent over an hour talking through Dylan's grief. Once again, God took care of Dylan and our family.

Dylan would remain at Sweetser for ten days. Meanwhile, he had been involved in a play with the Children's Theater of Maine. We were not sure how to handle it because the play was only a week after he was admitted to Sweetser so it was way too late for them to find another actor. We talked to the people at Sweetser and they gave Dylan permission to leave for the play. Amazingly, he knew all his lines and he knew exactly where he needed to be in every scene. Despite missing all of the week's dress rehearsals Dylan performed without a flaw in all his scenes. No one watching the play would ever have guessed that his life was crashing all around him. It was classic Dylan, stepping up and surprising all of us again with his bravery and resiliency. When the play ended we brought him back to the crisis unit. A few days later he was released but with no school to attend and no one to guide us, it was only a matter of time before he crashed again. Two weeks later, he was back at the crisis unit for a few days. This pattern would continue for several weeks until he started at Spurwink for their summer program.

Spurwink School

Dylan started seventh grade at Spurwink School in South Portland. He had spent the summer there trying to get assimilated with their program and also trying to get caught up on some of the schoolwork he had missed at the end of sixth grade while we were trying to figure out where he was going to go and what we were going to do next. His primary teacher was a woman named Traci Korman who was a single woman in her early thirties. She looked older than her years. I don't know if it was working with special needs children all the time, something in her personal life, or just her genetics, but she definitely looked older than she actually was chronologically. She was used to dealing with kids that had more severe special needs than Dylan. When I say that, what I mean is a kid who could not or would not talk back. They may resist her efforts to instruct them but they wouldn't be talking back or arguing with her at the cognitive level that Dylan would. This created a challenge for her and an opening for Dylan to try to manipulate the situation to get what he wanted. He did not want to be at this school. He wasn't happy about spending the summer there and he was very upset about the idea of not going back to the public middle school. Unfortunately going back to the public school wasn't even an option at this point. There was no indication from the public school that they would even take him back until he showed significant improvement from when he left in April.

Spurwink would turn out to be what we call, "the wasted year." Dylan learned very little academically or socially. He and his teacher fought all the time and he knew how to get under her skin. That was Dylan's specialty. He was very good at seeing people's weaknesses and then exploiting them verbally. When the teacher would challenge Dylan or end up in some confrontation with him about something, he would call her an old maid and ask her how she felt about her limited chances of ever marrying and having children now that she was over thirty. During our meetings she would tell us about these interactions.

She would imply that it didn't bother her but Dylan knew instinctively that it did. If he didn't think it was an effective method of throwing her off her game, he would have stopped and pursued another verbal jab. But he knew that whenever he would go after her about her marital status she would get more and more upset, raise her voice, and lose her patience quicker, and Dylan thrived on that. He was the seventh grade equivalent of Michael Jordan, who used to get inside opponents' heads on the basketball court to gain a mental advantage. Michael Jordan was the best player and so if he could get inside the opponent's head, he could separate the gap between him and the other players even more. Dylan used that same strategy with teachers.

It was November of his seventh grade school year at Spurwink when we had a teacher conference similar to what you would have in a public school, and Dylan sat in. They talked during this conference about the need for him to be involved in a social skills group. Dylan insisted that there was nothing that he was going to learn from a social skills group. He had been in many of them and was no better making friends than he was when he started. They explained to him that all of the kids at the school who were diagnosed with social defects took social skills groups and many benefited greatly from them. Dylan said to the director of the school, "And what kind of things do they learn at these social skills groups?"

The director sat up in his seat with confidence and told Dylan that they learn how to say hello to someone, shake their hand, make eye contact, and ask their name. "These were the kinds of things," he said, "that help you make friends."

It was almost as if Dylan was anticipating the answer, and with the skill of a good trial lawyer, set up the witness to answer the question the way he wanted it answered so he could pounce in response. It was this kind of scene that started making us think at this point what an incredible lawyer Dylan would be if we could only get him through school. His argumentative skills along with his large vocabulary and ability to read people's deficits would have served him well as a trial lawyer. As much as we talked about that, we knew it would probably never happen. We were just trying to get him through seventh grade in a school for special education students. Law school was a dream we knew would never happen.

So, the school director answered the question just the way our son wanted him to. Dylan sat up just as tall in his seat, leaned over the table, and with his finger pointed, said, "*That* is exactly why I don't need a social skills group. I know all those things. I know how to ask for someone's name and tell them mine. I know how to shake hands and look someone in the eye, and I know how to ask them about the weather. But that's not how you make friends—that's how you meet people. Making friends is much harder and takes much longer than those simple tasks."

Then Dylan used an analogy that blew me away and is something I'll never forget because it so beautifully explains the challenge that he has and that so many thousands of kids with Asperger's, higher or lower on the spectrum than Dylan, battle with every day. Dylan said, "What you're talking about is like me going to the beach and putting my toes in the Atlantic Ocean. I can do that, I can put my toes in the Atlantic Ocean. That's what shaking hands, smiling, and looking someone in the eye is doing. But making friends is like swimming to England." This incredible analogy reached deep into the psyche of Dylan, explaining just how overwhelming it was for him to make a true friend.

It was mid-December and as with many schools that time of year, Spurwink would hold a "holiday party" which included a "holiday concert," which we all used to call a "Christmas party" and a "Christmas concert." Without trying to sound like a complete insensitive jerk, the holiday concert at Spur-wink would be one of the lowest moments I would experience as a parent of a special needs child. It's hard to tell this story without coming across as a snob or an insensitive bore, but I'm going to risk that and explain how I felt at this concert because until that evening, I'm not sure I really knew in my heart that I had a child with serious special needs. After this concert, there was no getting around it.

We sat down in the little auditorium at Lyric Theater in South Portland right around the corner from the school. The students came out, including Dylan, and began singing Christmas carols.

It's hard to describe our feelings at this moment, and I can't speak for Amy when I say that I just wanted to cry. I wanted to curl up in a ball and cry. The kids on the stage were all doing the best they could. They were singing, some of them much louder than necessary and they were all enthusiastic, but they were all over the stage. Some of them didn't even realize what was going on around them, some of them were spinning in circles, and their hands were flapping. This was a group of special needs kids. When I was young, we would've called them "retards." That's not a politically correct term anymore. It is now considered mean. I can't remember the last time I even heard it used, but for those of you who are reading this book over thirty-five years old who grew up before political correctness, you know what I'm talking about. My son, my only son, was on stage singing with a bunch of "retards" and it was one of the most overwhelming and depressing moments of my parenting experience with Dylan. I know I sound like a complete jerk. And I feel like one as I read these words myself. It had nothing to do with the kids on the stage. They were kind, caring and happy kids all enjoying a Christmas concert. I was ashamed at my thoughts as I felt I was probably the only one in the room feeling such negative and mean things during such a festive event. Who did I think I was that my kid was supposed to be better than those other kids? Who am I to judge them? After all, my kid is right up there with them. Some of the parents there were thrilled to see their son or daughter up on stage singing but I had to come to grips hard and fast with the situation that I was in. Although it had been almost five years since his diagnosis, it had never hit me as hard as it did that moment. Even more than when we checked Dylan into Spring Harbor and drove away, there was something surreal about this holiday concert. It just reached deep inside me and slapped me across the face with reality, as if screaming at me saying, "Wake up, you have a son with *a lot* of issues. You better man up and handle what's ahead of you." I remember saying a quick and quiet prayer right there in the theater. "Lord, forgive me for thinking such awful thoughts about those children of God. I am going to need to lean on you a lot to get through this. Please help me and guide me to be the dad I never thought I would have to be for a son I never thought I would have."

The concert ended, and there was a social hour. Dylan thought being up on stage with all those kids was hysterical. This was not an uncommon reaction for Dylan. We should have expected it. He laughed and laughed as he talked about all the kids who were out of control on the stage and how the teachers had to pull them back to stand in line and do what they were supposed to. I tried to see the humor in it as he did, but any laughter that I had was for Dylan's sake and was completely insincere because all I really wanted to do was cry as I had just finally come to terms with the reality I was facing.

Dylan's First Comedy

Dylan always loved comedy. He usually was drawn to the most outrageous characters when he watched TV shows. His favorite shows were *Gilligan's Island*, *Saved By The Bell*, and *Seinfeld*. All the shows had one character that was uniquely goofy and often over the top in their comedic style. This appealed greatly to Dylan. When most kids watch TV shows they might be drawn to the coolest character but Dylan felt a connection with the character that was different from the others. He laughed hysterically at Gilligan, Screech, and Kramer. He would often start taking on some of their body movements and even voice fluctuations, tone and pitch. I remember when we would be having a conversation with him and we would have to say we are not talking to Screech we want to talk to Dylan because he was impersonating a *Saved By The Bell* character.

When Dylan was in eighth grade and told us that he wanted to try stand-up comedy it was not surprising. We had seen his comedic talent a couple of years earlier with some hysterical prank phone calls so we knew that he had the capability to be very funny. We remember thinking if he could find a way to talk about his unique views on the world from a young man with Asperger's he might have a niche in comedy that nobody else had discovered. But Dylan was not ready to out himself like that. His comedy had no reference to his disability. We understood that and suggested to him that maybe at some point down the road he might want to use it to his advantage. Now we had a fourteen-year-old interested in doing stand-up comedy but no opportunity to do it. A couple of years earlier Dylan had been involved with an improvisation group through the Children's Theater of Maine. While he showed moments of success with the improv group it was often challenging for him because it required very quick thinking on a variety of topics.

Dylan's world was focused intently on just a few topics, so we would sit in the audience and watch as he tried to weave every suggestion from the audience into something he liked instead of keeping with the topic at hand. We saw during these improv and theater performances that he had great capability to make people laugh. His role as the aunt in *James and The Giant Peach* had the audience cracking up, as well as his role as California Cowabunga in the middle school play, *Groovy*. His most impressive comedic performance would be during a middle school performance of *Aesop's Fables*. Mariah was in this play as well. It was one of the few times they were on stage together. Dylan stole the show with one hysterical line after another. Many of his lines were ad-libbed. It was nothing short of brilliant. Several people commented that he reminded them of Robin Williams. We were so proud of him and realized he had a special gift. We were wondering how to harness it and make the most of it. I was so disappointed when I found out that the person that was supposed to be recording the play did not do it correctly and we would never get a copy of Dylan's incredible performance. All we have are a few still shots to remember a wonderful night for Dylan, Amy and me. We cherished nights like that one. We loved any nights, days, moments, and events that would give us an opportunity to beam about the son we had so many challenges with but who had so much potential.

The Church of the Holy Spirit had recently opened a small monthly coffee house in the back of the church. Once a month, Deborah King, the wife of the pastor, did a wonderful job converting the back room into a quaint and cozy coffee house. The coffee house was dedicated to promoting local Christian bands and artists. Most nights it would be just music at the Holy Grounds Coffee House, but Deborah had a big heart for Dylan. She wanted to give him an opportunity to perform his comedy, as long as he promised to keep it rated PG. With genuine enthusiasm she invited him to perform at the Holy Grounds Coffee House once a month. He could do a five-to-seven minute set. Dylan was only fourteen so most of his jokes were clean. His jokes revolved around his life experiences and his unique thoughts on the world around him. The first night Dylan preformed he tried to take on a persona that was not really him. He put on a tacky sport jacket that we picked up at Goodwill and a shirt that didn't match. His goal was to be visually quirky.

Although his jokes were pretty successful, the adults that gave him feedback all suggested that he lose the sports jacket and wear something more age appropriate. We all suggested he be himself. Dylan resisted this advice and for one or two more performances he donned the sports jacket but eventually came to the conclusion that it was distracting and unnecessary. He finally realized that his jokes were funny enough without the strange get up. Some people might wonder how a child who had been through so much already could be willing to put himself out there doing stand-up comedy. Stand-up comedy is something that takes tremendous courage. When you get up on stage and sing a song, you know the chords and you can sing okay or well, you know the performance will be no worse than acceptable. When you are doing stand-up comedy everything comes down to whether what you think is funny will be funny for an audience. How you deliver it, the timing, tone, and facial gestures all have an impact on whether the audience laughs or not. It was a lot of pressure but Dylan didn't seem to feel that pressure, he genuinely thought his jokes were funny. In fact, he thought they were hysterical and if the audience didn't laugh it was because they "just didn't get it." To him, the pressure was on the audience to be able to understand his humor.

Years later, we sat with Dylan and watched *Man on the Moon*, the story of the late Andy Kaufman, as played by Jim Carey. We were taken aback, while watching this movie, at how similar Andy's approach toward comedy was to Dylan's. I was amazed at the similarities between Andy Kaufman and Dylan. Kaufman was even more outrageous and over the top but we figured by giving Dylan some time, he had that potential. I noticed the commonalities from the very beginning of the movie. In the first scene Andy is about six years old and he is up in his bedroom performing for his stuffed animals. His dad, much like I was many times when Dylan was little, is frustrated that he is not outside playing sports with the other kids in the neighborhood.

His dad was not angry or insulting, just confused about why his boy would want to be inside when the other kids were having so much fun outside. I could almost hear my own voice coming from the screen. Andy tells him that he is performing. His dad explains that he needs a real audience to perform, with "live people, that breathe." So Andy drags his three-year-old sister in to watch his show. When I saw this scene I remembered many days when Dylan, with no one to play with as the kids in the neighborhood were outside playing sports, would do a show or a skit or teach a class about his special interest to Mariah. Mariah would sit and give Dylan her full attention, attempting to learn all about birds or laughing hysterically at his silly antics.

She was always his best audience. If you open a Volk family photo album from 1996 you will see dozens of pictures of Dylan making some kind of face or in the midst of some scene and on the side of him you will see his adoring little sister, Mariah, smiling ear to ear at her big brother whom she called "Nini."

The next scene jumps into Andy Kaufman as an adult performing in a club. He is doing the same exact routine he did in the previous scene with his three-year-old sister, but the adult audience is not nearly as amused. When the club owner tells him that he is no longer welcome at open mic night because no one is reacting to his comedy, Andy tells the owner that people are reacting, one guy was really upset and several stormed out. He cannot seem to understand that people getting upset is not helping the nightclub's business. Andy finds it entertaining to get a rise out of his audience, to elicit emotion from the crowd. Dylan's approach was often not much different. In my opinion, Dylan was funnier, but I may be biased.

One of the most interesting scenes in the movie was when Andy had just performed at Arizona State University. Instead of doing a comedy show he read the entire book, every word, of *The Great Gatsby*. When his manager, played by fellow *Taxi* co-star Danny Devito, confronted him the next day, he said words that reminded me of Dylan's comedy going back to his days making prank phone calls. He said, "You have to look inside, and ask this question, who are you trying to entertain, the audience or yourself?"

Dylan enjoyed this brand of humor in his off-stage life as well. When he was sixteen years old, Amy and I were in a long line at the register of our local drugstore when Dylan exclaimed, in the most audible but perfectly calmed and well-timed voice, "Wow, Mom, I am so glad that you are finally off meth!" Needless to say, that created quite the collection of head turns and eyes down as people awkwardly tried to pretend they didn't hear him say that. Amy and I just quietly laughed as it would have made it worse to walk up and down the checkout line explaining Dylan's unusual method of comedy. Another memorable moment took place when we were out for dinner as a family in Florida. The restaurant was in a strip mall and next to it was a pet store. As soon as we ordered dinner, Amy and the kids went over to see the dogs and cats in the pet store. So it did not look like we abandoned the restaurant, I stayed at the table. Dylan was the first one to return and as he arrived I was talking to the waitress. She had a thick New York accent so I was asking her where she was from. Dylan saw this as a great opportunity to try out some comedy at my expense. He didn't miss a beat as he blurted out to me, making sure the waitress clearly heard him, "Oh, jeez, don't tell me you're going to have another affair!" The poor young lady serving us could not get away quickly enough and Dylan had a big laugh as she awkwardly scurried off. Amy and I were getting accustomed to his humor, so we usually laughed it off as Dylan being Dylan.

Dylan loved to push the boundaries which is why he enjoyed making those prank phone calls. It is also why he often had Tim Ferrell at the Comedy Connection and Deborah King at the church coffee house on egg shells during his performances. They were just waiting to see if Dylan would say something unscripted and outrageous. Dylan performed about a dozen times within the next year and a half at Holy Grounds but eventually he felt that the audiences there had come to listen to music and many times they weren't in the frame of mind to hear jokes. Quite often when the music stopped people used that opportunity to chat, eat, and clean their table. All the commotion would go on while Dylan was trying to perform. He found it distracting and eventually stopped performing there.

Dylan was not the first comedian in our family. My father's mother, Charlotte, had spent many years performing stand-up comedy. She never had an agent or even attempted to make her act professional but she was never happier than when she was up in front of an audience telling jokes. Every year at our company party she was the entertainment and everyone looked forward to her act. My grandmother was a comedian in the tradition of Buddy Hackett or Jackie Mason. She told stories, often in a fake Yiddish accent, with a punchline. Her punch lines were mostly rated R. The older she became, the funnier it was to hear her tell jokes that made my truck drivers blush. My grandmother passed away in June 2005, just before Dylan started performing comedy. It would have made her so proud to see him entertaining an audience and I have no doubt she would have been his biggest fan.

Dylan and Nony, as we called her, were kindred spirits. They had a special bond.

Mariah was always Dylan's best audience and biggest fan

Transition Back to Middle School

Dylan was determined to get back to the middle school before his class graduated. And when Dylan sets his mind on something, he is almost impossible to stop. The transition, however, was anything but easy. The first step was convincing the decision makers at the middle school that Dylan was ready to return. We had a P.E.T. and, as usual, there were almost a dozen people in the room including our special advocate, Lou McIntosh. The one thing we knew with Lou there was we wouldn't have our rights trampled on like in the past. Lou would ask for specific markers to determine whether Dylan could or could not return to school. The problem with such "data" is that it is almost all subjective. For example, one of the goals was listed as "Dylan will demonstrate the ability to have five appropriate conversations with a peer or adult (with Dylan taking at least three conversational turns) in a small group setting each by January." Another one was, "Dylan will choose a calming strategy 100 percent of the time for five consecutive trials and follow through with using it 80 percent of the time for five consecutive trials." Amy and I did not have much confidence that this level of data could be accurately and consistently tracked in a public school setting. The teachers had enough on their plates without adding the extreme detail of tracking the conversational turns or calming strategies being utilized by our son.

At the meeting in early September, the education director asked the group, "Does anyone here feel that Dylan is ready to rejoin the public school with success at this time?" No one raised a hand or spoke up in the affirmative. Even though it was a public school we did not seem to have the ability to say, "Take him back now." Dylan had to earn his way to Scarborough Middle School. There was no question in anyone's mind that he was determined to return to the public school. In an interview during some testing he told the psychologist, "Socially, I'm tired of annoying people or saying inappropriate things and then suffering the consequences. If I could stop myself, I would." He told us, in no uncertain terms, "There is no way that I am not graduating eighth grade with my class. No way."

* * *

They suggested that Dylan start by attending the first couple of periods of the day. After the first couple of periods they suggested he could go outside and get on a small bus that would take him back to Spurwink for the remainder of the school day. Dylan was there but was instructed to be on his best behavior or he could ruin his chances of getting back to the middle school. When they suggested he get on a small bus right in front of the school he couldn't help but speak up. Dylan explained, with calmness and reason, that he was trying very hard to gain back some semblance of social status and that would be virtually impossible if they made him climb on a small bus during the school day. None of the school administrators appeared to appreciate Dylan's concerns. They basically reverted back to the same argument that Mrs. Little gave us that got us into this situation in 2004, "you could if you wanted to." We were quick to stick up for Dylan. We asked if they were willing to compromise and come up with another option. Dylan wanted a car to pick him up, but they said that was simply impossible. There were insurance and liability issues that they could not avoid. It had to be a small bus.

Dylan was quick to come up with a solution. He said, "I will agree to get on the small bus if you let me go out the side door near the gym and have it park on the side of the building." They looked at each other as if they were trying to find a way to reject his plan but there was really no logical reason to shoot him down. They agreed to Dylan's plan and he began the process of working his way back into the middle school.

DYLAN'S TAKE: *Lots of these unpleasant memories I had forgotten about, but the first thing that comes back to me when I think about this time was the same shock and genuine awe I remember feeling back in 2006 when this all went down. Those professional adults working in the educational field could not understand or respect the very healthy desire of a kid in middle school (especially one with Asperger's) to blend in socially with his peers. It was simply a reality that arriving outside the enormous double-doored entrance to our school in a short bus was a social taboo. It is one that would have completely ostracized me in middle school. It was so obvious to me back then, and still seems obvious now. And I was the one with the social understanding disorder! Those presumably college-educated individuals, however, couldn't seem to understand this concept. It seemed to me that if you are working in a public school, the knowledge and appreciation of the social dynamics of young teens should be imperative to that profession. What always separated me from the majority of people on the autism spectrum, as a kid and now, was an honest desire to fit in. This desire should have been recognized by the people at the school, and appreciated. Instead I was left desperately trying to explain to people three times my age why rolling up to school in a neon-yellow short bus would have basically been like walking around the school with a huge sign on my shirt that said, "I'm weird!!"*

Mission Accomplished!!

When June arrived, announcement for the eighth grade graduation came out and it included a dance. Dylan had his first girlfriend and was very excited to be going to the dance. She was a sweet kid who seemed rather shy but seemed to genuinely like Dylan, and he was on cloud nine. Attending the ceremony was an extremely emotional event for us. We got there a little late, as we were not expecting the gym where the graduation was being held to be quite as packed as it was, and found our way to a seat at the top of the bleachers. It gave us a nice perspective of the whole room. I remember looking around at all the parents in the gym. There wasn't a parent in the room that wasn't visibly happy and proud to be there to watch their child complete middle school and begin the journey of the next phase of their life into high school. And as I looked around at all those faces, many of them very familiar, I became emotional. Turning to Amy I said, "There is not one kid that's going to walk into this gym that went through as much as Dylan to be on that stage." Amy teared up as I had a hard time even getting the end of that sentence out.

As the music began and the Scarborough Middle School eighth grade class of 2006 walked into the room, Amy and I both broke down, crying more tears of relief than tears of joy. There were other moms and dads that were crying or tearing up, but we were full out sobbing as if we'd been holding it in for months. The moment just overwhelmed us. We started this middle school journey in 2003 not knowing in our wildest imagination that during the next three years we would walk away as we checked our son into a mental institution and several crisis units; Dylan would be pulled out of school and not even attend his entire seventh grade year within the middle school walls and then claw his way back with grit and determination when everybody doubted, *everybody* doubted, that he could do it, and that he could be a full-time student when his eighth-grade year was completed. He didn't doubt it and maybe his mother believed it as well, but I can honestly say that I didn't think that he could do it. I sat there in that gym with tears pouring down my cheeks and my shoulders shaking, trying to avoid drawing too much attention to myself but unable to control the flow of emotion as Dylan walked into the room in his blue shirt and tie, ready to stride up to the front of the stage, collect his diploma, and then attend a dance with a girl he called his girlfriend who didn't have special needs, who looked at him like just another kid. I wanted to give that girl the biggest hug but I was afraid I'd look like some kind of freak because she barely knew me. She made Dylan feel so special. Amy and I knew their relationship wasn't going to last a long time. School was going to end and probably so was their relationship. However, for that one night, Dylan was just another kid. There isn't a dollar figure I could put on it or a way that I could thank that girl for what she gave Dylan and us that night. She had no idea idea how she was impacting our lives. On that night, Dylan was very close to grabbing that rabbit.

The Wedding Crasher

In the spring and summer of 2006, Mariah was back on the ball field playing for the Southern Maine Flame and I was again managing the team. I was also president of the organization so I had a lot of responsibility, both on and off the field. Mariah was playing U-12 for the first time, and she was excited about her upcoming season. Some of the girls were the same girls she had been playing with since she was nine and some of the girls were new to the team.

It was a little bit different for us this summer because Dylan was at the age where he was very difficult to leave home with his grandparents, but he was definitely too young to be left home alone. For the first time, if Amy wanted to come to the tournaments, Dylan had to come along.

Every year on Mother's Day weekend, there's a tournament in Chelmsford, Massachusetts, called The Mother's Day Massacre. It's a tournament that we had been in, in the previous couple of years, and played in every year after that up until 2014 when Serena played in her first year of Flame softball. We had a lot of memories from these games. One of the things that Amy finds funny is my ability to remember dozens and dozens of games in great detail. When I go to those fields in Chelmsford I can just stare out at the three fields and memories and visions flood into my head of former players, former parents, game situations, and great stories.

One of the stories from this particular weekend in Chelmsford was not a story of softball, but about Dylan. We had an afternoon game and did not get back to the hotel until around 6:00. We made the mistake of going to the pool before dinner. We went down to the hotel restaurant as a team. The Radisson Hotel in Chelmsford is very large and they have a pretty nice restaurant. It also is a popular choice for many wedding receptions in the spring and throughout the summer.

We all sat down to have dinner. Serena was two at the time and not very patient. Lilly was eight and Dylan was almost fifteen. Dinner was taking an extraordinarily long time, taking us after nine o'clock before we finally ate. The lesson I learned was that you can control when the girls get out of the pool, but you can't control when dinner comes out to the table. From then on, we always ate dinner first and then, when it was time to go to the pool, we were able to decide how long they got to swim based on how long dinner took. Sometimes, the girls didn't get to swim at all. But, one of the special things about travel softball, especially when they're fourteen and under, is the pool time, so we tried to at least get them fifteen minutes in the pool after a long day of softball.

As we sat around waiting for dinner to come that evening, Dylan was getting very impatient so we suggested that he go for a walk around the hotel and come back in about ten minutes. If dinner came, somebody would run out and find him. But the waiter had told us we still had another ten minutes, so we figured at the rate it had been going that evening, he'd be back in plenty of time.

Dylan left and about ten minutes later our meals did come out. We waited a few minutes for Dylan to come back but when he didn't, I volunteered to go look for him. I went to the main part of the hotel and walked around everywhere but could not find Dylan. There was no sign of him. I was not worried that he was kidnapped, that's for sure. One thing we always joked about was that if anybody ever kidnapped Dylan, they would be calling us, offering the ransom money as opposed to asking for ransom money. With no luck, I went back and sat down to have dinner with the team.

About ten minutes after that, Dylan came back, grinning and excited. We asked him why he was laughing so much as he approached the table and he told us how he had crashed the wedding that was being held at the hotel. He went into the reception hall, actually sat down to a table to eat, talked to a bunch of people, and even got himself in some of their photographs. When we asked him what he would have said if somebody asked who he was, he said that he would ask them before they had a chance to talk to him,

"Are you with the bride or the groom?" And then he would say he was with whoever they were not, so as to avoid the chance that someone might think that this fourteen-year-old boy had crashed a wedding party because his dinner meal was taking too long with his little sister's softball team.

Everybody at the table got a huge kick out of listening to Dylan tell the story. He told it with great excitement and animation. He was an amazing story teller and was able to captivate a group of people.

The Prank Caller

The Dylan stories in the summer of 2006 did not end with the wedding crashing. We were at the ASA State Championship Tournament in Waterville, Maine. We had competed well on Saturday and we were in the single-elimination games on Sunday. The Saturday games can be stressful, but no matter what happens during the three games on Saturday, all the teams know they are still playing on Sunday. However, if you lose on Sunday, you are immediately eliminated, and nobody likes to go home early, especially my group of competitive players.

We were playing our first game at 9:30. Dylan really did not have any interest in watching girls softball, so he requested permission to stay in the hotel, which was right up the street from the fields. Between games, when check-out time arrived, if we were still in the winner's bracket, Amy would go pick him up. We reluctantly agreed, giving him several rules about staying in the hotel by himself, but we didn't think of all the things he could do alone in a hotel room.

Around the third inning, the score was close and I was doing my best to give our girls any advantage that I could when my phone rang. I usually put it on silent during the games, so when it buzzed I didn't even look at it at first and just felt the buzzing in my pocket. Amy was at the fields, so I couldn't imagine who could be calling me so early on a Sunday morning. But then, a couple of minutes later, it started buzzing again. This time I knew I had to at least reach into my pocket to see who it was. I pulled out my phone and the name on the screen was the Holiday Inn in Waterville.

I knew the people at this hotel very well because for four-and-a-half years, my sales territory for Volk Packaging included Waterville and Bangor so I often would stop at this hotel to make phone calls or to do paperwork during the day. They had a nice desk set up there and a phone. In 2006, cell phone calls were still expensive, so whenever I could, I would try to find a place to make free phone calls.

Because of my time spent at this hotel, several of the front desk staff either knew me by face or by name. Darlene, the hotel manager, knew me by name. In 2006, we still sent and received faxes, as emails were not yet available on our cell phones, so I was at the front desk quite often asking to send or receive a fax. I knew her pretty well. When I picked up the phone, Darlene was on the other end. She said, "Derek we have a problem here at the hotel."

I said, "What is it?"

"Apparently, there have been a number of prank phone calls that have been made from your room."

It didn't take me any time to admit that my son was in the room, he was fourteen years old, and he was the culprit. I apologized and told them that I would either contact him immediately or that we would come back to get him.

Dylan loved to make prank phone calls and I have to admit, he was actually very good at it. He had heard the Jerky Boys, thought they were hysterical, and figured he could do something just as funny. The good thing about Dylan's phone calls was that they were not like the Jerky Boys in their vulgarity and inappropriateness. Often times, he would just call people asking them very silly questions as if he was extremely confused about one topic or another. He would call a record store, for example, and ask about one artist but pretend he couldn't remember the name, and then when they said the name, he would use that as some sort of a play on words to go to another artist, and when they said that artist, he would go to another, and the game would go on like that for a while.

He knew so much about music that he could do this for lengthy periods of time and keep these people on the phone to the point where they were not only confused, but very frustrated, which he found hysterical. He even bought a recording device all by himself at Radio Shack so he could tape his phone calls. We still have the recordings today. By his request, they were burned onto CDs. It created an awkward parenting moment for us because he would keep busy for hours in his room making prank phone calls and, while we knew it wasn't the right thing to do, he was not being vulgar or inappropriate. For a kid who had no friends and no social life, it was hard to say no to this relatively harmless activity. Plus, they were funny, very funny. He would run downstairs and tell us, "Listen to this one, listen to this one!" We could not help laughing as we tried to tell him not to do it again. One thing we learned with Dylan is that traditional parental lines are blurry and gray. While we knew we shouldn't encourage him, we also respected his talent. He was hysterical and we were happy to see his joy at his ability to make us laugh.

Amy did go back to the hotel to get Dylan, and brought him to the game. It was one thing to make phone calls from our home, but it's another thing to do it from a hotel that tracks every phone call they get.

The softball team went on to make it to the championship that day, but unfortunately lost against our rival team from Augusta. Despite having to deal with Dylan, it was a great weekend of softball.

DYLAN'S TAKE: *Creating premises and characters to use in these prank calls was a pastime that gave me something to be happy about during a relatively dark and awkward period of time in my early teenage years. Like my dad wrote about, it is true that I had really no friends, no social life, and just wasn't really fitting in with any of my peers as a thirteen-and-fourteen year-old adolescent boy. I hadn't really come into myself yet and just didn't know the right way to present myself to the world. I always knew how to be off-the-wall and over-the-top with my comedy. The former Comedy Central television show, Crank Yankers, had me so awed at the idea of doing real prank phone calls as comedy. And, like most teenagers, the way my parents at first strongly disapproved of it made the calls much more exciting to do when they weren't looking. I learned from hearing these professional comedians that the key was to be funny and outrageous, but also keep it just believable enough that the person on the other end doesn't hang up and end the call. It's harder than it sounds to take a prank call from just goofing around to bona fide comedy. I would tell everybody in school about it and even eventually managed to get a teacher (who always supported me), Mr. Townsend, to play one of my tapes for all my classmates over the sound system in a study hall. That gave me pretty boss status and made any conflicts about them with my parents well worth it.*

— 6 —

The Rabbit Gains Ground

Freshman Year

Every kid starts high school with a mixture of excitement, anxiousness, and varying levels of enthusiasm. Dylan was no exception. He had worked really hard to get himself back into the public school to finish eighth grade, and he was determined to make high school a success. He was assigned primarily to the special education room, but he had a couple of mainstream classes as well. It seemed like a good mix, and the special education teacher seemed to be very understanding, patient, and knowledgeable about Asperger's. It was a very different and refreshing change from middle school.

Freshman year, for the most part, was a successful one. It was one of the better years we have had. Dylan was relatively happy in school and not overwhelmingly shunned socially. We tried to keep him busy with activities he would enjoy. He joined an improvisation group through the Children's Theater of Maine and had a really good time attending the improv training classes and practice sessions on Saturdays.

Although Dylan has always been very funny and still was working on his comedy, improv was not something that came naturally to him. We were surprised by his struggles with the improv performances. He had a great time at the practices, and he did okay during the performances. But what we noticed, that others probably did not, was Dylan's small scope of topic that would reoccur over and over again during his improv performances. He had tremendous knowledge about certain topics—music, for example—but little ability to turn an improv scene into something entertaining if it was a topic that was completely out of his "topic of interest." Like with many of his conversations going all the way back to when he was little and only wanted to talk about birds or *Star Wars*, that pattern continued in his improv class.

Whatever the topic was that the audience helped create, Dylan would somehow bring it back around to what he wanted to talk about. This was not obvious to most of the people in the audience because they didn't know

Dylan, so they didn't see the pattern like we did. However, to Amy and me, it was very obvious. We tried to talk to Dylan on several occasions about staying on topic during the performances, but he had a hard time with that idea.

Nonetheless, we were very proud of him for trying improv comedy. It's a very challenging and demanding form of theater. Unlike the TV show, *Whose Line Is It Anyway?* the objective in true improv is not always just about being funny; it's about taking the topics presented and performing a scene that's as real as possible based on those topics. Dylan saw it as a way to work on his humor, and for the most part, he was pretty funny during the shows. He was also still performing some comedy when the opportunities arose. They were there to hear music, not comedy, and they rarely laughed or even paid attention. Yet, Dylan maintained his interest in comedy and continued to write jokes, and we did everything we could to try to encourage his interest.

Dylan in the Spotlight

In September of Dylan's sophomore year, his interest in pursuing a comedy career, or at least a comedy hobby, continued. Portland's only comedy club, "The Comedy Connection," was holding a class for people interested in pursuing a career in comedy or advancing their skills as a comedian. We signed Dylan up for the class. He had already taken this class once before and really enjoyed it, so when it came around to doing it again, we signed him right up. They preferred students to go through the class only once but were willing to accept Dylan. They knew him and how much he liked doing stand-up comedy. Once again, he was the youngest in the class, as most of the students consisted of people in their twenties and thirties and even a couple of senior citizens. Dylan was the only high school student.

When he arrived at the first class, there was an attendee there named Pamela Cragin. She was a writer with the plan to do a story about the comedy class and stand-up comedy in Portland. After sitting in on one class, she made a decision, if it was acceptable to us, to change the focus of her story to Dylan, and she called to ask us if we would mind. She said that she found him very intriguing and thought there was more than enough there to write a story about him. When we explained to her about his Asperger's, she became even more interested. We checked with Dylan to see if he was okay with this idea, and not surprisingly to Amy and me, he was very enthusiastic about it. The magazine was called *Salt* and its focus was Maine human interest stories. She needed to have permission to follow Dylan around as much as possible for a couple of months, maybe even visit him at school, talk to people that knew him, and spend time in our home, interviewing us, his siblings, and of course Dylan. We were okay with this, as we knew how much Dylan was excited for it, and maybe it was an opportunity to educate people about Asperger's and perhaps give him some publicity about his comedy. It also gave Dylan something to feel special about, and in his life, that didn't happen very often.

The one caveat that Dylan had for her in writing the story was he did not give her permission to say that he had Asperger's. She was really challenged by this, especially after getting to know Dylan and spending time with him because she learned very quickly how much his Asperger's affected his life on a day-to-day basis and how much it was such a part of who he is. She even called us on a couple of occasions and even asked us if we could convince him to allow her to talk about his Asperger's. We did talk to him about it but he was adamant that he did not want the article to include the word Asperger's and he refused to participate if it did. Pam even contacted Tim Ferrell, the instructor of the comedy class that Dylan was taking, to see if he would be willing to talk to Dylan in an effort to sway him to change his mind. I don't blame her for wanting to talk about the Asperger's aspect of his life because without it, the story was definitely missing something.

Tim didn't get any further than we did with Dylan, although he finally did allow her to say that he had a neurological disorder that impacted his social skills in the hopes that people would draw their own conclusions. However, in 2007, there were still a lot of people who didn't know much about Asperger's. This would have been a great opportunity to educate them.

Pam followed Dylan around to his job at Jim's Pizza, cleaning tables and sometimes preparing salads. Jim's Pizza had hired Dylan and he seemed to be doing pretty well keeping the job, but it was not without challenges. As she would report in her article, Dylan often made inappropriate comments which caused problems for his coworkers. He would make references to his female coworkers' anatomy, particularly their breasts, in an effort in his mind, to be funny and edgy. Dylan's comedy when he was on stage was frequently inappropriate for his age. It was something that his instructor, Tim Ferrell, often talked to him about. In addition to teaching the class, we hired him to be Dylan's private comedy coach. Dylan was sixteen but had a "baby face" and looked fourteen. Tim explained to him on multiple occasions that audiences are uncomfortable with someone who's sixteen telling sex jokes, much less someone who looks fourteen. Tim said those jokes wouldn't work until he was older. However, Dylan really struggled with this advice because he so desperately wanted to push the envelope on stage the same way he liked to push the envelope off stage.

On one occasion at work, a black man came into the restaurant. Maine is over 98 percent white and Scarborough is even whiter. There's very little ethnic diversity in our town, so when a black man came into Jim's Pizza, Dylan thought it would be funny to ask him if he was Barack Obama. As one can imagine, this did not go over well with the customer, the uncomfortable patrons who witnessed it, his coworkers, or his boss. Dylan didn't really care. He only cared if he thought something was funny and, if it made somebody uncomfortable, then it became even funnier to him.

Pam shadowed him and spent hours talking to him, taking him places, and it was really nice in many ways. She seemed to genuinely like Dylan, and he sensed that. Because of this, he wanted to be around her more and never minded when she would ask to infiltrate his life. He saw it as a positive in almost every way. She even talked to a couple of kids at school about Dylan, including Dylan's friend Patrick Damicis, who was on Dylan's Little League team. Later when Patrick was in high school and the pressures of the social food chain became too great, he rarely called Dylan anymore or wanted to hang out with him. The same theory that Dylan had in fourth grade when he said, "Why would anybody want to hang out with me?" when referring to the fact that he had an ed-tech, became even more common in high school, as kids that were once his friends deserted him. And when I say, "deserted him," I don't say that in a disparaging way. I was in high school once too. I understand those pressures, so Amy and I both knew that kids like Pat were not turning on Dylan out of malicious intent. Instead, it was out of sheer survival instinct in the battle grounds of high school. Pat was a good friend to Dylan and we appreciated his role in Dylan's life.

Dylan would eventually lose his job at Jim's Pizza in the course of Pam's writing the article. It would be the first of many, many jobs that Dylan would lose because of his Asperger's.

Amy was home on the computer one day in her office when she received a call from the owner of Jim's Pizza. He told Amy that he had to fire Dylan because he was worried about a lawsuit from all the inappropriate comments he was making. He had warned him repeatedly but Dylan seemed uninterested or incapable of stopping himself. His boss had no choice; he had to terminate Dylan's employment. But then, he surprised Amy by asking her to tell Dylan. In fact he didn't even ask her, he basically told her to let Dylan know that he didn't need to come into work anymore. Amy was very quick with a response and said, "Absolutely not. I'm not going to be the one to tell Dylan he's fired. We've also been warning him about his inappropriate comments and he hasn't listened to us. He's not going to believe me when I tell him why he was fired. He's going to take it out on me and he's not going to learn a lesson if I fire him. It's not my responsibility—it's yours."

I was so glad that Dylan's boss called Amy instead of me. She's always better in situations like that. I think I would've been more likely to go along with a plan to tell Dylan myself. So when Dylan came home from school, Amy didn't say a word. When it was time for him to go to work, she gave him a ride to Jim's Pizza and waited outside, knowing he was going to get fired. Dylan was very angry about losing his job, but handled it in a surprisingly mature way and knew he had nobody to blame but himself. Yet, at the same time, he knew that it was, at least at the time, more about being incapable of stopping himself, than being uninterested.

A couple of weeks later, Pam was just about done her time with him when he took a turn for the worse, and Amy and I were going to have to make some big decisions regarding what our next step was in the crazy and unpredictable parenting of Dylan.

Boarding School? Is That an Option?

When sophomore year started, we were cautiously optimistic that things would go okay. We were cautiously optimistic because we never knew what would be around the next corner. But freshman year had gone by without too many major glitches. Academically, Dylan was doing well. He seemed to have a good connection with the teacher in the special education room, Mr. Townsend. And socially, he was surviving, which is not really success in any way, but he was navigating the challenging high school food chain the best he could. The problem was, of course, that he was barely on the food chain.

It's one thing to be on the top of the high school food chain where you're a star of something in some way or when you are considered valuable in the eyes of the other high school students. But there are very few kids who fall into that category. There are very few captains of the football team, stars of the soccer team or head-cheerleader, which in Scarborough is not really considered the top of the food chain. In Scarborough, to be popular you have to play sports, so a girl who's the star of the soccer team is of higher value than the captain of the cheerleading squad. And then there are the majority of the kids in school who fall in the middle ranks somewhere. If there's a school with a thousand students, there would be a significant bell curve with the most popular on one side, the least popular on the other side, and the bulk of the students in the middle. Dylan's problem was that he didn't fall anywhere on that bell curve. If anything, he was on the low popularity side, but to him, he felt that he was *below* the least popular kids, that he was completely unnoticed altogether. And sometimes, that's the worst place to be. Even unpopular kids are noticed or have other friends who are in the same boat as they are. It only takes one or two friends to feel that you have someplace where you are cared for. Dylan really didn't have anybody at the school that cared whether he showed up the next day or not, and that's an extremely difficult place to be. As a parent, it is brutal to watch your child experience it. We knew all along that if he could just find one friend, one person that liked him for who he was, it would make such a difference. He didn't find that person in his sophomore year. As a result, he slipped further into despair. Although it was never clinically diagnosed, he was probably suffering from clinical depression.

I remember many times when he was younger, therapists would say, "I think Dylan's depressed." Amy and I would say, "Well overall he has a pretty good attitude about things, given the fact that he has no friends, no social life, and no real hobbies that give him a lot of joy. So, why wouldn't he be a little depressed? Wouldn't you be?" In fact, most people, given the circumstances that Dylan faced throughout his life, would be much more depressed than Dylan ever was. I've mentioned this before, but his optimism was sometimes beyond what was reasonable. He felt like things would always turn out better, eventually.

But then we reached October of his sophomore year, where nothing seemed to be going right, and Dylan lost, or seemed to have lost, the most important thing that we all need to keep going during tough times, and that's hope. He seemed to have no hope that things were going to get better. I remember going in and saying goodnight to him one night, and it was more than one night that this happened, but I remember him looking at me and saying, "When you come in the morning, don't be surprised to see me hanging from the ceiling fan."

I said, "Dylan, why would you say something like that?"

He quickly responded, "Why wouldn't I? Every day I wake up seems to be worse than the day before. Nothing is getting better. It's just getting worse and worse."

Terrified he would actually hurt himself, Amy and I took all the wires and belts out of his room before he went to sleep that night. We took them out of his computer, the outlets, even the bathrobe belt he had hanging on his bathroom door was hidden away from him. He had talked about suicide in the past, but on this night, it seemed to be more than just an idle threat or a reach for attention. He was getting to the point where he wasn't a kid anymore and we couldn't take these kinds of threats lightly in any way.

Amy and I didn't know what to do. We were at our wits end as to what our next step should be. Sometimes, God puts people in a certain place at a certain time to do or say just the right thing that changes your life. I met someone who changed the course of our lives only a couple of days after that terrifying night.

* * *

When we got married, Amy gave me a cross necklace as a wedding gift. I wore that necklace every day and never took it off. That previous summer we were up on Sebago Lake visiting our friends, Kim and Drew Mader, who had rented a cottage on Sebago Lake for a week. We put our boat in the water and rode over to spend the day with the Maders and their kids, Katie who is the same age as Mariah, Charlie who is a couple of years younger, and Maggie who is Lilly's age. We got along very well with them and it was nice to spend a day up at the lake.

One of the things we do when we visit Sebago Lake is go to a place called Frye's Leap. The eighty-foot rock wall is named after Captain Joseph Frye. Legend has it that the Scarborough, Maine, native was being chased by Indians when he got to the end of land. He looked over into Sebago Lake. Not knowing what to do or how to turn back, he jumped and swam across to what is now called Frye's Island. Today, it is illegal to jump off the top of Frye's Leap but occasionally people do. It is a risky jump because you have to jump out, not just down. You have to clear some rocks that jettison out from the rock wall. There are smaller, lower-level rocks that are safer to jump from. Some are eight to ten feet, some are about twentyfeet. They are fun and a lot safer to jump off. However, there's no place to park a boat. Someone has to stay in the boat while everybody jumps off and swims over to "the Leap." As we were doing that, I was swimming with our youngest daughter, Serena, who was four at the time. The waves were pretty rough that day, as they often are on Sebago Lake, and she was getting tossed around. Even though she had a life jacket on, she was scared. In a moment of panic, she reached out and grabbed my necklace, which ripped from my neck and sank to the bottom of the lake. That was the end of the necklace that Amy gave me when we were married seventeen years earlier.

What did that story have to do with anything? I had not gotten around to getting another necklace until that fall. A couple of days after the incident with Dylan saying he was going to hang himself, I went into Cross Jewelers on Congress Street in Portland to look at some cross necklaces that could replace the one Amy gave me. I had been trying to find one that was similar but hadn't had any success. The woman who came out to help me make the decision was a woman named Lynn Ouellette. I went to church with Lynn back when Dylan and Mariah were little, and Amy and I were attending Woodford's Congregational Church in Portland.

After picking out the necklace that I liked, she was writing up the paperwork and for no reason other than just to be polite, I asked her how her two daughters were. She told me her older daughter was doing well at some college somewhere, and her younger daughter was doing really well now that she was attending a boarding school. I asked, "What do you mean she was at a boarding school?"

Lynn said, "Well, she was having a lot of problems in school socially. Academically she was doing fine, but socially she was very challenged and it was really starting to get to her." Lynn went on to describe Dylan's life, explaining how her daughter had never been invited to any birthday parties or school get-togethers outside of class, and that her daughter, who was a junior in high school, had felt very sad and alone most of the time.

As I listened, she told me about the impact that going to this boarding school had on her daughter. She said she was now like a different person. It was like a flower had bloomed that had been sitting and rotting. I asked some questions and she told me the school was in Connecticut. After buying the necklace, I went down and sat in the car not moving for what seemed like hours, and I thought to myself, "Is that an option?"

Amy and I had often talked, jokingly, about sending Dylan off to military school. It was always in the back of our minds, wishing that it was a possibility on those days when it felt like it was too challenging to go on any longer. But the idea of boarding school for a child with special needs had never really occurred to us as a serious option. We always kind of thought of boarding school as something that the ultra-rich go to, like on the seventies sitcom, *Facts of Life*. After this woman, who was a single mom in Portland, Maine, realized that her daughter's life was in a situation that she couldn't get her out of, she had sought boarding school and it actually worked. I picked up the phone and called Amy. I told her the story of how I had just run into

Lynn, and then I asked her the question I was asking myself, "Is that an option for us?"

Amy was home that day and got on the computer to do some research. As it turned out, there were several options for boarding schools for kids that were going through difficult times, and even a couple for kids on the autism spectrum. The problem was that most of these schools were *very* expensive. After hours of research, Amy had narrowed it down to several schools that were a possibility. It was not as if there were dozens to choose from, but of the ten or so options that she found around the country online, she narrowed it down to three or four that might be viable options for Dylan.

One of them was in Arizona. This was a school primarily for young people on the autism spectrum, but the challenge with this school was that they all lived in one house, and we were not sure how that would work out. Dylan is very challenging and often very difficult to live with. Our concern was that after a month or so, he would have alienated everyone in the house one way or another, and then what? That school was also about $70,000 a year, which was not really the price range we were looking for. There was also another school in Connecticut right about that same price range that was also an option as far as accepting him into the program, but again, it was more than what we felt like we could handle financially.

Amy's first choice for a boarding school for Dylan was a place in North Carolina, just outside of Asheville called Southeast Journeys. The problem with that school, despite being far away, was that it was basically like boot camp for autistic kids. It was a converted summer camp that they turned into a school-year program, and it was definitely a place that Dylan would not choose for himself. There were no TVs, cellphones, or computers allowed, and you lived in basically a summer bunk house that you'd see at a summer overnight camp with eight to ten other kids on the autism spectrum. We knew he would absolutely hate it, but it was an option.

The school that seemed to be the most likely fit for him and for us was a school in northwest New Hampshire called Oliverian. It was about a half an hour from Dartmouth College, which is pretty much in the middle of nowhere. It's a very rural setting, but the school seemed to be able to fit all the needs that we had. Amy called and we made an appointment to go visit there.

A couple of days later we were on our way to Pike, New Hampshire, which is about three and a half hours from Scarborough through the White Mountains and almost on the Vermont border. We pulled into the parking lot of a very rural set-up. There was a barn and various other buildings. It was a cool day in Scarborough and probably ten degrees colder in Pike. We got out of the car, all very anxious about the meeting we were about to have. Dylan didn't have a lot of questions on the way up, which is probably good because we didn't have a lot of answers. We really didn't know a whole lot about what this process would look like.

We went in and sat with a couple of the admissions advisors, who tried to make Dylan feel comfortable and we asked them some questions. They seemed to have the right answers to tell us that Dylan was a good candidate for the school. However, the thing that made us the most nervous was that they had not actually had another student on the autism spectrum and were not aware of any with Asperger's. They said they thought they had some students over the years with Asperger's looking back, and may even have had one or two at the time. But they had not had a diagnosed student with Asperger's Syndrome. Nevertheless, they claimed they knew enough about Asperger's to be able to handle Dylan and his challenging behaviors.

We entered the living area first and Dylan was immediately unhappy, feeling like it wasn't an option for him. It was actually a pretty nice set-up as it was quite comfortable living conditions. But the two things that set Dylan off were the fact that the carpets were old and appeared dirty, and the fact that the TV did not have VH1, the music station that played music videos and some of his favorite reality TV shows. The school insisted they clean and vacuum the carpets on a regular basis. But to Dylan, they were "filthy." They were old; there was no question about it. The carpets were old because the buildings were old, but they were in good shape and for the most part the living area was clean and tidy. The lack of VH1 was actually an even bigger issue for Dylan.

Dylan spent most of his time alone. He didn't have friends or much of a social life. So in an unusual way, those characters on his favorite VH1 shows were his "friends." He would watch some of them, such as *I Love the '80s*, a series covered fad by fad and everything to do with the 1980s. Most of it had nothing to do with music, but he found it fascinating and very entertaining because most of the comments that were made on the show were made by comedians, so they were funny. They took every fad, every '80s' style, and made sarcastic, comedic comments about it, and Dylan would laugh and laugh and then watch it again and laugh and laugh some more. He also liked to keep up with the top music of the day, and he did that through music videos. So the idea of not having VH1, while to most people would be something they could make accommodations for, was an impossible reality for Dylan to grasp.

We had finally settled him down after he basically said there was no way he would go there without VH1. The tour guide said they had never even looked into the possibility of the TV having VH1 and maybe there was a chance they could get VH1 on the TVs with a different cable package. That slight accommodation to Dylan's concern was enough to calm him down to a point where we could at least move on to the next building.

As we walked around the campus, we headed over to the building where the classes were held. There was not any really large building on the campus. There were a number of small buildings, so you had to go outside and go from building to building. Dylan did not like that idea either because he did not ever like to be outside and was wondering what it would be like in the middle of winter trying to navigate from building to building. They were all within walkable distance but Dylan didn't like the whole idea of it. He was resistant, as most kids probably would be, to the idea of leaving home and going to a boarding school. But somewhere in his heart, I think he knew things needed to change.

When we reached the main building where the classes were held, we saw kids roaming around from class to class, which became Dylan's next objection. The kids that attended the school, without being too stereotypical, looked like they had been the outcasts from their schools. Although Dylan was an outcast at his school, he tried very hard to assimilate and look like the "popular" kids, the kids everybody wanted to be around. The kids at Oliverian school appeared to Dylan to be the kinds of kids who marched to the beat of their own drummer. There were kids with different colored hair and piercings. There were more all-black outfits, black fingernail paint, and some tattoos. These were generally not the kind of kids that Dylan thought he would fit in with. The truth is, they probably would be the most kind and accepting of his quirkiness. They were not kids who worried as much about fitting in and looking like everybody else. They were not kids who felt like they had to act like anyone else. They were kids that knew how to be themselves. So, Amy and I felt like this was a good thing and a place where Dylan *could* make friends. We were trying to look at things with the glass half full while Dylan was seeing everything with the glass half empty.

His next comments focused on his hopes for romance. When he saw the girls at the school, he did not feel like they would be girls he could be attracted to because they were different from the stereotypical teenager with the stereotypical outfit and looks. While we only saw a handful of girls in the short time we were visiting, they did tell us that the ratio of boys to girls was very heavy on the boys, which made Dylan feel that his odds of finding a girlfriend, something he had always longed for, would be limited with so many guys and so few girls.

We finished up with the classrooms and went to the recreation room, which was like a social hang out. It was nice. There were some big TVs there that *did* have VH1 which made Dylan very happy. There was a ping-pong table and a pool table and a couple of video games. It seemed like a warm and welcoming place where Dylan could hang out and maybe find some acceptance. And then they told us about the barn.

Once a week, each group of students, as they are broken up, had the responsibility to wake up early to take care of the animals, which includes milking the cows, brushing the horses, or cleaning out the manure. This had to be done all year long, no matter how cold it was, and it was to be done early in the morning. None of this appealed to Dylan in any way, at all. But surprisingly to us, he did not seem to have as many objections to dealing with the animals or waking up early as much as he did to the carpet, the VH1, and the peculiarity of the girls in the school.

Finally we went back to the main office where we could ask questions and they could ask us some questions as well. This was not a school that you could simply sign up for. They had to accept you. I'm not sure if acceptance simply meant you were willing and able to write a check, or whether there was an actual process to decide if your child was a good fit for the school. Nonetheless we got all the information and on the way home told Dylan that we had every intention of applying and should he be accepted we planned to send him to Oliverian School.

We stopped at the area around Dartmouth College to have lunch and to talk to Dylan some more about the possibility of attending the school. We figured speaking to him in a restaurant would hopefully limit the possibility of him having a meltdown. He handled it all pretty well, however, and accepted his fate.

We formally applied to Oliverian and, not surprisingly Dylan was accepted several weeks later. They seemed quite confident they could handle whatever Dylan threw their way. We were, of course, cautiously optimistic. It would be the perfect time for Dylan to start because he would only be up there for a couple of weeks before it was time for him to come home for Christmas break. It would give him time to get used to living up there and it would give us some time to figure out if it was definitely the direction we wanted to go.

High School Talent Show

Dylan was registered to begin attending Oliverian in northern New Hampshire. A few days before he left, the high school held a talent show. Dylan decided it would be a great opportunity to perform his comedy. This was without comparison the biggest and riskiest comedy performance to date. Unlike his performances at Holy Grounds Coffee House or even at the Comedy Connection, this performance was in front of his peers. There was clear stress for Dylan in preparing for this act. We certainly couldn't blame him for being nervous. We knew that a successful set would show a lot of the kids in the high school that although Dylan was not a star on the athletic fields or in the class room he had a talent that made him special.

We worked very hard with Dylan the week leading into the talent show. Amy and I felt a lot of pressure as well knowing that this was potentially his farewell to all the kids he had been in school with for many years. We didn't know at that time whether he would be successful at Oliverian, or return to the high school. A funny comedy routine would allow him to leave the school on a high note. Dylan went over his jokes, some were brand new and some were jokes he had told in previous performances. He hated repeated jokes, Amy and I debated with him many times about his insistence on telling all new jokes with every new performance. We explained to him that even professional comedians repeated jokes over and over again. He had it in his head that he always wanted to tell jokes no one had heard before. This performance was different and he knew it so he was more flexible in his self-imposed rule. He agreed to retell jokes from past performances. His best joke, almost a lock for a laugh, was one that he would tell about how he was sitting at our "cottage on a lake" when his third cousin walked in the door and took his breath away only to discover that they were related and that would be too weird. He tells the joke with great expression and perfect timing and I could never do it justice in this book but trust me, it's funny. It's very funny.

Friday night came and Dylan got up on stage after some singers, piano players, and a band. The audience roared as Dylan came on stage but then fell silent as he began to tell his jokes. That sound is very eerie in comedy, a rousing round of applause of cheers followed by dead silence as the comedian begins to talk and the audience thinks "Okay, make me laugh." Dylan's first joke was a home run. That first joke is very important, it sets the tone for the performance. If you can get them laughing early, you can roll the laughter from one joke to the other and Dylan nailed it. He rolled the laughter from joke to joke to joke. The crowd was awesome. They laughed and they cheered. Then Dylan paused and asked them for a minute as he turned around, put on a jacket and told them that he was going to do an impression of one of the most popular teachers in the school. Mr. Muncasci was a social studies teacher for mostly freshmen at Scarborough High School. According to Dylan he had very unique personality traits and mannerisms that Dylan thought he could impersonate. He was leaving the school anyway so he had no fear of repercussion. Just in case, he did run the idea by Mr. Muncasci prior to doing it and his teacher thought it was hysterical and looked forward to seeing it.

Dylan's impersonation was brilliant. The audience went wild. I don't remember anything else about the performances that night. I'm sure there was an excellent singer, musicians, maybe a dance, but it really didn't matter to us. In that moment during that special evening, Dylan was the star of Scarborough High School. It was a night we will always remember with great fondness.

DYLAN'S TAKE: *It should be said that Mr. Muncasci was one of the greatest teachers I had ever had. His class was entertaining and educational and I looked forward to it every day. He was a young, cool, very hip white guy, despite that confusing name. On day one of his class I decided I would get in front of my class and do an impression of him before the school year ended. Some of the other jokes I did that night were material the politically-correct, left-wing staff working at this New England high school would never have signed off on. I performed a bit about a car radio being racist which included doing cartoonish-impressions of the music of different races. Another joke was about how I wished one of my teachers was cooler hoping he would come into school on a Tuesday with a hickey and a hangover. After the show a group of about fifteen guys from the popular jock crowd in my class came up to me and started screaming my name and high-fiving me telling me how awesome my performance had been. It was the first time in my life when I saw that comedy could really bring people towards me.*

Oliverian

There was already snow on the ground in Pike, New Hampshire. Because it is in the White Mountains, it snows quite a bit. In fact, Dylan would later report that it snowed almost every day he was there. We went into the house and met the people that would be his host family. Each building had a family. Dylan's house consisted of a husband and wife and a couple of young kids, ages one and four. The students didn't have a lot of interaction with the family other than the parents, as it was their job to make sure the students in the buildings were doing their chores, following the rules, and coming in at the appropriate curfews.

Leaving Dylan and driving away was probably the second hardest thing that we had ever done. I think leaving him that April day in Spring Harbor was still harder to do. In this case, we felt we had no other choice and we were doing something that was in Dylan's best interest. When we left him at Spring Harbor we had no idea what was going to happen. We didn't know where we were going to go from there and we didn't know if they were going to do anything to actually help us.

Leaving him at Olivarian felt like a more permanent situation and, while we held it together as we said goodbye to Dylan, we didn't even get a mile up the road before we had to pull over because we were both bursting into tears. We ended up stopping five or six times on that ride home because we just needed to hold each other. I get teary just writing these words and thinking about that ride and how difficult it was. As difficult as Dylan was, and as many times as we wished he didn't live in our house, he was still our son and we loved him very much. And it wasn't that we didn't want *him* in our house because we desperately wanted him in our house. We just wanted him in our house in a way that we could all live in peace and that he could be happy. Not only were we sad leaving Dylan, but we felt like failures. We felt like we had failed him as parents and we felt that we may never be able to provide him with what he needed. But at the same time, we were thankful that the one thing we did have were the financial resources to enter him at Olivarian. We talked many times about what a blessing it was that we were in the situation we were in, so that we could get Dylan into the programs he needed to be in. We wondered on occasion what his life would be like in another home. Now, please understand that we were not saying we were the best parents or that we had the answers because we certainly didn't. We certainly were not the perfect parents. But we were lucky enough to be born into our situation and to have the resources to provide him with what he needs and the background from our parents' role modeling to get through those tough days without physically or verbally abusing Dylan. In many homes, with the challenges that Dylan put in front of a parent, he would have been violently abused. We wondered if he had been born into another home, if he would be thrown out of the house on the street, in jail, or even dead.

Dylan quickly reported to us that there was a lot of drug use going on behind the scenes at Olivarian. There were a lot of kids that were up there for drugs and alcohol, a much higher percentage than we were led to believe.

According to Dylan, virtually everyone was there due to drugs and alcohol, and many of them were still secretly doing it out in the woods behind the school. That was very frustrating for us, but we were going to stick with the school because we felt, at that time, we had no other options.

Dylan made it through the first couple of weeks, but it went anything but smoothly. It was only a matter of a week or two into it before many of the students in the school did not like Dylan. He was very brash and he alienated others. He had been there about a week and a half when he got one of the most popular students in the school so angry that the boy punched a glass window and was suspended from the school. This earned Dylan a great deal of unpopularity.

The boy that Dylan pissed off was very well liked and was making progress, and Dylan, with his ability to find a person's weakness and attack it as a means of defense against his own insecurities, had found this boy's weakness and played him like a fiddle.

When I went to pick Dylan up for Christmas break, I met with Dylan's main counselor, Brian. The school was not sure what they were going to do with him. They couldn't really suspend him because technically, he had not broken any rules. I talked with Brian for a while and he seemed to genuinely like Dylan. However, he was not able to convince Dylan of that and thus was not able to get through and connect with him. He made a great analogy that I still remember.

He tried to explain to Dylan how to get into a conversation with other people because Dylan had completely the wrong approach. He described it like opening a door. Every time you enter a conversation, it's like opening the door into a room. He said when most people enter a conversation, or open a door to a new room, they slowly turn the handle (approach a group of people), crack the door open (walk up to people who are already in a conversation), slowly enter the room one foot at a time, and then bring their body in (enter the conversation with a comment, laughing at something funny, etc.). That's the normal way to go about joining a conversation with people—slow, casual, and unexpected.

Then Brian explained, "However, when Dylan joins a conversation or enters a room, the analogy is this . . ." Brian then held his hands like a machine gun and proceeded to stand up and act like he was kicking a door in and then firing a gun. He said, "That's how *you* enter a conversation, Dylan. You walk up and start talking about something that's completely offensive in an effort to be funny or shock people so they pay attention to you."

It was a great analogy and I've used it many times over the years to describe Dylan's social challenges. He has gotten better over the years at entering conversations. He eventually learned that kicking the door open and shooting a figurative machine gun was not the best way to effectively join a conversation.

At the meeting, we continued to talk about what would happen after Christmas break and how they could better work with Dylan to successfully get him through the school year and their program. I asked Brian if Dylan seemed scared when that boy punched the glass. Brian told me he asked Dylan the same question and he said he wasn't scared at all. The boy was much bigger than Dylan, so Brian was surprised by that answer and asked him, "Why weren't you scared when a boy much larger than you, much stronger than you, was so angry with you that he actually punched his hand through a glass window?"

Dylan responded in a way very few people would. He said, "Sure, he's bigger than I am, he's stronger than I am, and he could probably kick my ass. But I'll heal from those wounds. I can hurt him with my words in ways that are much more damaging than anything that he can do to me with his fists."

When Dylan was younger, we knew that statement to be true and we knew that he probably knew it as well. But it took me aback to hear that he verbalized his ability to use words to hurt people because at that moment, I realized that the words that he said to people over the years may not have always been the words of an Asperger's child with no filter. Some of those words, including words to Amy and me, were intentional, malicious and meant to hurt. That realization made me sad.

While I was actually a little impressed that he had such courage to not be afraid of a boy much bigger than he was it also felt discouraging to think that maybe Dylan, the sweet boy that I knew he was inside, had a real mean streak. The question I asked myself was, "Is he mean or is this just the defense he has created after years of loneliness, isolation and rejection from his peers?"

Dylan and I drove home that day in a horrible snow storm. The three-hour ride was almost five hours in the heavy snow and given that Dylan and I were not in the best place as a father and son at the time, it seemed like ten hours.

DYLAN'S TAKE: *The thing about Asperger's is that you mature more slowly than neurotypical people. Looking back on this time, I was sixteen years old but I was much younger mentally and emotionally. If I went back and re-lived this experience now, I would have no problem but back then I was just so blind to* *the wrongness of all my behavior. I knew that acting in a brash, outrageous way around my peers wasn't right and clearly wasn't working for me, but I had no idea what to do instead. I can still see why I didn't understand the advice being given to me by the school's counselor. The analogy about busting into a conversation like entering into a room didn't make sense to me for a long time. I frequently don't understand explanations for my actions. It is often because older people tend to try to explain my behavior in a very high-concept, abstract and in an intellectual way. I hate that. I know he was trying to be helpful but was he serious? Did he really think a kid as socially retarded as I was at that time would suddenly see the error of my ways with the aid of this complex metaphor? He could have just said something like, "You're going up to this group of kids and saying X,Y,Z; but what you should be doing is saying Z,Y, and X" and I might have had a chance of understanding. Throughout my life people have tried to explain things to me that I wasn't seeing because of immaturity in big, intellectual, college-professor ways. That doesn't work for me and it probably doesn't work for most kids on the spectrum. I figure these things out by hearing literal specifics, and then stepping back and seeing the whole picture. And sometimes that takes time. At least I know how I learn now. I learn it the hard way, through real life experience. This is not to excuse the way I was back then. I was totally a mess. I was out-of-control and I don't even know what the solution could have been because I wasn't smart or mature enough yet to see things for how they really were. The only thing that changed me was time and maturity.*

Southeast Journeys

Christmas break with Dylan went better than expected. There were no major fireworks and no major explosions. Shortly after the girls went back to school, it was time for Dylan to head back to Pike. I drove him back and dropped him off with a lot less tears but more apprehension about him being able to make it at this school.

It was about a week later that we got a call from the school that things had gotten worse. Dylan had basically alienated every student at the school and there was nobody there who didn't want to hurt him. They told us that they actually had a staff member sleeping outside Dylan's room at night because they were fearful someone would come in during the night and hurt him. We wondered how long this was going to last, how long were they going to put up with Dylan. We were stressed beyond belief in wondering what on earth our next move was.

We decided that our only option, our *only* option, was to be proactive. We couldn't wait. We called down to the school in North Carolina, the boarding school specifically for kids on the autism spectrum, mostly Asperger's, and we asked them "Is there any way that Dylan could get into your program?" They told us that school had already started. It was Thursday of that week, already four days into the new semester, and they really couldn't take a student after Monday. We had one day to make a decision and one day to get Dylan to North Carolina.

We called the school in New Hampshire and told them our plans. We knew it was only a matter of time before they had enough and kicked Dylan out of the school. And while they tried to tell us that was not the case, their words and their tone were quite unconvincing, so we knew we were making the right decision. We knew that there was a very high chance they were going to kick him out and they probably already had several meetings about when and how they would do it. If Dylan got kicked out of that school a week later, it would be too late to enter the program in North Carolina. Amy and I would be stuck with Dylan angry, humiliated, depressed, and bored in our home. It was a nightmare that we could not take a chance on.

We told the people from Oliverian that we would be coming up first thing Friday morning. The plan was to pick Dylan up, take him directly to the airport in Manchester and fly him directly to Asheville, North Carolina, where we would enter him immediately in the school. As I mentioned earlier, this was a boarding school that was like a boot camp for autism. It was *not* something that Dylan would be happy about, and because of that, we asked the school in New Hampshire to not tell Dylan we were coming. We didn't want them to have to deal with his explosion, and we didn't want him to have any time to run away and ruin our chances to get him enrolled in North Carolina.

With a very heavy heart and a lot of anxiety, Amy and I took the trip up to Olivarian. We were armed with Seroquel, which is an anti-psychotic medication that often is used as a sedative. We knew that it might calm Dylan down just enough to get him on the plane if we could even get him to take one.

We arrived at Olivarian when Dylan was still in class, and we waited outside his room. While we were waiting, we packed up most of his stuff so when he came back, we could just get him in the car. But we knew that was not going to be easy to do. Dylan approached the car and as soon as he saw us, he knew something was up and began to yell and scream about us being there. He knew that he was being kicked out of the school and insisted that he could make it work. He wanted to stay there because even after only a few weeks and even though people were sleeping outside his door to keep him safe, he had grown a level of comfort there and didn't want to go somewhere else. We told him he had no choice and he had to come with us. He refused to go. I tried to physically get him in the car but he put up a fight and I didn't want to wrestle him into the car, so we continued to talk to him and explain that this was his only option.

He became more and more hostile and more and more agitated. We told him he had to take one of the Seroquel and he refused. We argued and argued and there was yelling and screaming. In the meantime, the minutes were ticking because we had to get him on a plane that afternoon.

We finally convinced him to take one of the Seroquel. I can't even remember how we got him to do it, but we offered him something in exchange. It barely made an impact at first, and he continued his outburst. But after much convincing that he had no other options, he finally got in the car. About half way to Manchester, he lost it again and started screaming and kicking the back of my seat, making it almost impossible to drive. I pulled over on the side of the road and basically forced another Seroquel into his mouth. If what you're picturing is a father out-of-control and a son out-of-control, you are picturing the right scene. But the second Seroquel luckily did the trick and within the next twenty minutes, Dylan had settled down enough that we could continue our trip.

We arrived at the airport and Dylan was in rough shape. He could barely keep his head up. The Seroquel had kicked in pretty hard and he was very drowsy. Our biggest concern at that point was someone thinking we were kidnapping him or that he was drunk and not letting him on the plane. We checked all the bags, waited at the gate, and when it was time to get on the plane, we walked him between us to hold him up and get him on the plane. It was an indescribable moment—our son, heavily medicated, being dragged to a school in North Carolina a thousand miles from home to enter a program he did not want to enter at a cost we could barely afford. Our emotions were about as high as they had ever been on that flight.

We arrived in Asheville and grabbed a hotel room. It was late in the day at that point and Dylan would be joining the school the next morning. He remained calm most of the night. At that point he had realized there was no turning back so there was no point in arguing with us. The next morning we drove the half an hour from Asheville to the school, which was directly at the state line between North and South Carolina. In fact, just beyond the parking lot at the school, there is a sign that says, "Welcome to South Carolina."

The visit to Southeast Journeys couldn't have started off worse. As we pulled into the parking lot, Dylan saw a short bus, a school bus that was smaller than the standard size school bus, and he flipped out. He shouted, "There's no way I'm riding anywhere in a short bus!"

The short bus in Maine was only used for special education kids. It was the bus he refused to ride on in sixth grade and now, as a sophomore in high school, very concerned, as all sophomores are, about his image, the idea that he would have to ride around town in a short bus was unimaginable. We tried to explain to him that nobody knew him for a thousand miles around so it didn't matter whether he was on a short bus or not. Nobody was going to see him that knew him or cared. However, that made no difference to Dylan. He felt it was humiliating to ride on that bus and that he would refuse to go anywhere. That would be a major problem because the Southeast Journeys program takes a lot of trips. They not only take day trips around town but they go on two-or-three week trips, camping down rivers, exploring the area. So if Dylan refused to get on the bus, there was no way he would be able to participate in the program. Amy and I tried to keep the argument to a minimum, hoping that in time and with no other option, he would be forced to ride the bus like the rest of the students.

We walked into the office of the school. The school was just a summer camp converted for the fall, winter, and spring into a school. In the summertime, it would be filled with special education kids all summer long. But during the school year, it was Talisman's Southeast Journeys School for kids on the autism spectrum. Therefore, the office and all the buildings were very rustic, basically winterized camp cabins. We sat down with Michael Dorris, the director of the program, and started talking to him more about Dylan. We could not have been happier with how he responded. There was nothing that we said—and we told him everything he would be facing with Dylan— that seemed to shock, startle, or even concern him in the slightest.

We had become experts on reading people and how they react to what we tell them about Dylan over the years, going back to our experience in middle school when we took him out of the public school to enroll him in a private school and, six days later, he was kicked out. They also told us that they could handle Dylan.

Michael talked about all the kids at the school, what they deal with and how they would handle Dylan. Dylan was listening too. Michael asked if he had any questions, but he had nothing to say. He asked again, "Are you sure you don't have any questions for me?"

Dylan was still in shock by what he was experiencing and didn't have anything to ask. He had had a meltdown up at Olivarian a month before because the school didn't have VH1 in the residences, only in the rec-room and now, because of his behavior, he was at a camp in rural North Carolina with no TV, no cell phone access, no ability to use a computer, and permission to call home only ten minutes per week at an assigned time. He felt like he was in jail and, as you often see from prisoners in war movies, they're in such shock they have nothing to say. For maybe the first time in his life, Dylan was speechless.

Michael walked us around the campus, which didn't take us very long. It wasn't very big. There were a dozen or so cabins but they weren't using all of them. Some were for boys and some were for girls. Some were for mildly autistic kids and some were for severely autistic kids. Other than a basketball court and a small pond that they wouldn't be using much because it was too cold, that was about it. The lunch room was nothing special, but it was relatively clean so Dylan didn't have too much of a problem with it.

We then approached the first cabin that would be the one Dylan was going to live in. Michael said that he would bring out a couple of the students to meet him so he would feel comfortable that there were other kids like him. We had explained to Michael that Dylan was relatively high functioning Asperger's and had a hard time with the idea that he was going to be around kids that were lower functioning than he was. He assured us that there were other kids there who were also higher on the spectrum, and he went inside to get a couple of the students to come out to meet Dylan.

The two boys who met Dylan that day were nothing like we expected. They were visually autistic at an instant. Neither of them looked us in the eye. One of them kept waving his hand over his head in some kind of autistic type motion, and they both spoke very limited sentences and very choppy word formation. It was exactly the opposite of what Dylan, Amy, and I were hoping was going to come out of that cabin. Michael asked the boys a couple of questions that they awkwardly answered, and then they went back inside. After they left, there was a moment of silence. Michael didn't realize how thick the tension was but if the expression is "You could cut the tension with a knife," I think I needed a chainsaw.

Dylan looked at us, paused for a second and said, "You have got to be fucking kidding me," in a slow and deliberate tone.

I knew immediately where this was going and tried to calm him down before he got too worked up. I said calmly, "Dylan, take it easy."

He looked at me again and he looked at Amy and said, "You have got to be fucking kidding me if you think I'm gonna spend the next four months with those kids."

It was at that point that Michael stepped in and said, "What's the matter, Dylan?"

Dylan stared at him straight in the eye and said, "Those kids are way lower on the spectrum than I am."

"What do you mean?" Michael asked.

There's one thing you can never do with Dylan and that is try to bullshit him. He has an incredible "bullshit radar" and can detect bullshit from a mile away. Michael, at that moment, made a big mistake by trying to bullshit Dylan and pretend he didn't know what Dylan was talking about.

Dylan said, "What do I mean?? You run a camp for autism and you don't know what I mean when I say those kids are lower on the spectrum than I am? What the fuck are you doing running this camp if you don't understand that sentence?"

Michael said, "Dylan, there's no need to use that kind of language. Let's try to have a civil conversation."

The conversation went on for a few more minutes, but we told Dylan that while we were sorry that he was in this situation, there was no turning back. Amy tried to give him a hug, which he pushed away. We continued with the tour, Dylan still insisting there was no way he could stay there, no way he could ride the short bus, and there was no way that this was going to work.

We went back to Michael's office and sat down. When Michael told us it was time for Amy and me to leave and that they were going to go bowling that afternoon, the first thing Dylan asked him was if there were other buses or another means of transportation. Michael asked Dylan what the concern was with the bus and I don't think there was any bullshit at this point because he said, "We're a small private school. There are private schools all around the south and they all use small buses because they can't afford or don't have enough students to be using a big bus."

We explained to Michael that in the north, the small bus was not only just used for special education kids but that it was actually a source of comedic humor. Comedians often talked about riding the short bus. It was the punchline to a joke that Dylan did not want to be a part of. He again insisted to

Dylan that that was not the case in North or South Carolina and they would just look like a private school like any other private school in the area. I don't think Dylan believed him but he didn't continue the conversation, and just insisted it didn't really matter what other schools were doing. There was no way he was going on that bus. Period. End of story.

Michael told us not to worry about it, that it wasn't our problem, and it was time for us to go. Amy and I hugged Dylan goodbye, got in the rental car, and drove away. To both of our shock, we didn't cry. Possibly it was because at that point, we were out of tears. However, we talked about the fact that neither one of us felt like crying and we both agreed that it was because of Michael's confidence in his ability to handle Dylan. We felt that maybe for the first time, Dylan was at a school that could help him. And, in a strange sort of way, leaving our child someplace he was absolutely miserable at was comforting.

Amy and I went to go get some lunch and walked around for a little while in downtown Asheville, as we had time to spare before our flight back to Manchester. It was about two hours after we left that we received a call from Southeast Journeys that the group had decided they were going to go bowling that afternoon and since Dylan did like bowling and he realized he really didn't have much of a choice, he ended up getting on the short bus without a whole lot of arguing. That fact gave us even more confidence that Dylan was going to be okay at this new program.

The first week was really hard while Dylan was away in North Carolina because there was no contact with him whatsoever. It was the first time we had ever had so little contact with him since he had been born. A whole week went by and we didn't speak to him at all. About ten days after we left him, it was finally his night to make a phone call. All that was allowed was a ten-minute conversation. And Dylan, of course, spent the majority of those ten minutes telling us what a huge mistake we had made, how he shouldn't be there, and we needed to come down and get him. He said he didn't like any of the students there, any of the faculty, or the living conditions. There was literally nothing he told us that was positive, but we kept promising him that if he just stuck it out, he would be better off in the long run. It was really difficult to hear him sound so desperate and apologizing for his past behavior, promising us that if we just bring him home, everything would be fine. However, we had been down this road too many times and we knew better. We held our ground, tried to ask him questions that didn't lead to arguments, and the conversation went by very quickly before we were told his time was up.

The following week, we didn't even speak with him at all because they went on a trip. One of the reasons the program is called Southeast Journeys is because they go on trips all over the south, and most of these trips are pretty rugged. They don't even bring tents. They put up lean-tos with a tarp, and that's what they sleep under. This is camping to the extreme, especially for a kid who had never been camping in his life and had never slept outside.

They went on a trip down a river right outside of Asheville. It was just a weekend trip. Dylan got access to a computer to send us an email after he returned. The email started out, "I just spent two days in hell. It was the worst experience of my life. But I saw how over the last two days, I saw myself in a lot of these kids and I saw the way that I act. Now I know why everybody hated me. I hope when this is over and I can come home, I don't act like that anymore."

Amy and I were in tears as we read his email. For the very first time, he was coming face to face with his disability, and for the first time, there was a cracked window that he may actually open and try to get inside his head and learn why he does what he does and acts the way he acts. Maybe just maybe, we might make some progress.

DYLAN'S TAKE: *It was beneficial for me, for the first time, to be around other kids with my disability. In hindsight it was very necessary for me as it allowed me to see what I had been doing all those years. Many of the kids at Southeast Journeys were much more obvious in their disability so it just amplified what my issues looked like. The kids at the school were "lower-functioning" so they had similar behavioral tendencies but their actions were right in your face in a way that couldn't be ignored. Most of the learning from that program came from observing. The camping trips and living conditions were definitely a challenge but the whole time at this school was an adventure. I have always enjoyed adventures even if they are negative. It was a rustic place to live so my time in North Carolina made me appreciate really simple things I love like drinking a soda from a gas station or watching music videos on YouTube.*

Dylan at boarding school in North Carolina

Salt Story Release

When Dylan came back from North Carolina that spring, the article that Pam Craigin had written was published. They had a big grand opening of that edition of the magazine. It was a magazine that only came out a couple of times a year, so when they did come out with an edition, it had many stories in it and they made quite a fanfare around the printing of this magazine. *Salt* had some space rented in downtown Portland on the corner of Exchange Street where they had a big open house. Each of the authors of the stories in that edition spoke about their experiences writing the articles, and there was an entire wall of pictures of Dylan and our family from the time that Pam shadowed him. It was a very exciting evening for Dylan in the midst of a pretty dark time. But for one night, he was a celebrity. We were so proud of him, not because he was the subject of a magazine story, but for taking the step to "out" himself and his Asperger's. It was a monumental step forward for a kid who just a year ago insisted he did not have Asperger's; he was "just eccentric."

The one change in the article from when it was drafted and approved by the publisher was footnoted at the very end. While Dylan was at Southeast Journeys in North Carolina, learning to accept himself for who he was, he contacted Pam to let her know that it was okay to mention his Asperger's. It was too late to change the article, but it was footnoted at the very end of the story.

Dylan would end up spending the rest of his sophomore year and his entire junior year of high school at Southeast Journeys. He gained a tremendous amount of maturity and independence while at the program. When he finished his junior year he was convinced that he was ready to come home and graduate with his class, just as he had done in eighth grade. The staff that was originally at SEJ had transitioned into all new people whom we were not as confident in. His primary mentor while in North Carolina, Matt Thompson, had moved on to another location. We felt Dylan had taken the program as far as he was going to take it and they had made as much progress with him as one could reasonably expect of them. There comes a point of diminishing returns and we had reached that point. We all agreed it was time for Dylan to come home and finish his schooling at Scarborough High School.

— 7 —

The Many Adventures of the Greyhound

Dylan's Car Adventures

We knew that Dylan home with his own car gave him freedom and independence like he had never experienced before. I decided that if Dylan was going to be driving around southern Maine we needed to know where he was going. We could ask him but in the words of the great Ronald Reagan during his negotiations with Mikhail Gorbachev, "Trust but verify." I purchased a small GPS tracking device that could be installed in his car. It allowed us to not only find out where Dylan was at all times but it had a feature called Zones that told us when Dylan went in and out of any of the nine established Zones. We set up Zones called Home, Old Orchard Beach, the Mall, Sanford, and also created a couple for his friend's homes. Any time Dylan entered or left the Zone we could receive a text message. This tool was extremely helpful and I recommend it for all parents of teenagers.

The first time we used it was when Dylan had a friend in the nearby town of Gorham that we did not approve of. He was trouble and we knew it. One night Dylan went out for the evening. Before he left, Amy and I specifically told him we did not want him hanging around his friend, Mick. At about 9:00 I checked the GPS and sure enough, Dylan was in Gorham. I called him and told him I wanted him to head straight home. He said he would. I said, "Where are you?"

He didn't hesitate, "Biddeford."

"Okay," I said, "I want you to come home." Biddeford is twenty miles southeast of Gorham.

Dylan came home at almost 9:45. It only takes fifteen minutes or so to get home from Gorham and about twenty-five minutes from Biddeford. When he arrived home I very calmly asked what took him so long to get home. He said, "I stopped at that Kennebunk rest stop for gas."

Kennebunk is next to Biddeford, where Dylan claimed he was, but it is south of Biddeford. Dylan did not think of that geographical detail when concocting his lie. For him to have gassed up his car in Kennebunk he would have had to get on the Maine Turnpike and driven the opposite direction of our home. It made no sense at all and was a terrible lie. Because of the GPS I knew it was a complete lie. I had been following his path all the way home from Gorham. I said, "Okay, Dylan, I am going to ask you again where you were, but this time I want you to think really hard before you answer. Where were you tonight?"

Without hesitation and with complete confidence he said, "I was in Biddeford."

"Shoot," I said, "I figured you might come up with a better answer."

"Why do you say that? I was in Biddeford."

"Dylan, I know you were in Gorham hanging out with Mick despite us specifically telling you not to go there." Now I was in a quandary. If I told him I had a GPS in his car I was blowing my undercover surveillance method. If I did not tell him, I would have to come up with a quick lie. I decided that my covert tracking was too important to give up so I lied. I told him that a friend of mine was in Gorham and saw him and he remembered he owed me a call. Dylan believed me. He lost his car for a week. I felt bad having to lie but once he knew I was following him via technology I knew he would figure out a way to avoid being tracked.

In a later incident, when Amy and I were away for a night, we told Dylan to call us when he arrived home for the evening. We told him to call us from the home phone so we knew he was home. As we suspected might happen, he called from the home phone, said he was going to bed, and then hung up and went out. He did not return home until 5:30am the next morning. When I confronted him about this deception he said, "How did you know that?!"

Again, I was faced with lying or losing my competitive advantage in the dad versus teenager cat and mouse game. I chose to tell him that a friend was out for a morning run when he saw Dylan's car pull in at 5:30. He knew we were away so he was concerned and called me. Dylan not only was busted again but he was starting to feel like I had eyes everywhere. That was a good thing for us and it proved to be effective as Dylan was much more honest about his whereabouts, for a while anyway. But it was just the beginning of Dylan's car adventures.

On New Year's Eve 2009, our friend Andy Campbell, who was Lilly's soccer coach, held a big event at his karate school. It was a chem-free dance for New Year's Eve that he put on every year so that kids had something fun and safe to do that night. Andy's a great guy and was always very under-standing of Dylan. Andy was DJ-ing this big dance. He knew that Dylan was really interested in getting into the radio business. Andy was very agreeable when I asked him if Dylan could shadow him just to get an idea of what that experience would be like, playing, picking out music, and managing a crowd. As I expected, Andy was very open to the idea. Dylan had a blast that night. I thought that he would just watch Andy and learn, but Andy took it to the next level and let Dylan pick out some music, talk to the crowd, and really become part of the evening's entertainment. It was a great night. Andy texted me a couple of times, telling me how awesome Dylan was doing and how fun it was to DJ with him.

As Amy and I were lying in bed waiting for Dylan to come home at about 12:30 New Year's morning, Amy was just about asleep and I was fading as well. We could never fall asleep until we knew Dylan was home safely.

I remember telling one of my sales reps one day when we were out on the road that I can't go to sleep until Dylan comes home and how people think it's hard to have little kids and babies, but teenagers are the worst of all. They stay out late and you cannot go to sleep until they are home safely. My sales rep laughed and said, "Oh I won't have that problem. As long as I know he's coming home, I'll go to sleep just fine."

His son was eight years old, so I laughed and said, "Yeah, we'll see in a few years if you still think that way."

So as we were in bed waiting to see the lights of his car come up the driveway and watching the New Year's festivities, while trying to keep our eyes open, the lights came around the corner and up our driveway. I whis-pered to Amy, who was laying on my shoulder, half-asleep, "Dylan's home."

Almost without pause, the whole house shook. My next sentence was, "And…he hit the house." Our tired bodies jumped out of bed and ran downstairs.

Dylan ambled into the house as we were both standing there in the kitchen. He said, "Goodnight," and walked right by us.

"Whoa, whoa, whoa, Dylan. What the hell? You just hit the house!" I said.

He turned to us, "Oh…not that hard."

"Not that hard?! The whole house shook! We were upstairs and we could feel it!"

"Oh, it wasn't that bad."

I went outside to see a big dent on the corner of my garage bay and a big scratch down the side of Dylan's car. Fortunately, it was Dylan's car and he hit mostly the wood of the garage door frame. He couldn't understand why I had a problem when he hit the garage door with his car.

That same thought process would repeat again a few months later when Dylan was moving Mariah's car to get it out of the way for his car and he again hit the garage, scratching up and denting the door of Mariah's car. Mariah was extremely angry with Dylan. As he would with any other situation, Dylan played down the whole thing, accusing her of overreacting.

We told Dylan that he would be responsible for fixing them, and he went ballistic, calling Mariah spoiled and saying we were being completely unreasonable. We went around and around and around about Mariah's car for months until we finally had Dylan pay for the car to get fixed. It was $500 and it's very possible that if I asked him today, he would still say that she was unreasonable to want her car fixed.

It was a very difficult situation to handle whenever Dylan, and his lack of ability to generalize, created conflict. One would be better off talking to a wall because what you're saying to Dylan goes in one ear and out the other. He just cannot understand or even begin to comprehend how someone can feel different from him. It is extremely challenging to have a conversation, debate, or an argument with a teenager who has a complete inability to put himself in another person's shoes, to see something from a different perspective. Those conversations have all been very frustrating for us and frustrating for anyone who has worked with Dylan when he is in one of those mental blocks that prevent him from seeing another viewpoint. Nobody—not us, not any professional or counselor that he's ever worked with—has ever been able to break through to the point where he just turns to them and says, "Oh okay, now I can see how you would feel that way." It makes it very difficult to discipline him because he doesn't appreciate the consequences of his actions on other people. He does understand that others are upset, and he often feels bad that someone is not happy with him, but he cannot put himself in another's shoes to understand where that other person's feelings are coming from.

Laptops Stolen

In the Spring of 2010, Lilly and Mariah were both playing travel softball, so many weekends sent Amy and me in different directions. I was coaching Lilly's ten and under travel team as well as her Little League team, so if Lilly and Mariah both had softball tournaments, Amy would take Mariah and I would take Lilly.

In May of 2010, it was one of those softball weekends. Mariah was off to one tournament with Amy, and Lilly and I were heading in a different direction. When the weekend was over, we came home, hoping that everything was okay at the house. We never knew because Dylan was there alone. We both got home relatively late on Sunday because Lilly and Mariah were both playing for very good teams on the Southern Maine Flame, teams that won a lot and would go deep into tournaments on Sunday. When we arrived home, we unpacked the cars, took showers, and got the kids ready for bed. Everything seemed to be fine until the next morning.

We got up the next morning and had to look around because Dylan couldn't find his backpack. We looked everywhere, but it was nowhere to be found. And then we heard a scream from upstairs. Mariah's laptop was gone. It was then when we realized that my laptop was also gone. We started screaming at Dylan, "Who was here?! Did you have a party!? What happened?? We need answers!"

Dylan told us he had only had a couple of friends over, but they brought some friends. Apparently, at some point during the visit, they had gone upstairs, grabbed Dylan's backpack, loaded up my laptop, Mariah's laptop, a few pieces of Mariah's clothing, some of Amy's jewelry, Lilly's jewelry, and some of my jewelry, including a tie-clip that was my grandfathers and several Indian-head pennies from the 1860s and 1870s that my grandfather had given me. They were all gone. These "friends" had gone through our doors, had gone through our home. We were robbed and felt violated, but nobody was more upset than Mariah.

Not only was her laptop gone, which could be replaced, but the contents of it were gone. This was a time before "the cloud," before everything was so easily backed up. Back in 2010, to back something up, you usually had to burn it onto a CD. There were no thumb drives. On Mariah's computer, she had a book that she had been writing.

She had over eighty pages written in this fictional book about a young girl who loses a father to cancer, and it was really good. It was actually amazing. She had read several chapters to me as we drove to softball tournaments, and I was always blown away by her writing skills and the detail that she put in the book while making a very interesting story come to life. I was so proud of her, and I couldn't wait to help turn the book into something real. But now, it was gone. She was so upset, and I had no way to comfort her. There was no way to get those eighty pages back, unless we found that laptop, and I knew there was very little chance of that.

We asked Dylan who he thought took the laptop, and he knew immediately. He only had three people over to the house—an African American friend from Old Orchard Beach and his neighbors, a girl who lived next door and her twenty-year-old boyfriend. He trusted his friend and felt that it was the neighbors. Dylan said they were not nice people and in fact, the twenty-year-old even branded a gun and was showing them, in *our* home, his gun. I immediately told Dylan that we were going to get in the car and drive down to confront them because he knew where they lived. However, he did not want to do that because he was scared of retaliation. I told him, "Well, we are either going to call the police or we are going to try and get our stuff back."

So we got in the car and drove to OOB. We knocked on the door, and the girl's father answered. We explained what happened and told him that we believed his daughter and her boyfriend had our laptops and we wanted them back. We even told him that Dylan's friend informed us that after he dropped them off in Old Orchard, he saw the girl and the boyfriend go out to the shed behind their house, and he thinks they might have had a backpack in hand. The father was indignant, insisting that his daughter didn't do anything wrong and demanded for us to leave his doorstep.

I said, "Well if they didn't do anything wrong, just take us out to the shed and then we'll know that they didn't take the laptops." As expected, he refused to oblige. I said, "I don't want any trouble. We just want the laptops back. We won't call the police if we can take back what they took." He continued to insist that that couldn't have happened, and then the girl came to the door and said that they didn't do it. We called the police but had very little expectations that they would pursue it. We told them where the laptops were, who stole them, when it happened, and what their address was. We told them about the shed and begged them to go down to Old Orchard and get our laptops. However, the police department did absolutely nothing to help us, and we never saw our stuff again. And sadly, Mariah would never re-write her story.

The Hitchhiker

There are many Dylan stories that are entertaining. My company CFO, Doug Hellstrom, used to stick his head in my office when he needed a break from staring at his computer screen and just say, "Any new Dylan stories?" I usually had something to share. The winter of Dylan's senior year of high school offered Doug almost daily mental breaks. One of the best Dylan story was what we call simply, "The Hitchhiker."

We always had a curfew for Dylan because without one he would come home in the morning hours instead of the evening hours. In his senior year the curfew was 11:30pm. We would often lock the doors and close the garage bays so Dylan had to ring the doorbell to get inside. This allowed us to make sure we did not fall asleep and miss him arriving home, and it prevented him walking in after curfew with a crowd of people, as he was prone to do. One night during the previous summer I made the mistake of saying to Dylan, "You need to come home by curfew, I don't care if you have ten people with you but you need to be home." The next night when he pulled in at 11:28pm and came into the house he had about ten people with him. It was tough for me to kick them out as we both remembered my words from the night before. They were finally all told to leave at 2:00am when they were just too loud for me to get any sleep.

On one particular cold night in early December we were just about asleep when the doorbell rang. Dylan was home just in time. It was 11:29pm. I went downstairs, in my t-shirt and underwear because that is what I sleep in, and opened the door. Dylan breezed past me heading to the living room and as he passed he said, "I made curfew, bring her home."

He then proceeded over to the couch and turned on the TV. I stood there, in my underwear, staring at a rather attractive twenty-eight-year-old woman I had never seen before who was wearing no shoes! She was "the hitchhiker."

"Dylan," I called from the mudroom, "come over here please."

"What?"

"Who is this?"

"Oh, she is a hitchhiker. I picked her up because she needed a ride to South Portland and didn't have any shoes on. It's cold. Give her a ride home,"

"Why didn't you give her a ride home?"

"I needed to make curfew."

"Dylan, making curfew means you come home and all the people that need rides are already dropped off. I am not going out at this hour and I am not taking some strange lady with no shoes home."

"Fine, I'll take her home."

Now I was in a pickle. Dylan had tricked me into staying out later than curfew by picking up a hitchhiker knowing I would not want to go out at

11:30pm to bring her home. Little did I know that standing at the stop sign at the end of our street were three or four of his other friends who needed to get rides home. It was a brilliant move.

An hour later, he returned. When I asked him why it took him an hour to bring one person to South Portland, he admitted that "a couple others needed rides, too." It was too late to do much about it other than punish him which, at eighteen, wasn't going to get me very far. He had outsmarted me that night and I was actually impressed with his cleverness.

The Runaway

This may be the best Dylan story ever. It is the story that inspired me to write this book because just about every time I tell it to someone they end up saying the same thing, "You need to write a book!"

It was July 2009 and Dylan was between his junior and senior year of high school. He had recently returned from Talisman in North Carolina to resume and complete his high school career at Scarborough High with the classmates he had known since second grade. He was spending a lot of time, as usual, in Old Orchard Beach. We would call it "hanging out" but his expression was "Straight Scummin' it." I have no idea where that expression came from but he thought it was so funny he put it on his senior t-shirt. Every year the seniors at Scarborough High had a word that they all put on t-shirts followed by something that describes them. They have used words like Totally, Shamelessly and Absolutely. The word for Dylan's senior class was Absolutely. Dylan was very proud of his shirt that read Absolutely Straight Scummin' It.

We were at home for a quiet evening without softball, a rarity for us in the spring and summer. I was just about to sit down with Lilly to watch the third Harry Potter movie. We had just finished reading it together so she wanted to have a movie night with just the two of us. The phone rang and it was a woman I had never spoken to before. She said, "Have you seen my daughter, Julie?"

I said, "No, I have no idea who you are talking about. How did you get my number?"

She replied, "The last call I received from her was from 604-2561. The outgoing message was someone named Dylan and he said if he doesn't answer to call your 883 number. He must have been with my daughter."

I told her that Dylan was in Old Orchard and there are tons of kids that hang out down there in the summer. He may have just loaned her a phone because her name didn't sound familiar as one of his friends. I offered to call him to see if he knew where she was. Julie's mom seemed quite concerned. She told me that Julie was supposed to be sleeping at a friend's house but she talked to the friend's mom and Julie was never there that night. She wouldn't be the first kid to lie to her mom about a sleepover on a nice summer night so I urged her not to panic. I told her I would call Dylan and then call her right back.

I called Dylan on his cell and he answered. I said, "Dylan, are you with a girl named Julie?"

He said he was not. I explained what her mom said and that she was very worried about her. I said, "If you know where she is you need to tell me."

He said, "She was with us earlier and used my phone but she took off. I haven't seen her in a while." I believed him.

I called the mom back and told her what Dylan said. She did not seem as convinced as I was that Dylan was being truthful. Lilly and I sat down to watch Harry Potter. It was only about ten minutes later when the home phone rang again. This time it was the Sanford Police. They wanted to know what I knew about Julie's disappearance. The word "disappearance" concerned me. She was a kid that lied to her mom about a sleepover and now they were practically calling her kidnapped. I went over my conversation with the mom and with Dylan. I was very clear with the police officer that I had expressed how serious this was to Dylan and he had not seen her in a while. I said, "Sir, if Dylan knew where she was I am sure he would have told me." Ouch, those words would bite me later!

Before Lilly and I sat down to start up Harry Potter again I made another call to Dylan. "Dylan, I just got a call from the Sanford Police. You need to tell me if you know where this Julie girl is." He swore he had no idea.

I said, "I want you to come home now. I don't like this situation. If that girl ends up in a ditch somewhere they are going to come right to you because your cell is the last contact anyone had with her. Come home right now." A few years prior there was a girl from Saco who was killed and left dead on Pine Point Road in Scarborough. They know that she was with two brothers at the boys' house until late that night and then she wound up dead on a street in Scarborough. Almost everyone is convinced those boys killed her or know who killed her but the police could never prove it. No one was ever charged with her murder and the case remains unsolved to this day.

Dylan agreed to come home, which surprised me, but I was happy he was being compliant so I didn't think too much about it. Lilly and I sat down, again, to watch our movie.

About twenty-five minutes later Dylan came in the house and immediately went upstairs. About five minutes later he went out into the garage. Five minutes after that he came back in and went upstairs. And then shortly back down and out to the garage. I was watching the movie with Lilly so I was not paying any attention but Amy was and grew more and more suspicious with every in and out of the house. On his third trip to the garage she quietly followed him.

A few minutes later, as Lilly and I finally started enjoying the movie, Amy came out of the kitchen and said, "Honey, I have something to show you."

I turned around toward the dining room and there was Amy, Dylan and a young girl about sixteen. My head slumped and then I said, "Let me take a wild guess, you're Julie."

Dylan then explained to us that she was a runaway. Her step father was abusive and she was not going home again. He was just being nice because he felt bad for her. I tried to tell him that, while that was very kind, her mother was extremely concerned when she wasn't at her friend's house and I had emphatically told her, and the Sanford Police, that he had no idea where she was located. He insisted she would not go home and if we tried to take her home she would run away from us. We couldn't send her back to an abusive home. I would feel bad if it were true she was being abused, but she certainly couldn't stay hidden in our house. I called the Sanford Police. They said she makes these claims all the time. They said the Department of Human Services has investigated the home and her but there has been no evidence of abuse. They told me to call the Scarborough Police Department. I did.

The first thing the Scarborough cop told me, after explaining the whole situation, was "take her home." I told him that there is no way on earth I was going to force a sixteen-year-old girl into my car and drive her almost an hour back to what she says is an abusive situation.

The policeman said, "Call the parents back and have them come get her." Again, I said no way. I am not going to have her parents show up here at 11:00pm all pissed off at her, and at us, for lying to them about her whereabouts.

He said, clearly getting frustrated with my lack of cooperation, "Bring her to us." My response was again, "Nope. I am not bringing this kid anywhere. She is a sixteen-year-old girl I have never met claiming she is being abused. You want her? You come get her." He said they would come for her. It was now almost 10:30pm. Lilly and I would have to watch our movie another night.

Amy and I put Lilly to bed and waited in our room for the Scarborough Police to arrive assuming they would be there shortly. The police station is less than ten minutes away. Dylan and Julie sat on the living room couch watching TV. And we waited, and waited and waited.

Finally at around 12:30am the police arrived with Julie's parents and grandmother in another car. It was nice of them to let us know they were going to wait for the parents to drive up from Sanford before coming to get her. They knocked on the door and we called to Julie. She insisted she wasn't going with them but the police officer convinced her to come outside. Her step father, dressed in ripped shorts and a "wife beater" shirt was visibly angry. The mom smelled of cigarette smoke even at a distance of fifteen feet away. The grandmother was literally in curlers. It was like a scene from *Cops*.

I said, "Come on, Dylan, let's go inside, it is very late and this isn't our problem anymore."

We walked inside, closed the door and, before heading up to bed Dylan calmly turned to us and said matter of factly, "You gotta admit, the drama is pretty exciting." We had to laugh. Our evening with the runaway was over and the idea for this book began.

It was not surprising to us that Dylan would bring Julie home. Dylan was always sensitive and empathetic to people who were down on their luck or outcasts in some way. When he was ten years old we started volunteering through Woodford's Church at our local soup kitchen. Dylan loved serving the homeless in Portland. When we changed churches and our new church did not have enough people to provide the manpower for a weekly soup kitchen, Dylan kept going. On many occasions Lilly or Mariah had other activities on Saturdays, so we would simply drop Dylan off at the soup kitchen and then return later to get him. He would get in the car with great excitement telling us about all the people he served food and coffee to that day and how much they appreciated it. When he was even younger, we took a trip to New York City. He had saved up all his allowance and, instead of buying any souvenirs, he spent the weekend handing out five dollar bills to random homeless people we came across while walking the city streets. He wanted no recognition or praise for his actions. There was no Facebook or Twitter for us to brag about him. He just wanted to do what little he could to lift someone's day.

We spent much of our lives when Dylan was young battling him through meltdowns and temper tantrums but we never lost hope for him because we always saw that he had a big heart for others. Underneath the anger and frustration that led to the meltdowns was a caring and loving boy. As we look back now, we see that many of his emotional issues were the result of his attempts to cope with a world that often didn't make sense to him, was frustrating or simply moved too fast for him to keep up.

DYLAN'S TAKE: *In addition to me being a humanitarian who enjoys helping out the downtrodden and unfortunate, there was definitely a little bit of additional motivation with the story of "the runway." During that summer I was really making up for lost time. I had a car and I had developed a social circle outside of the kids, especially the girls, that I went to school with at Scarborough High. I was working on developing my social skills so I could have friends of high social status. I was particularly determined to get as many girls as I could to like me. You'd probably think, "That is not too different from most teenage guys." The difference is that for my life it was a much more serious ambition. I met Julie on MySpace and we started talking on AIM (talk about a blast from the past right?) and after some talking and some flirting, I got her to hang out with my friends and me. Julie was a petite and very cute blonde girl and I was doing pretty well with her. I was picking up many signs I had learned to read that she was attracted to me. When she told me about her situation with her parents and not wanting to go home, I jumped at the chance to try to sneak a pretty girl in to my house for the night. Even though the night didn't go as planned, she told me later that she really just didn't want to go home just because she wanted to stay with me! I spent so many years not having a clue when it came to girls, so that feeling of accomplishment was pretty awesome. And yes, I loved the drama.*

Assaulted

Many Asperger's kids are bullied. They tend to be easy targets because they so badly want to be liked they will go along or do anything to make friends. We were blessed to have made it through elementary school and most of middle school without many bullying experiences. That would change when Dylan got to high school. Bullying in high school is not always what you see on TV or in the movies. It is often more subtle than those images. Dylan was bullied by people making him drive them around wherever they wanted to go. He was often used as a personal chauffeur for his friends and acquaintances. He was often tricked into doing things he would never have thought of on his own.

And he was manipulated into letting people into his home where they would steal from him and our entire family.

* * *

When Dylan's senior year began we would learn how bad bullying could get for a kid with no natural ability to defend himself. Dylan was now about 5' 8" and probably close to 175 lbs. but he was not an aggressive person by nature. He had no brothers to roughhouse with and never played any sports beyond the minor Little League baseball at age twelve so he had never had the experience of using his body to gain physical advantage over another person in a situation. It was mid-October of 2009 when Dylan would experience his first hard dose of bullying. I was on the road making sales calls that day. Generally, when I made a sales call I would bring my cell phone with me and keep it on vibrate in case someone needed me.

In a recent sales meeting my sales reps told me they wished I would keep my phone in the car when I visit customers with them because, since it buzzes constantly from calls, emails and texts, it is distracting and the customers notice it. I took that advice so I did not have my phone on me when my sales rep and I visited a customer in Auburn, Maine, that fall afternoon. It was a lengthy visit, about an hour, but that is not unusual in our business. When I came out and grabbed my cell phone I saw that I had ten missed calls from Amy and a few texts to call her immediately. When I reached her she was very upset that I had been so unavailable. I had never mentioned my sales reps' recent request to her. She told me, "Dylan was attacked on the school bus. I am with him at the ER. He may have a concussion and a broken arm."

Dylan had been riding on the bus from the high school to the vocational school where he was taking a video class when another boy just opened up and started wailing on him. With no altercation prior to give him any advance notice that a fight was going to start, Dylan was taken completely off guard. It was only a couple of minutes before someone pulled the boy off him but he was hit pretty hard. Dylan was okay but very scared to get back on the bus again.

It was only a few days later, while Dylan was walking through the halls of Scarborough High School, a boy jumped out from behind a locker and cold-cocked him with a fist right to the face. Dylan went down hard. Luckily, he was not seriously hurt in either incident and both boys were caught and suspended but Dylan no longer felt safe at school. For a kid who had spent his whole life feeling emotionally unsafe at school it was devastating to now also feel physically unsafe. I called a good friend of mine, Andy Campbell, to see if he could be helpful. Andy is a world champion black belt who owns the local martial arts school where Dylan helped him DJ a dance for the previous New Year's Eve. We asked Andy if he could give Dylan some basic defense skills in case he was ever attacked again. He needed some simple moves to defend himself. As I expected, Andy was extremely generous with his time. He met with Dylan a couple of times, providing him with some basic self-defense tactics.

It was on the day after Christmas 2009 when Dylan's experience getting bullied reached a new level. They call it Boxing Day and that was a fitting name for this year because by the end of the day I felt like I had been twelve rounds with Muhammad Ali. We had a puppy so I was up early that morning when the dog let me know that she needed to go out. Since I figured she would want to come back in shortly I just crashed on the couch. Over an hour later I woke up with a terrible pain in my back. I went upstairs and said to Amy, "Wow, that couch is incredibly uncomfortable. My back is killing me!" I took a few Advil and the pain subsided. Lilly was going to do some ice skating so Serena and I decided to take the puppy to the dog park in Portland. We had a nice time and my back seemed fine. About an hour later she was hungry, so we decided to visit Subway sandwich shop near the park. We had just finished getting our sandwiches and were headed outside to my car when I suddenly doubled over in pain. It was almost indescribable and I knew almost instantly what it was. A kidney stone! I had experienced pain like this twice before so I knew it was not from an uncomfortable couch. We got in the car to get Lilly but by the time we made the mile or so to the ice rink, I crawled out of the car and lay on the sidewalk unable to move another inch. I called Amy and begged her to come get me and bring me to the hospital. She arrived about fifteen minutes later. I climbed into the car and, while rolling around in the back seat, she rushed me to Mercy Hospital's Emergency Room. I literally crawled on my hands and knees into the ER as Amy parked the car. They brought me in and drugged me up quickly, greatly alleviating the pain. I spent the whole day in the ER and was finally released at about 7:00pm with some heavy duty pain meds and praying that it would pass quickly. I thought my excitement was over for the day but it was just beginning.

At about 10:30pm the phone rang. The phone number popped up on the TV with the words, "Biddeford Police" next to it. I said to Amy, "Well, this isn't going to be good news." The police officer on the other end of the phone informed us that Dylan had been assaulted in Biddeford. He was in rough shape but okay at Southern Maine Medical Center in Biddeford. We immediately got dressed, jumped in the car and drove the twenty-five minutes to the hospital. When we arrived we were shocked to discover Dylan lying in bed, with a neck brace, his face extremely swollen and black and blue. We gave him a hug and asked him what happened. He said he didn't remember. He was standing next to his car in downtown Biddeford when, all of sudden, he was being tossed around, punched, slapped and kicked. He didn't see who did it or how many of them there were. His friends, scared they would suffer the same fate, took off. Dylan was left on the sidewalk bleeding and almost unconscious. A neighbor saw what was happening and called the police. The EMT that brought him in, Jason Crocker, was a former Volk Packaging employee so he took extra care of Dylan. Dylan was released once the X-rays came back that there were no major broken bones and no neck damage. Once again, God was looking out for Dylan because he could have had eye damage, a broken nose, a broken jaw, lost teeth or even been killed or brain damaged. He doesn't have any skills or instinct to fight back so he was easy prey. He told us he just covered his face as best he could hoping it would end soon. He did end up with a broken bone just under his eye but it was nothing that required surgery. A visit to a specialist a few days later was a relief when he said it would mend on its own within four to six months.

We went to the Biddeford Police Department the next day because they wanted to get a statement from Dylan. He told the investigating officer that he didn't know who did it. He told him he knew where it happened and who was with him at the time. The police officer was very determined to find the person who did this and, it seemed to both Amy and me, had a pretty strong suspicion of who was involved. There was no ambiguity that he wanted to nail the culprit or culprits. A couple of weeks later we were informed that they had made two arrests in the case, a twenty-year-old man and a sixteen-year-old boy were in custody and charged with assault. They told us someone that was there that night turned in the attackers. Both of them quickly admitted to the crime and were sentenced. The teenage boy was given five years in Long Creek Juvenile Center and the adult was sentenced to eighteen months with two years probation. We were asked by the district attorney's office if we were satisfied with the sentences and if they should accept the plea arrangement. Amy and I discussed it and felt it was acceptable but requested one more stipulation. We asked them to require that neither of the convicted offenders be allowed to initiate any contact with Dylan for at least five years. The DA's representative felt that was a reasonable request so she added it to the plea deal. But the story does not end there.

Mariah and Amy, along with the worship band at the Church of the Holy Spirit regularly attended Saturday morning service at Long Creek. They would not only perform music for whoever attended the non-mandatory service but they often shared a testimony or message to the boys and girls in lockup. An interesting interaction occurred about nine months after the incident that landed Dylan in the hospital. One Saturday that Mariah and the CHS band were performing at Long Creek, the gentleman who arranges the event asked Amy to be the speaker for the day. When the music was over, Amy took the mic and spoke for about fifteen minutes about her experience, as a mom, raising a child with a disability.

She talked to the kids about how God is always there to lift us up when we feel we can't handle it anymore and that Jesus has never left Dylan's side, always protecting him from serious harm even when serious harm was right at his doorstep. In the middle of her talk, unbeknownst to her, a boy got up and left the room crying. It turns out that the boy who beat up Dylan was in the service that morning. After leaving the room he asked one of the staff at Long Creek if he could speak privately with Amy after the service. She was nervous about the meeting but agreed to talk with him. The boy told her what happened that night and apologized for attacking Dylan. He said he had no idea what Dylan had been through and would never have done anything to him had he known. Amy thanked him for his apology and reminded him that, regardless of his disability, there is never a reason to attack someone physically for no reason. It was a powerful moment for all the people in the room and it led the boy to confess that there was actually a third attacker, his girlfriend. The boy told the Long Creek staff that it was his girlfriend who hatched the plan to beat Dylan up and it was she, who, when the boys had Dylan down and covering his face out of fear, kicked him repeatedly. The staff reported this new information to the police. The girl was later arrested, convicted and sentenced to six years in youth jail. Both she and the boy were now safely off the streets until they turned twenty-one years old. We pray for them and hope that they used that time and the resources of people like our friends Dan Mercer and Ken Hawley of Straight Ahead Ministries to turn their lives around so they re-entered society as better people than they were when they walked into Long Creek as teenagers.

Robberies

One of the challenges we always struggled with was the fact that we were very busy parents. With three very active girls involved in sports and school activities, it was impossible to be home all the time to monitor Dylan. The problem was that constant monitoring is what was required to keep our home safe from his friends and their sticky fingers. The only time any justice occurred when it came to our home robberies was because of the quick thinking and awareness of a couple of Dylan's female friends who knew what to look for in untrustworthy people. One day Dylan was home with a couple of young ladies he liked to hang out with. They were, as most of his friends were, from Old Orchard. They were not from the best of home situations but we had met these girls many times and they seemed to not only be pretty good kids but they appeared to like Dylan for who he was. That was a rare combination so we were okay with him hanging out with them.

However, on this day a couple of boys from Scarborough stopped by the house. One of them was a boy named Hector, whom Dylan had been hanging out with quite a bit. Hector also seemed like a decent kid. He wasn't exactly who we would hope Dylan would have for a friend but he could have been a lot worse. At this point it was all about the degree of unhappiness we had with Dylan's choice of friends. We were not happy with any of them, so on that scale, this kid rated better than most. The other boy was someone we had never even heard of and Dylan barely knew as well. They were just laying around the house doing the typical teenage nothingness when the boys started wandering around the house looking in drawers and cabinets. Dylan was hardly paying any attention, as usual, to what his guests were doing in our house but this behavior caught the attention of the girls. They quietly said to Dylan, "We think those guys are casing out your house." Dylan did not believe that was possible as Hector was a boy Dylan considered a good friend. The girls persisted in their efforts to convince Dylan that something wasn't kosher about what they were doing. They suggested to Dylan that they tell the boys they have to go but instead of driving away, Dylan and the girls would drive around the corner and see what happened next. Dylan agreed to this plan, still believing it was a waste of time and energy.

They told the guys that one of the girls had to go home so everyone had to leave so Dylan could drive her home. Dylan offered to drive the boys wherever they needed to go, but they told Dylan they were fine walking and started off down the street. As soon as Dylan and the girls turned the corner

Hector and his friend did a 180 and headed back to our house. Dylan and the girls watched from a distance as the boys went around back and climbed in a window, an unnecessary extra effort as the house was probably left unlocked anyway. The girls immediately called the Scarborough Police to inform them that Dylan's house was being robbed as they speak and someone needed to come right away. The next move was the one that showed their immaturity. They went back to the house, before the police arrived, and confronted the boys. They told them they had called the police so they better get ready to be arrested. One of the boys left the house and went outside where he proceeded to kick a huge dent in the side of Dylan's car. The police did come and the boys were arrested.

They would later be charged with theft. The boy we didn't know would get fined, put on probation, and spend a few days in lockup. Basically, they received nothing more than a slap on the wrist. With Hector, who was a minor, the situation was different. He would be assigned a youth officer who called us because Hector and his parents wanted to meet with Amy and me to apologize. We would have a significant role in determining his fate. We met with Hector, who apologized for robbing us and apologized for taking advantage of Dylan. We told him that it was not really the stuff that he stole that upset us or the fact that they went through our personal belongings; we were used to such invasions of our home and privacy by this point. What really hurt us, and what we have a hard time forgiving him for, was the way he let Dylan down. We explained to him how Dylan's life has been full of friends who give up on him, turn on him or just simply start ignoring him until he gives up trying.

He considered Hector a real friend, someone he trusted and someone who actually liked him enough to not be one of the many who would take advantage of his vulnerability. He did more than steal our stuff and invade our home, he hurt our son in a very painful way and, for that, we were very angry with him. He acted as if he understood but the truth is that he didn't. He could not understand, his parents could not understand, and the youth officer could not understand. No one reading this book can understand what we felt unless you have had a special needs child who has spent a lifetime being bullied, taken advantage of or simply cast aside as if he had no value.

Some of you reading this with neurotypical kids may be thinking, "Hey, I know how you feel. My kid doesn't have any special needs but he has his feelings hurt and has been taken advantage of." I am sorry but you are wrong. I have three very neurotypical girls and they had similar experiences. It is

NOT the same. If I could find the words to describe the hurt in seeing your child reach and reach for something they can never attain, that simple dream of being a normal kid with a friend, I would write those words. I have no words for it. Hector ended up with probation and a fine. He did not get sent to lockup because it was his first offense and we wanted to give him a shot to redeem himself. I have no idea what he did with his life after that second chance. The older boy, ironically, ended up working at the local Tim Horton's breakfast restaurant. The Scarborough Tim Horton's also had inside it a Cold Stone Creamery and I had become addicted to their blueberry/pineapple smoothies. I stopped there at least a couple of days a week on my way to work, on my way to a softball game or when I wanted a healthy snack. Dylan had told me that he was working there. On my next visit I quickly figured out which employee was the young man who had been all through my house collecting my property. He had taken my order before and was about to take it again. This time, I had one of my softball jackets on that said, "Coach Volk" very predominately across the chest. He took my order and then said, "Mr. Volk, do you know who I am?"

It was as awkward as you imagine it would be. I said, "Yes, I do."

He said, "I am sorry for what I did."

I looked him in the eye and said, "I forgive you. Now, do me a favor and do something good with your life. There is still plenty of time to be a better person than the one who robbed me." He just nodded and walked away.

He worked there for a few more months and then I never saw him again. I pray he took my advice. In fact, I keep a prayer list inside the cover of my Bible and his name, and Hector's, are on it to this day.

DYLAN'S TAKE: *Many people meet me and see I have a well-off, stable family background and assume I've had an easy life. They don't feel like they should care about anything I go through because I have a loving family and money. These chapters were examples of how struggle comes in many different forms. Some people grow up poor, their parents suck or aren't there for them at all and they have that as their adversity. On the other hand, they may have lots of friends and people outside their family who care about them. They may have a great, healthy social life to keep them going through rough family times. They can't imagine what it must be like trying so hard to make friends and win people over that they get taken advantage of for their generosity. They do not understand the difficulties that come with not having good judgment due to a neurological disorder—the challenges of discerning people and looking out for things like friends plotting to* *rob you blind. Family is great, I am thankful for my family. But at the end of the day I always knew they have to love me as I am linked to them biologically. They do not love me because of anything to do with who I am as a person. It sounds cold, but just logically, family was never a replacement for peers who have chosen to be a part of my life. I'm not saying my adversity is worse or harder than people who grew up poor. I am saying that if given the choice throughout my childhood I would have happily traded living in a big house in exchange for having tons of real friends. Most people generally agree that having material things is not as good as having people.*

It should also be noted that here is another story where my poor judgment in people and attempts to reach out and build friendships caused my family and me to be robbed and our property to be damaged. What was even more frustrating is that the police did absolutely nothing to help us. My family members and I learned the hard way that the police are not interested in small crimes. If somebody decides to kick a dent in your car or steal thousands of dollars of electronics out of your house, they basically can. This is especially true if you let them in the door to do it. The police of suburban Maine never held these people accountable by helping us get our things back. And it is not just the Maine police officers and detectives. I had the exact same experiences when I moved out of state with the police in Florida and Utah. It has always been a source of great frustration that my family, who gives so much to their community, was completely ignored when they needed help from the local police.

Dylan's Friends

Dylan has always struggled to maintain friendships, but that does not mean he has never had friends. Over the years there have been people in his life who could be considered real friends. Sometimes they were people Amy and I were glad Dylan had in his life and sometimes they were not. They rarely stayed his friends for long, but we do not feel it was because Dylan was a bad friend. Many times over the years we have seen Dylan be a caring and generous friend. There were moments when we felt he was being taken advantage of, and some of those times we were right. Yet, as we look back, we now realize that there were times that we did not give him the credit he deserved. His friends from Little League, Eben Bradley, David Ornstein, Pat Damicis and Adam Saltz were real friends. In high school he became friends with a young man named Tony Stanley who was not always a good influence and frequently got Dylan into trouble, but could definitely be considered a friend.

Another young man named Mike Josephs was also a good friend to Dylan and seemed really sad to see him go when he had dinner with us the night before Dylan left for Utah. Dylan also had some female friends in high school that cared for and looked out for him. He had one female friend, Annalee, who was from a dysfunctional home but was a sincere friend to Dylan. He always tried to help her through her personal difficulties and never gave up on her, even when she found herself in legal trouble. Many of Dylan's friends will be forever unknown to us. He spent much of his summers in high school doing things and spending time with people we will never know about. To all those unnamed friends who cared for and watched Dylan's back during those days, whoever and wherever you are, Amy and I thank you and hope you read this knowing we appreciate your role in Dylan's life.

DYLAN'S TAKE: *What many people, especially older people, don't seem to understand when they're looking at my social life from the outside and throwing up air quotes to tell me that my "friends" are just using me for my car is that it's not such a black and white thing. There seems to be this perception that anyone you would refer in conversation to as a friend, should be a "REAL friend," and anyone who might be more inclined to hang out with you because of the huge advantage of having a vehicle to be able to actually go places and do things with you, must not be a "REAL friend." The thought is that they must be using me. First off, people always seem to assume that any friend you have, you have known for years, neglecting to realize that many people in your life you may have just recently met. Imagine you are a teenager, and just met somebody. It's the summertime and you are bored and without a car but you know a kid that has a car. It is completely natural that you would hit up that person to come hang out. Does that mean over the course of hanging out with that person you don't eventually spend enough time with him and get acquainted enough to consider him an actual friend? Or maybe the same situation except you kind of like that person, but maybe they wouldn't be your first pick if not for the car. But still you enjoy hanging out with him. Does that mean you are a fake friend and using that person? It is a gray area. There were lots of people that I hung out with that thought I was hilarious and enjoyed being with me. If I didn't have a car maybe I would not have heard from them as much, that is true. And there were many people who still would have wanted to be around me even if I didn't have a car. I generally knew who was who. The social interactions of teenagers are not so formal that I would tell somebody I met two weeks prior, "I don't wish to see you anymore because you are not a real friend." I took it for what it was, and went with the flow. Sometimes I was right* *about people and sometimes I misjudged them. When I lost my car many months later I found out who my real friends were, and there was nothing much to be surprised about.*

Peeing in Cape Elizabeth—Wrong Place, Wrong Time

This may be one of the strangest Dylan stories in the book. I am not sure how it happens but sometimes it seems if there is any luck at all for Dylan it is bad luck. In the fall of Dylan's senior year he was driving in the coastal town of Cape Elizabeth. "The Cape," as the people who live there like to refer to it, is a very high income community. The town has done a nice job maintaining strict ordinances preventing chains like McDonald's and Subway from moving in. The problem, on this night in fall 2009, was that Dylan had to relieve himself. It was late at night and with no chain restaurants or stores to stop into he pulled over on the side of the road. In an effort to not take a chance he could accidentally urinate on himself while taking care of business on a dark night on a dark road, he found a street light to aid him visually.

As he was peeing under the streetlight a policeman drove by. Seeing Dylan under the light he switched on the blue lights and asked him what he was doing. Dylan explained his thought process to the cop but he was not sympathetic to Dylan's strategy. Instead he wrote Dylan up for "indecent exposure." This is a serious charge that in Maine is considered a sex crime. If found guilty Dylan would be listed on a statewide website as a registered sex offender!

The thought of Dylan on a list of Mainers convicted of sexual crimes was daunting and terrifying. The list, which is accessible by website and searchable by town, would not explain all the detail and background. It would just say that Dylan had been convicted of exposing himself, indecent exposure. To think that they would ruin Dylan's life over an act that takes place on every golf course, every hour of every day in this country—a man having to go to the bathroom and finding a tree to do it—seemed ludicrous and grossly unfair. It was one of the scariest times that we went through with Dylan because the long-term impact would have been devastating. That list is often referred to when people move into neighborhoods or are hiring. It was essentially an internet scarlet letter.

I called our corporate attorney and asked him if he would send someone from his office to represent Dylan when he had to appear in court. The attorney said that he'd make sure Dylan was taken care of and we would review the files. A few days later, I received a call from one of the attorneys in his practice. He told me not to worry—it was a bogus charge and there was no way they could convict him of indecent exposure. Not only had he not intentionally exposed himself to anyone, he hadn't exposed himself to anyone at all. You cannot be convicted of indecent exposure if you don't actually expose yourself. He was on a dark road late at night, just trying to relieve himself. He just happened to pick the wrong spot in the wrong moment. The attorney said that policemen don't always know the law and sometimes they write the wrong charge on the ticket. He would talk to the district attorney, and he was confident that the charges would be dropped or at least reduced to something with a much smaller consequence, such as a "misdemeanor for urinating in public."

About a month later, Dylan's court date came up. He dressed up nicely and appeared in court. The attorney did a nice job representing the facts of the case and assured them that there was no intent to expose. It was just a young man picking the wrong spot to take care of nature's business. They charged Dylan with public urination with the stipulation that if he stayed out of trouble for six months, the whole case would be scrapped, as if it never happened. We were very relieved. We paid the fine, and six months later, the charges vanished, thanks to Dylan staying out of trouble. Once again, what could have been a terrible outcome ended up as a valuable lesson for Dylan with no long-lasting negative impact.

These are all bumps on a very rocky road, but Dylan has lived. Some bumps seem higher and take longer to get over, but it does always seem to be one bump after another. Just when we get over one bump in the road, if we don't hit another one, we can see it in the distance.

Hit and Run

I was sitting in my kitchen reading the newspaper one late winter evening in March 2010 when there was a knock on the door. I opened up the door and my heart sank when I saw a policeman standing on my porch. I opened the door and said, "Can I help you, sir?"

He introduced himself as a South Portland police officer and told me that my son was involved with a hit and run. My heart sank even lower as I feared the worst. Did he hit a runner? Biker? I had immediately said, "Was anybody hurt?"

The situation became instantly better when he said, "No one was hurt, it was a parked car."

I called Dylan from the other room when he was sitting on the couch calmly watching TV. "Dylan, this policeman says that you hit a car and took off."

Dylan looked at us without so much as a moment of hesitation and said, "Yeah I did." The police officers jaw dropped and looked at me as if to say "Did he actually just admit that he hit a car and took off without so much as an apology for what he did?"

I looked at Dylan, "Honey, you can't just hit a car and drive away. That's a crime."

Dylan said without any concern, "It wasn't that big a dent."

The police officer disagreed and said that the dent on the woman's car was pretty significant. It turned out Dylan had his car parked at the Maine Mall near the food court where people often come outside and wait for rides or take smoke breaks. It is the most crowded outside part of the mall so when Dylan backed out of his parking lot and smashed into a parked car, and then proceeded to stop his car, get out, look at the car that was hit, and get back in his car and drive away, he gave everyone witnessing it plenty of time to write down his vanity plate that read "DIELAWNN." Dielawnn is the nickname his friends gave him a couple of years earlier. If this were an episode of *Law and Order* it would be over by the first commercial break.

The officer said, "You understand that I could arrest you for what you did right?"

Dylan became argumentative as he often did when he was confronted with something he didn't agree with. He argued, "It wasn't that big of a dent! What is she getting so worked up about?"

The officer just looked at me in shock that Dylan would seem so unconcerned about the situation at hand. I'm not really sure how most teenagers would react when confronted with a police officer telling them they could be arrested, but I'm pretty sure that Dylan's reaction was outside the norm.

I said, "Well did you even leave a note?"

"I didn't see the point…It wasn't that big of a dent," he said again slowly, "I have way bigger dents on my car." This was true. Dylan's car had several dents on it and although, like everyone else, he would like to have a car without dents, he was getting by just fine with his dented Oldsmobile. He really could not understand what the big deal was. Why would this person have such a problem with one relatively small dent when he was getting by with several much larger dents.

"I looked at the dent, it's a pretty good size ding," the officer said, "And I also looked at your car when I pulled in here and can see the white paint marks from where you hit her, and it's clear to me that it was a sizable impact."

I told Dylan that whoever this person was, she probably did not have any dents on the car and didn't want any, and it was his responsibility, if he hit the car, to either find her or leave a note with his information on it because he would be liable for repairing the car to its original condition.

Dylan said, "Oh well that's just ridiculous."

It was at this point that I told Dylan to go back into the other room and asked the police officer if I could talk to him privately. We stepped outside and he said, "What's the deal with your son? He doesn't seem to understand the seriousness of this incident."

I was glad that the cop recognized that there was "a deal" with my son. It was almost as if he knew that something was different about him and there must be an explanation. I can only assume that this officer, who was in his mid to late thirties, had presented similar information to many teenagers during his career, and he had rarely seen a reaction like Dylan's. I don't know if he had any experience or training with Asperger's, but he knew that something was out of the ordinary.

I explained to him that Dylan had Asperger's Syndrome and part of his disability was what they call "an inability to generalize." I told him that Dylan has a difficult time seeing things from other people's perspective. In fact, it's almost impossible for him to step out of his world view to see through someone else's eyes. Even when you say to him something like, "Can you see how it would be difficult for someone without a dent in their car to just accept a dent in their car when they had no responsibility in putting it there?" He wouldn't be able to put himself in that person's shoes to see from a different angle. I told the police officer that we would do whatever it took to resolve the situation, and I apologized that Dylan did not seem to take it seriously but reiterated that it was not due to arrogance or the fact that he was uncaring. He just could not understand why, if he could live with dents, someone else couldn't just as well. The officer was very understanding and told me he would contact me later with the name and phone number of the woman who owned the car that Dylan crashed into.

Later that evening, I gave her a call and apologized for Dylan hitting her car and told her that we would take full responsibility for the cost of any repairs that were needed. I even explained to her the interaction Dylan had with the police officer in the event that he told her about it but didn't get the information accurately conveyed or that someone at the mall told her how Dylan got out of the car, reviewed the situation, and yet still drove away. I used it as an opportunity to explain Asperger's Syndrome to someone who probably had no experience with it. She was very kind. As it turned out, she was the daughter of a good friend of one of my sales reps. A few years earlier, her dad had been hunting with my sales rep, Chuck Fabian, when he fell out of a tree stand and broke his neck. Because of that accident, he became a quadriplegic and was bound to a wheelchair for the rest of his life. It's a tragic story, and he's had a really difficult time dealing with his life in a wheelchair. I think her experience with her dad might have had an influence on her patience with regard to Dylan and his disability.

I recommended that she obtain a couple of estimates and give me a call in a few days so we could arrange for her car to get repaired. I have no idea how, to this day, Dylan continues to get so lucky with every incident that he has, but Amy and I do feel that God has a hand in keeping Dylan from getting in too much trouble. Once again, Dylan had learned a lesson without any serious repercussions. This would go on to happen over and over again, to the point where there was no way that you could explain it without believing that God was looking out for our son.

The young lady called me a few days later and told me that the estimate was almost $2,000. I was not surprised by the amount. However, her next comment really shocked me. She said, "I think this is a ridiculous amount of money to take to fix my car. It's completely unnecessary. There's no way that I would pay $2,000 dollars to fix this dent."

I told her that car repairs are very expensive. I had had some bodywork done for various reasons over the years, and it doesn't take much to rack up a $2,000 bill. She said she understood but still felt it was not right to ask me to spend that amount of money on a car that wasn't worth much more than that. I'm not sure what kind of car she had or how old it was, but she didn't seem to think that it was worth putting $2,000 into it. Instead, she suggested that she take it to a local shop that does car washes and detail work primarily. She said, "I'm pretty sure that they can suction cup this dent out, buff it up, and it'll look fine."

I reiterated, "I don't mind paying for the full repair of the car."

But she said she wouldn't hear of it and would go get an estimate to buff it out and let me know how much it would cost. She called me a couple of days later and told me that all the work could be done for only about $200, and she made an appointment. I thanked her and called the car wash with my credit card number. She took her car in, and that was the end of it. What could have been a very expensive and potential legal situation for Dylan turned out to be a $200 bill and a good lesson learned.

Two More Cars Bite the Dust

The weeks leading up to and around graduation were not very good weeks for us with Dylan. Just a couple of weeks before he graduated, he had been on his way to school in the Buick that his grandmother had given to Mariah. My mother had a Buick that she looked into trading in but it didn't have a lot of value and she knew Mariah would be getting her license soon, so she had offered the car to Mariah. This was a very generous offer that Mariah appreciated, as did we because it saved us from buying a car for her. Dylan had been driving an old Volvo we had recently purchased, but eventually it had too many problems to spend the money repairing it, so he started driving my mother's Buick. One morning, as he was driving to school, he decided to reach down and grab a mirror that he had on the floor to make sure his hair looked good. Why he didn't look in the rearview mirror at his hair, I'm not sure.

Apparently, he wanted a larger mirror to get the full effect of how his hair looked that day. What he did not do was wait until he approached and stopped at the traffic light that was less than a mile away to get the mirror. So, as he reached down to the passenger side of the car, he continued to travel up Black Point Road toward the high school where he smashed into the car in front of him, sending that car into the car in front of them. Fortunately, no one was hurt in the accident and fortunately, the girl that was driving the car Dylan crashed into had been on my Little League team and we were friendly with the parents.

They were very patient about the whole situation. We obviously had to pay for the repairs that went through our insurance. But they never threatened to sue us or take any other legal action for the damage that Dylan did to the car. The car in front of them was not damaged, luckily, and they were able to drive off. In the process, however, the Buick my mother had offered to Mariah was smashed beyond reasonable repair. The whole hood was compressed and crushed and there was no way that we could spend the amount of money that it would take to repair it. This left us without a car for Mariah when she started driving, and it also landed Dylan completely without a car, which made him very frustrated.

The first thing that happened when Dylan didn't have a car to drive people around is that some of the kids, the ones that were not his real friends, stopped calling him. His pipeline of friends dried up very quickly when he was no longer able to act as a chauffeur. He had become very used to driving his friends all over the place, oftentimes making money doing it by charging them well beyond the gas required. Kids would call Dylan up and need a ride that was five minutes away and he would charge them ten dollars for gas. He saw it as a win-win. Not only could he make money, but it was an opportunity for him to have social interaction with other teenagers. He saw many of these kids as his friends but also realized that some were using him. However, it was still a win-win because it gave him the opportunity to get out of the house and hang out with kids his own age.

When he lost the ability to drive them around, some of those "friendships" disappeared very quickly. However, when we pointed that out to Dylan, he would get *very* upset with us and turn it around, accusing us of seeing him as having no value and no qualities that would allow someone to want to be his friend. We tried to explain to him that that was not our intent in talking about how nobody was calling him, but instead to point out that some of those kids were not his friends. It was not a matter of him not being a good and valued person. In fact, Dylan was a terrific friend and we often felt bad that more kids did not give him a chance to prove what a good friend he could be to them. The ones that stayed in touch with him proved to be true friends but it was clear to us that others were using him for his car.

To this day this conversation creates tremendous conflict with Dylan. He really feels that we think he wouldn't make a good friend and has very different recollections of this time in his life. There also may be a part of him that knew we were right and his defense mechanism was to take that anger out on us and turn it around as if we were the ones who didn't care for him. We had these conversations frequently and they were always very frustrating and loud. Looking back on those conversations, I can see how he could take it that way and it hurts me to think how that must have felt for him. But we didn't know how else to tell him that these kids were not his real friends, and in a lot of cases, were very bad influences on him. It was not that he lacked value, it was that they were simply unkind people. His argument to the fact that his friends were bad influences was always the same: "Bad friends are better than no friends."

Now you and I, and the average person reading this book, could argue that is not the case. I would rather not have that person for a friend at all. But after seventeen years of loneliness and rejection, Dylan felt differently and it was hard to blame him. Without a doubt, without hesitation, in his mind, a bad friend was indeed better than no friend. There was nothing worse than those days I have talked about in earlier chapters where he would spend all evening on Friday and all day on Saturday begging people to hang out with him, only to find himself all alone on those Friday and Saturday evenings. So for him, any friend, even if he knew in his heart and sometimes probably in his head that they were using him for his car, was still better than no friends at all.

Since he could no longer drive the Buick, Amy found a used 1996 Oldsmobile Ninety-Eight for Dylan. It was only $1,800 and in excellent condition. Dylan was driving to school one day in mid-May without Mariah. This time, he was in the proper lane in a three-lane intersection. One lane goes right and straight, the middle lane goes straight, and the left lane is left only, which takes you to Route 1 and Scarborough High School. Dylan was in the left-only lane. As he sat there waiting for the light to turn, he suddenly decided that he needed to pull into the local Mobil station, which was all the way across the three lanes, to get some cigarettes. Impulsively and without looking, Dylan whipped his car out and drove at a ninety-degree angle to the right to get to the Mobil Station. In fact, according to the man who hit him, he drove at more than a ninety-degree angle. He was actually driving the wrong way down Black Point Road away from the intersection and the gentleman coming up over the hill had no way to stop from hitting Dylan almost head-on.

The gentleman in the truck hit Dylan's car at enough force to drive the corner of the car and the hood into a mangled mess. The pickup truck had some front-end damage as well. I received a phone call shortly after that Dylan had crashed his car, and I immediately drove up to Oak Hill. There, in the parking lot of the Mobil Station, was Dylan, the other gentleman, and a policeman who was very agitated because Dylan could not find his driver's license or his registration. My first goal was to settle everybody down and find the documents needed to fill out the paperwork. I found them, gave them to the police office, and assured him that Dylan did have a driver's license even though he did not have his wallet on him.

I didn't even know what to say to him because I was so upset. I was furious! Not only had he crashed and totaled two cars in under a year but he was now responsible for destroying the free car that my mother had given to Mariah, leaving Mariah without a car, and now the new car we bought him.

It would cost us almost as much to repair the Oldsmobile as we had originally paid for it. And, to add insult to injury, he did this looking to buy cigarettes, which was a habit that made Amy and me very upset and disappointed in him to begin with. Smoking was not a fight we could win so we did whatever we could to discourage it but didn't battle him about it. We had learned to pick our battles.

I exchanged information with the gentlemen who owned the pickup truck. Fortunately, he was very patient with the whole situation, and told me he would get an estimate and call me in a few days. As I had done before and would later do with Dylan's frequent car accidents, I told him that we would take full responsibility for any repairs needed.

Dylan was very shaken up by this accident because he knew he had really screwed up. He knew how angry his mother and I would be, and he knew that it might cost him his driving privileges because, without an extra car in the family, he had no way to get around. He also was upset because I kept telling him how irresponsible he was and how it seemed clear he was not mature enough to drive.

After the information had been exchanged and the paperwork was done, I drove Dylan to school and went to work. Later that day, I received a call from the owner of the pick-up informing me that the estimate was almost $5,000 to fix the damage. There was no way that we could pay for that out of pocket, so we would definitely have to put it through our insurance. But then the man on the other end of the phone said something that took me by great surprise.

He said, "I don't think it's necessary to pay $5,000 to fix this truck. I have a buddy who's really good with cars and bodywork. He looked at it and told me he thinks we could do it ourselves for about $1,000." I almost fell off my chair. This man had no responsibility for the damage to his car. It would not cost him a penny out of his own pocket to have it repaired professionally, to its original condition, and yet he was offering to do the work himself and felt it could be done for $4,000 less than what was quoted.

I said, "It's not your responsibility to fix the car. My son is the one who crashed into you and we will get your truck professionally repaired."

But again, he responded, "No, I wouldn't hear of it. Like I said, I think $5,000 is an excessive amount of money for these repairs. My buddy and I can take care of it."

"How do you want to handle it going forward?" I asked.

"We'll do the repairs and then just send you an itemized bill for what it costs us."

About two weeks later, he called me and told me that they had the car all fixed up for $1,200. He asked if I could mail him a check, which I did happily. Somehow, Dylan seemed to get into accidents with the nicest and most generous people in southern Maine.

DYLAN'S TAKE: *From the outside looking in, it might have looked like all the time I spent in high school going on adventures with friends and having a big crazy social life was just a teenager wanting to party. But I always looked at it as a strategic endeavor; this was the first time I really had opportunities to have a social life with people I chose, (people outside of who I went to school with in the town of Scarborough). And I got to see what kids were like in other towns, and found that there were certain types of people who were not as judgmental and more accepting of me and my unique personality. These tended to be kids who partied and did things like drink and smoke, but I found that they weren't as intimidating as I always thought and some of them actually made good friends. The strategic part comes from the fact that having Asperger's like I did, being social with my peers in the expected way doesn't come effortlessly to me as it does with many nuerotypical people. It's always something that I have to consciously and deliberately do. Therefore this was a time in my life I was working every day to learn all the do's and don't's essentially of how to act around "cool" people my age that had some social status, and how to be a part of these social circles, which I had never been before. I had to learn from making many mistakes and paying attention to feedback I would get. The thing is that I don't have the appearance of having any type of mental diagnosis like I have, so me saying or doing things that were unexpected just came off funny most of the time. Knowing this, I definitely played it up sometimes for comedic effect, which is how I found my role of basically being the comedian of the group, and using that as my way to make friends. That's why I, and my parents as well I'm sure, see this time period as a time of learning and taking on challenges, even though most people would mistakenly see it as a teenager just having fun.*

Tour of WBLM

Dylan had many special interests over the years but no interest has been as consistent as his love of music. When he was a little boy as young as four we would marvel as his ability to memorize songs. He always had very clear and logical explanations for why certain music was more popular than other genres at the time. He loved to listen to Casey Kasem's Weekly Top 40 and would often spend the three hours writing down all the songs as they were announced and then re-writing them in the order he felt the forty songs should be in that given week. At that time, he owned six or seven books that were full of countdowns going back to the fifties, and he had an amazing ability to tell you what songs were hot in what years, what genres were popular, why they came and why they faded. As with most things that Dylan became interested in, he absorbed himself in data. When he was also extremely focused on *Star Wars*, we were shocked at his ability to distinguish one musical piece from another, scene by scene, as the soundtrack played in the car. Most of his special interests came on like a hurricane but eventually faded away, yet his passion for music remained.

It was spring of 2010, and Dylan was seriously considering attending the New England School of Communications in Bangor where they have a program for radio broadcasting. He didn't really want to be a DJ, although if the opportunity arose, I'm sure he would take it. What he really wanted to do was learn how to have a career as a program director. His dream was to run a radio station where he could pick out the music. Dylan has an incredible sense of music. He often knows when an artist is going to be "hot" as soon as he hears the first song. He told us about Nikki Minaj, Lady Gaga, and Justin Bieber before they were popular.

So when Dylan said he wanted to work in the radio business, I called the ex-husband of our former banker, a local gentleman named Mark Snowden. Mark not only works for WBLM, a classic rock station based in Portland, but Mark has two children on the autism spectrum. Thus, he was very accommodating in helping Dylan figure out what he wanted to do in the radio business. Mark invited Dylan to come to the studio for a tour. Dylan and I waited in the lobby looking at collectibles of artists that had come to WBLM and autographed pictures of album covers. There were some big names in the lobby and it was pretty cool to talk to Dylan about what he knew about each artist. Of course, he knew something about every one of them, whether he liked their music or not. Mark came out, introduced himself, and started giving us a tour. I hung back, so Dylan could get the most out of the visit. Before long, they were talking about things that I didn't even understand. Dylan knew all the lingo, all the buzz-words, and Mark was very impressed with him.

After a tour of the studios, he took us back to meet one of the most popular and well-known DJs to ever come out of Portland, Herb Ivy, known as "The Captain," who had a morning show dating back to when I was in high school. Herb was the program director as well as the DJ at WBLM, so Mark asked if he would sit with us.

Dylan knew who he was, but to me it was like sitting with a celebrity because I had been listening to him for twenty years. He started asking Dylan questions about what he was interested in but before long, it turned around and Dylan started asking him about different genres, his opinions about different artists, and how playlists were determined. Once again, I was lost as they talked radio lingo. It was an absolute pleasure to see Dylan in his element. These moments I cherish—Dylan presenting about birds to his first grade class, talking cars with Adam Lee at Lee Auto Mall on his eleventh birthday; and talking music with one of Portland's most famous DJs. It's so wonderful when other people appreciate what Dylan has to offer. The challenge continues to be how to make those "special interests" a marketable skill.

After the conversation between Herb and Dylan, Herb brought us back to Mark and told him how impressed he was with Dylan. We asked about possible internships, part-time work, or volunteer opportunities, but they both felt that there was unfortunately very little opportunity for Dylan at WBLM. The radio industry was a very difficult business. Satellite radio and iTunes have been a huge blow to mainstream radio. Radio is a tough market to enter, and although they were both impressed with Dylan, they were both honest and warned him it's a very difficult business to get into and not very financially lucrative. Dylan didn't care. He was so thrilled at his visit that he was riding high for days, and it was great to see him so happy and inspired. The stage was set for Dylan to apply to the New England School of Communication to pursue his dream of radio.

DYLAN'S TAKE: *I have had a lifelong passion for music. It has been a blessing but it has also been a source of frustration. There are millions of people that love music just as much as I do. However there are extremely few people (I have actually only met about four, all on the internet) who are interested in all in the aspects of music like I am. Most people say they like a wide range of music. What I always loved about music was beyond the sound or the beat. I was passionate about studying and talking about the marketing of the music. I loved predicting how well certain artists or songs would do on the charts and how much radio airplay they received. Any conversation you might be having about music dies instantly if you start a conversation with the average person by asking, "Can you believe they released THAT song as Katy Perry's next single? This one would have* *been picked up way more by radio stations." It was fantastic to be at WBLM that day so I could talk with Herb Ivy about music from a commercial point of view. My frustration has been when I try to ask the average American, "Do you think this Rihanna song will be a hit, and why?" Even if they love music I get a polite response and then a quick topic change. If you are reading this and want to prove me wrong, you have my permission!*

The Slow Transition to Adulthood

Visit to New Directions

It was May 2010. Dylan was only about a month away from graduating. We started to really get concerned about what we were going to do after he graduated. We knew there were not a lot of opportunities in Maine for him, and we really wanted him to get away from some of the bad influences that were negatively impacting his decision making.

Amy found a program in southern Florida called New Directions for Young Adults. She talked to them on the phone and they sounded like they could handle Dylan. The program is designed to help young people who have graduated from high school get through college. We were not really sure whether Dylan was going to be able to handle college, but many of the kids in their program went to community college. We thought that might be a better fit for Dylan. We helped Dylan apply to Palm Beach Community College and scheduled a trip to Florida in late May to visit New Directions.

We flew down to Deerfield Beach, where the school is located, in Southeastern Florida. Not only was it a really nice place to live, but Deerfield Beach is only about forty-five minutes from my parents. This meant that for most of the year, Dylan would have family nearby in the event that he needed somebody. My Uncle Roger also wintered in Boca Raton, which is even closer to Deerfield Beach, so there was a network for him in the event that something didn't go well. Knowing we had family in the area made us more comfortable.

We sat down in their office, which was basically an apartment converted into an office in a gated complex. It was beautiful. Amy and I were both very jealous at the opportunity that we saw for Dylan to move into these beautiful apartments and live in southern Florida. There was a small fitness center, a swimming pool, and lots of nice walking and biking areas all inside a gated community.

Our biggest concern whenever we considered moving Dylan somewhere was his living space. It was a matter of great anxiety. That anxiety disappeared very quickly when we visited Deerfield Beach because the apartment was very beautiful, very clean, and possibly best of all for Dylan, they allowed cats. This meant Dylan could bring his cat, Beautiful Boy, with him to Florida.

We sat down with Dr. Drew Rubin and his associate Dr. Michael Kellen to talk about how Dylan would fit in with their other students. Most of the students at New Directions were on the autism spectrum somewhere, some higher functioning than other students. And some with other issues as well. They told us they would match Dylan up with a roommate and if it didn't work out, there were other options. They could move people around. There was almost nothing they said that caused us concern or fear that Dylan would be too much for them to handle. They met with Dylan and found him, as most people do, entertaining and very engaging.

The most challenging part of the trip was not New Directions or convincing Dylan to move to southern Florida. The most challenging part of the trip was that Dylan was scheduled to complete high school within a couple of days of returning from our trip to Deerfield Beach, and according to his teacher before we left, he was failing almost every class. He had not completed a number of assignments and had not even come close to finishing the book that they were reading. If we didn't spend a significant amount of time with Dylan to help him complete his homework assignments, he would not graduate with his class. So the most memorable part of our whole trip to Florida was the hour after hour in every spare moment trying to get Dylan to complete his assignments. They were reading the book *The Pearl*, and Dylan had not moved past chapter two or three, and he didn't really have any idea what was going on in the book. So beginning on the plane, Amy started from page one reading the book to Dylan and going through each chapter assignment, helping him write out proper answers, sometimes having to read parts of the chapter multiple times to get them right.

This created an emotional conflict for us. Here we were flying all the way to southern Florida, not only signing Dylan up for Palm Beach Community College where he had already been accepted, but wondering how he could complete summer classes we had enrolled him in when he could not complete his high school homework assignment. The whole trip, the questions "What we were thinking?" and "How would we get him through college?" raced through our minds. We were really hoping New Directions would have the answers we needed.

Fortunately they offered virtually unlimited tutoring services in their offices and were willing to work with Dylan on his organizational skills to get through his classes. However, based on the difficulty that he had completing, what we felt were very simple assignments, that last month of high school, we wondered what had been going on the last four years that he was about to get a high school degree with such a limited ability to do schoolwork.

When the trip was completed, so were Dylan's homework assignments. I have to give Amy full credit for this accomplishment because my patience was very thin with Dylan at that time because I was so frustrated with his lack of effort in completing his work. The problem wasn't only that he had a hard time with the homework, it was his complete cavalier attitude. He really did not understand nor believe that they would fail him. He kept insisting that there's no way his teachers would fail him, as if he were entitled to a high school diploma, whether he earned it or not. I found that extremely frustrating and often took it out in the way I interacted with Dylan. Amy found it frustrating as well, but when push came to shove in situations like this, she was better at working with Dylan to get done what he needed to get done. I tried to do whatever else needed to be done on that trip so that she could focus on working with Dylan.

When we came back to Maine, he turned in his assignments and a couple of days later, we received an email from his teacher that Dylan had completed enough homework to get a passing grade. We did not really care at that point what that passing grade was, as long as ten days or later he would be up on stage with the rest of his classmates receiving his diploma.

High School Graduation

On June 7, 2010, we all gathered at the Cumberland County Civic Center in Portland, Maine, to attend Scarborough High School's graduation ceremony. There were a lot of kids on the stage that day who went through a lot to graduate. I'll never know all the individual stories of those 250 or so graduates, as we stood there watching Dylan in the processional with a cap and gown on, Amy and I were both so overcome with emotion it was hard to even breathe. There were so many times when we thought that this day would never come. There were so many times when we worried whether he would even be alive when his high school class graduated or whether he would be in jail when his high school class graduated. And yet, here he was, walking step by step up onto the stage to accept his high school diploma. We got some extra tickets so his grandparents could be there on this special day as well. Everyone had played a part in getting Dylan to that moment, and even his sisters were excited for him and realized what a big day this was.

When they called his name, it was hard to take pictures because the tears were flowing so profusely as he walked across the stage to take that diploma in his hand. Amy gave me a hug, and we knew that together, staying together, sticking together, we had all accomplished something great.

When the ceremonies were over, most of the kids ran around to find their friends to take pictures in their caps and gowns one last time before heading off to Project Graduation. As usual, Dylan's experience was different. He didn't take part in that post-graduation glee like the rest of his class. Dylan allowed us a quick picture, he took a picture with his grandparents, and then he went outside to have a cigarette. We waited until he was done smoking, talking with some kids we knew that had graduated and were planning to head off to college in the fall.

Dylan was also not headed off to Project Graduation with the rest of his class. He felt it would be loud and overwhelming for him, and, the truth is, he would have nobody to hang out with at an event like that. He didn't really have any friends at Scarborough High School. In all those years from second grade to high school graduation, there was nobody that truly was his friend. While it was disappointing to think about Dylan not going to Project Graduation and experiencing that traditional high school evening, it was hard to argue his point.

Instead, we all went down to a well-known eatery called Becky's Diner where we had late-night pancakes and waffles. It ended up being one of the most enjoyable and family-centered evenings we had had in a long, long time. We laughed, everybody got along. The funniest part of the evening was when Dylan announced that for a special graduation gift, he wanted everyone to tell their favorite Dylan story. We sat around one by one telling, in as much detail as we could all remember, our favorite Dylan stories. I still smile when I think about that night.

Stealing Amy's Credit Card

After graduation, we started preparing for Dylan to move to Florida. We booked a flight for Amy and Dylan to fly down in late June so they could get the apartment all set up. New Directions had already lined Dylan up with a roommate, a boy with Asperger's from New Jersey. And now we needed to furnish an apartment. The plan was for Amy and Dylan to fly down, take a few days to hit up some second-hand stores, and get all the things they needed.

The weeks before he left were challenging because Dylan had graduated from high school, felt that he was an adult now and could do what he wanted, yet he was still living in our house. We felt like he should still live by our rules, as most parents would, and he felt that he had the freedom to do as he chose, as would most nineteen-year-olds. The real conflict during this couple of weeks came from the fact that Dylan did not have a car to drive and was still very angry with us for suggesting that it was the car that made him popular.

But then, all of a sudden out of the blue, people started calling Dylan again. We couldn't figure out why Dylan's popularity re-birthed, but he used every opportunity to point out to us that he had a social life again and we were wrong. Although we didn't like his friends, we were happy for him that he wasn't sitting home all the time feeling sorry for himself and becoming depressed because he was almost nineteen and had no social life.

It was the day before Dylan and Amy were scheduled to fly to Florida that Dylan's renewed popularity all made sense. I was sitting in my office when I received a call from the Visa fraud department. My card had been hacked a year earlier so there were red flags on my Visa card already.

So, when they called me with another fraud concern, I immediately thought my card had been violated again. They started going through some of the charges and I said, "Nope, that's fine. That's fine. That's fine." And then, there was one at McDonald's that caused a red flag to come up for me because we never ever eat at McDonald's and it was for four dollars. Then there was another one at a gas station in Old Orchard Beach, and *another* one at a gas station in Old Orchard Beach, and then another and another. There were charges for Aeropostale, TJ Maxx, and other locations at the Maine Mall that I know *I* had not been shopping at. It did not take me very long to figure out that Dylan was using our credit card. I called Amy and asked her about all of these charges and if maybe she had taken the girls shopping lately. She said she hadn't and we knew what was going on. Dylan had stolen Amy's credit card and was using it to buy friendship.

Once again, our emotions were mixed. We were irate that Dylan had racked up over $2,000 in charges in less than two weeks, charges that we would be responsible for unless we told Visa that they were fraudulent. Obviously, we could not turn our son in as the hacker.

Dylan, at the time, was having lunch with my parents, who were saying goodbye to him before he left for Florida. I called my father and told him what had happened but told him not to say anything to Dylan because I didn't want him getting into the middle of it. I asked him to let me know when they were about twenty minutes away from finishing lunch and I would leave the office and drive to TJ Maxx where I would meet Dylan. Amy went up into Dylan's room and gathered up some of the clothes that she thought were from TJ Maxx, many of them still had tags on them.

Amy and I drove to the parking lot at TJ Maxx where my parents pulled up with Dylan. He had no idea why they were there. When we confronted Dylan about stealing the credit card and buying not only clothes, but gas and meals for his friends, he denied it at first. However, knowing the evidence was overwhelmingly against him, he quickly admitted it and then tried to come up with reasons as to why it was justified—we didn't get him a new car after he crashed his; we didn't give him enough money to go out with his friends; we didn't give him what he deserved. His feelings of entitlement were outrageous and aggravating. Instead of simply apologizing, he tried to blame us for his deception.

I made him take the clothes off that he was wearing. Amy brought him a change of clothes in case the clothes that he was wearing were stolen, and I walked in to TJ Maxx to return them. He refused to go in the store with me. I went in and told a sales clerk that the clothes had been purchased inappropriately and some were credited and some were not because they had been worn. She wanted to know if I wanted to keep the clothes that weren't credited and I said that I didn't. She could put them back on the shelf, donate them to charity, or do whatever she wanted, but I didn't want to leave the store with any clothes because Dylan would inevitably say he might as well keep them since they wouldn't take them back, and I didn't want that option for him.

While I was in the store, I asked to speak to a manager. The manager came over, a woman who seemed to be in her thirties. I told the manager that my son hangs out with some pretty rough crowds, and although I don't have any proof that he's even stolen anything, I know he's worn stolen clothes from TJ Maxx. He's told us he's wearing a shirt that his friend stole from TJ Maxx. I wanted her to know that these kids think TJ Maxx is a big joke because when they get caught stealing, they are just told not to come back into the store. The store never even calls the police so why would the kids be concerned about stealing again? All it would take was for them to prosecute a few of these kids and word would get out not to steal from TJ Maxx.

The store manager thanked me for my information and told me she finds it as frustrating as I do, but their corporate policy is that it would take more money to prosecute all these kids than the value of the product being stolen.

I said, "What kind of message are you sending to that entire generation of kids? You're telling them that stealing is not a crime that anybody takes seriously and the reward is much greater than the risk, so why not do it?"

Again, she agreed with me but said there was nothing she could do. It was a very frustrating conversation. I left TJ Maxx and went back out to the parking lot. One of the items of clothes I had not noticed had a Macy's tag on the inside, so I did take that shirt back outside and told Dylan to get in my car because we were heading over to Macy's to return it. Again, he refused to go with me. Voices were raised and I demanded that he get in the car. We finally got in the car and headed over to the mall.

When we got there, he absolutely refused to get out of the car and come into the store, so I took the shirt and the hat off his head. From what Capital One told me, he had purchased an Atlanta Braves hat at Lids. Dylan is *not* an Atlanta Braves fan, but for whatever reason he liked the hat.

I returned the shirt to Macy's and luckily got my money back because the tag was still on it. However, when I went to Lids they could not refund my money back because it had been worn but told me they'd give me a store credit. Anyone who knows me, knows that I like hats. If I have one vice in life, it's that I really like to buy hats and I have a lot of them. Every time I come back from something, my wife will smile and laugh and say, "That's good. You need another hat." I remind her that I could be a smoker, or a gambler, or a womanizer, which would all be a lot more expensive and damaging than a guy who likes to buy hats. Fortunately for me, that's a pretty strong argument.

When Lids refused to take the hat back, I saw this as a win-win. Not only could I return the hat that Dylan bought but I could walk out wearing a hat for myself. I knew my walking out with a new hat would piss him off and at that moment, pissing him off was worth more than the money. A few minutes later out I came with a brand new, flex fit, University of Maine hat with a black bear on the front. I sat in the car, turned to Dylan, and said, "What do you think of my new hat?"

As expected, he got pissed off, "Why did you get a hat?"

I said, "Because I paid for it."

"Well if they would not return my hat, you should have just given it back to me. What's the difference?" I had to explain to him again that he stole the hat, whereas I bought it. That was *my* money, not his. We went back and forth arguing for a while. When we got home was when the fireworks started because we pointed out that we had been right when we said his friends were using him. They were only calling him because he had a credit card and could buy them gas and food and gifts.

I guess the question looking back is, how necessary was that? He already knew that his friends were using him. I'm not sure we gained anything by getting in a huge argument. The problem was that you couldn't just say, as you could with most kids, the Pa Ingalls or Howard Cunningham model of very softly and slowly saying that classic one-liner of "We're very disappointed in you." With us, it always ended up in an argument. We have learned over the years that the calm, stern approach does not work with Dylan because unlike most kids who would just take that and walk up to their room with the burden of knowing that their parents were disappointed in them, Dylan would fight and fight and fight until our throats were sore from yelling. He always made sure that his position, as factually and emotionally inaccurate as it may have been, was fought to the very last breath. He would never back down or walk away. To be truthful, at times like this, when I was so angry at him for what he had done, I wanted the argument. I did not do it consciously but I believe that I actually wanted to make him feel bad about himself because I felt he didn't seem to feel bad for what he had done. Sadly, the night before he was moving to Florida, possibly moving out of the house forever, instead of having a nice, final evening with Dylan, we had one final blow-out. The next morning, we got up, went to the airport, and Amy and Dylan headed to Florida so he could join the program at New Directions.

Life in Florida Begins

Dylan was enrolled as a student at Palm Beach Community College taking a couple of basic introductory classes which we hoped would be manageable. The New Directions program offered tutoring, as did the school. We knew Dylan would have to access these services to be successful. The program planned time for him each week to meet with someone for tutoring and Dylan was doing a good job making the meetings. However, it was not long before we all realized that college was probably not going to be a good fit for Dylan. After thirteen years of public education Dylan was handed a diploma that was not worth much more than the paper it was written on. He was moved from special education class to special education class under the false assumption that he was on "the college track" when the fact is that college success was very unlikely for our son. One of the great regrets I will always have as a dad is my failure to march into the high school in Dylan's freshman year and say, "Look, I appreciate that you are optimistic that my son can attend college but the reality is that college is probably not in his future. What are you going to do for him so when he walks out of these doors in 2010 he does so with a marketable skill that allows him the opportunity to earn a living?" I did not do that. And the school failed in not reversing that statement to Amy and me. We found ourselves in 2010 with a son in Florida who could not get through college classes yet had no skills to earn a living. We were all extremely frustrated.

The Job Search

The only option now for Dylan in Florida was to work on getting a job. What would he do? He was determined to get into something in retail even though he had no success in the past with retail jobs. We encouraged him to get a job in a field where he had experienced more chance of success: sales. He had made calls for me at Volk Packaging as an inside sales representative and I told him he could do the same thing from Florida since he still had a 207 area code on his cell. I could send him lead lists and his task would be to get my outside sales representatives in the door for an appointment.

I would pay Dylan ten dollars an hour and ten dollars for an appointment as well as commission for the first year the customer bought from us. It would take some time to build up a base of business that would generate commissions because the sales cycle for attaining new business can be up to six months. Once he had a collection of customers he had generated, he would be able to earn commission every month without any additional work. From there he could simply grow the business. I was sure, if he put the effort into it, he could be successful and help me grow Volk Packaging as well. He was not interested but did make some calls here and there just to have a little money coming in. Mostly, he worked hard to find another job. Without a car it was a tremendous challenge.

Florida is vast and the public transportation system is unreliable. Dylan would have to take the bus or ride his bike to wherever he got a job. Within only a couple of weeks he landed his first job selling timeshares. The deal was almost too good to be true which made it hard to sell. For $300, people would get three weekends at three different timeshares in beautiful locations. The key to accepting the special price was that the people had to sit through a two hour presentation about the local timeshare opportunities when at each location. Dylan said it was an amazing deal but the price of $300 was actually too low. If the price were higher people might not be so suspicious. That job was not going well so Dylan started looking for other opportunities. In almost no time he landed a job selling ads for a golf course magazine that is handed out at local clubs. He had some success at both of these jobs but within a month he quit the timeshare job to spend more time on the golf ad job and then was fired from the golf magazine job for making inappropriate comments. During this same timeframe he landed a job selling septic tank cleaning systems. He actually did believe in this product but it was very expensive so it was not an easy sale. The other problem with the job was that he was supposed to call people at home and everyone knows people hate getting telemarketing calls at night. They seem to be particularly annoyed to get a call about cleaning their septic tank as they sit down for dinner. After about a month he quit the septic tank job because he was sure there was something better out there for him.

Dylan's next plan was to get a job selling cars. He lined up an interview at a dealership that was about forty-five minutes away. With no car we were not sure how he would pull this off and keep the job, but he insisted one of the co-workers was willing to pick him up and bring him back if he would pay for part of the gas. Since he had no money to pay his driver, Dylan expected us to foot the bill. We were so anxious for Dylan to be employed that we covered the gas money. Gas prices in Florida at the time were over $4.50 a gallon, so this proposition became very costly in no time. As we expected, his ride was not dependable. It took about a week for him to miss work or be late so many times he was fired.

Dylan is amazing at landing jobs. He is intelligent, speaks well and is extremely engaging. He knows what employers want to hear and is almost brilliant when in front of them during an interview. His ability to secure job after job after job is truly impressive.

Kicked Out of Wayne River Apartments

Dylan's first apartment in Florida was very roomy, clean and safe. There were security gates at every entrance and a nice little fitness room. There was a beautiful swimming pool area and a pond with a sidewalk around it. Unfortunately, he was not there for long. In early 2011, I received a call from the woman who ran the apartment complex. She said she had received a complaint from the people living below Dylan because he had urinated off of his third floor patio onto their barbecue grill. I don't think there are too many people that would not find that totally disgusting and call to complain. We called Dylan and asked him what he was thinking when he didn't just walk inside to go to the bathroom. He could not understand what the big deal was.

While he was sitting outside on his patio smoking he would sometimes have to go to the bathroom. He didn't want to bother to put his cigarette out just to go inside to go to the bathroom, so instead he went over the edge. We experienced the same kind of behavior at home. He would sometimes urinate on the driveway, occasionally he would even urinate in the garage and he was known to urinate out his second story window at home, sometimes not even taking out the screen and having his pee splatter all over the windowsill. He didn't seem to think much of it. It defied logic to us, but somehow he was able to justify his actions to himself and continue to do it.

I would get really angry when he would pee in the driveway and furious when it came to the garage. He didn't seem to care. I would yell "Dylan! Why would you piss in the garage when just inside was a bathroom literally thirty feet away." He had no explanation but also no regret. Now, he was in Florida and there would be serious consequences if he continued with his behavior. We were very concerned that Dylan would be kicked out of the complex. Not only did the complex hold all of the New Direction students, it housed the office and it was a terrific location for Dylan's cat, Beautiful Boy. There was a tree outside the patio that Beautiful Boy climbed to leave his apartment. Dylan could leave the patio open or leave food on the patio and Beautiful Boy could climb up and down the tree as he wished to explore. The apartment was situated in the back of the complex. Little traffic made it an ideal spot for a cat. We were very nervous that we would not be able to find such a perfect place for Beautiful Boy if Dylan had to move. The thought of something happening to the cat that he loved so much was of high concern. Despite all of our warning and another warning a few weeks later from the people at the Wayne River apartment office, Dylan continued to urinate off the patio. Just as she warned us, we received notice that Dylan was being evicted from his apartment. The people from New Directions were very upset and were unable to explain to us why he seemed incapable and unwilling to change, even when faced with a serious consequence. We had about a week to find him a new apartment and get him moved. Dylan's car was still in Maine, which made the options for his living quarters even more challenging. We had to find an apartment that would allow him to have Beautiful Boy within biking distance of the New Directions office where he had to make several meetings a week, significantly limiting the choices. A few days later we got a call from the staff at New Directions that they had located an apartment for Dylan. It was about four miles away, with no pool or pond, no fitness center and no security. It was on a dead-end street but it did allow cats. Dylan moved in and Beautiful Boy had new places to roam. Now we had to make sure Dylan had a decent bike so he could travel back and forth to his meetings at New Directions.

My father was talking to some of his golf buddies and happened to mention that Dylan had been kicked out of his apartment and needed a bicycle to get around. Two of my father's friends generously offered Dylan a bike. All they asked is that he take care of it and, in the event that he didn't need it anymore, he would give it back. He was given a bike and within a month it was stolen, most likely because he forgot to lock it. Dylan was given another bike, but this time he was careful to lock it.

Dylan was very happy with his new apartment. He lived alone so he didn't have to worry about getting along with a new roommate. He was the only white person in the entire complex, which of course made him delighted. Dylan was fascinated by the African-American culture, and because he also enjoyed hip hop and rap music he became quite immersed in black culture. I often joked that my son was convinced he was a black man. He dressed in "gangsta" clothes, wearing baggy shorts, extremely large shirts and a flat rim hat tipped just to the side. Once he got his car in Florida, he spent a large amount of time at flea markets where he bought "gangsta" clothes at bargain prices. Dr. Kellen from New Directions spent a lot of time talking to Dylan about his fascination with African Americans. It was essentially Dylan's new special interest and it was a long way from birds, Legos and *Star Wars*. As always, we tried to make the most of it which eventually included my attending a Chris Brown/T-Pain concert with him in Miami on one of my visits to see him.

Sears Theft

Dylan's experiences while watching his friends in Maine steal with no consequences even when caught, came to bite him in February 2011. Dylan was caught and arrested for stealing a shirt from Sears. He spent the night in the county jail and was charged with theft. In it, he is trying to look as tough as possible, unaware of how often or easily it would be seen with a simple search of his name.

Dylan could not believe that they had actually arrested him and made him spend the night in jail because he was under the impression that a store wouldn't pursue charges for anything stolen under $50. He actually thought that it wasn't even technically illegal to steal anything under $50. So, instead of being remorseful for his actions, he was resentful that they would charge him for such a "ridiculous crime." We tried to explain to him that stealing is stealing. He couldn't comprehend that the size or the dollar value was insignificant. We explained that you could be charged for stealing a pack of gum, just like you could be charged for stealing a shirt or jewelry. Taking someone else's property without paying for it is against the law, period. Our voices went unheard. Dylan was too hung up on this $50 theory to listen to anything we were saying.

Most nineteen-year-olds would be quite intimidated by the idea of spending the night in jail in southern Florida, but Dylan actually had a good time. During his brief incarceration, he told us he was "the hit of the cell block." He told us how all the other guys in the cell block with him that night were black and he was cracking them all up with his jokes. He told us that the guard didn't find them as funny as all his cell mates when he told them that he really liked his mugshot asking if he could get it in an 8 by 10. A couple of months later when we went to Florida during April vacation to spend some time with my parents and to visit Dylan, he would take great pleasure in showing us his mugshot and hung it on the door of New Directions with a hand written note that said stealing is not good. He thought that this was absolutely hysterical, and although we found it pretty funny ourselves, we had to play the role of responsible parents and frown on it. Dylan just found a way to make bad decisions comical. Much like the days of his prank phone calls, he had a special way of putting us in the position of either laughing with him or holding firm to disdain, in an effort to teach him right from wrong. He often made it so funny, it was hard to keep a straight face.

Dylan at Boston Market

We were very excited for Dylan in the fall of 2011. He had secured a job in the spring at Boston Market, right up the street from his apartment in Deerfield Beach. Although he was not working forty hours a week as we had hoped, we were very proud of him because for the first time, he was showing that he could hold a job for more than just a month or two. He had had the job at Boston Market for several months and seemed to be doing a pretty good job. We even stopped in and met his boss when we were in Florida for April vacation. Everyone seemed to be very pleased with what Dylan was doing. That wasn't uncommon after a month or so, but six months later, he still had the job, and that was a very exciting development.

In addition to maintaining his fifteen to twenty hours at Boston Market, he was regularly going to the gym again. In fact, he was going to the gym more than ever and when we arrived in Florida for Thanksgiving, everyone in the family was shocked to see what great shape Dylan was in. For many years, Dylan had battled with his weight. Some of his weight issues were because of the medications that he had been on years earlier. Those medications created baby fat when he was young and it was hard to outgrow. But for the first time, Dylan could be described as "jacked," "fit," "muscular." It was great to see him doing so well, in both his personal physical fitness as well as in the workplace.

"Has He Gone Crazy?!"

On Wednesday, October 19, 2011, I received one of most frightening calls I have ever received from Dylan. He said, very quickly and in a disoriented manner, "Okay, so now tell me what I am supposed to do today. Tell me. Tell me. Tell me. Okay, so you have three choices to choose from. Three choices to choose. I can A, make calls for you. B, go to the gym. C go look for a job because I was just fired from Boston Market. So, tell me, what do I do, what do I do, huh, huh, huh? What do I do?" I immediately became very concerned because I had not heard Dylan talk in this strange tone before. I asked him what happened at Boston Market, but he refused to tell me simply saying, "Oh, you know, you know you know, you just want me to say it and I am not going to say it. Nice try!" I honestly did not know. I had some guesses.

If I were to guess at that point I would have assumed that he either said something racially inappropriate or he slept through a shift. As it turns out, the latter was the correct guess. I tried to get him to calm down but he was so frantic and angry sounding that I was not getting through to him at all. I told him that he was in no mental state to make calls for me and not in the right frame of mind to go looking for jobs. I said that he needed to go get his car as it was ready after being damaged in a recent accident and he needed to return the rental car. I said, "Go to Enterprise on Powerline and return the rental and they will give you a ride to Sammy's Auto House where your car is done and ready for pick up. After that, go to the gym and work off some of this anger and frustration. It'll work out, you'll find another job. You always do." He was very brief with me, as he often is on the phone, said okay and hung up. I immediately called Amy and told her about my conversation and Dylan's bizarre tone. I was concerned, as I have been many times over the years, that Dylan would do something to hurt himself in the moment of self-pity and despair. I was also worried about his ability to drive through rush hour traffic in his current state of mind. I offered a quick prayer to God asking for his continued vigilance and protection over Dylan. I then contacted the staff of New Directions to let them know what happened and that I felt it was important that someone make contact with Dylan that night, preferably in person, to make sure he was alright.

And then, later that evening and the next day, things got worse and very scary. Amy received a Facebook message from Dylan and I started receiving texts stating that he knew what his problem was and it was that he was white and needed to be around more black people because they were clearly the superior race. His messages were garbled and confused. Dylan had previously had some unusual opinions but he had always been able to argue his case in a very clear and sometimes incredibly convincing manner. This was different. For example, this is the exact transcript of a series of short texts he sent me within a minutes of each other:

> 10/20/11 @ 11:15am Dont wanna trick idiots into helping there own anymore. Sorry
>
> 10/20/11 @ 11:16am U converted for a reason, guess what so am i
>
> 10/20/11 @ 11:16am Just did! Oh wait oh wait oh wait . . . can this mean I must accept what I need to?
>
> 10/20/11 @ 11:17am Before I must accept all this I feel I just must apologize to the others who are too to LEGIT see it MY way do u understand me yet? Do you know what you have in Amy Murchison Volk? Who she really is? The Nordic. Must I keep goin? I will warn u from here it does get graphic
>
> 10/20/11 @ 11:18am european history. Black people being bred by tricky. The evil blue eyed man, half jewish/half nordic. No matter what comes out of my mouth the white man continues to spin spin spin spin i'm not sure

What made Amy and me even more concerned is that I had just finished and Amy was three quarters of the way through a book called *Crazy*, about a dad's experiences with his son's mental illness. It was a terrifying yet educational book about the effects of mental illness on a family and, in particular, the treatment of the mentally ill in the Florida correctional system. So, we were both unusually aware of what mental illness could look like and it appeared we were seeing it in Dylan. As the days went on he became worse and worse. He kept talking, sometimes for what seemed like hours, about "Black Supremacy" and how the "Nordic people were the devil." He was saying that because Amy was a "Nordic" she could not be trusted, even as he continued to talk with her. We explained to him that his mother was actually Scottish, English and French Canadian and none of those are Nordic countries at all, so he could "trust her."

In his twisted thought process at the time he was saying that because she was so white he couldn't trust her. I, on the other hand, was Jewish so for some reason that was okay. He was saying that all the bad that happened in the world was because of white people and that he, included, was evil. It was terrifying and illogical. We tried to tell him about the Rwandan genocides, the Apartheid in South Africa and the mass killings in places like Sierra Leone and the Sudan as well as the Japanese atrocities in China during WWII and the Khmer Rouge in Cambodia to prove to him that people can be evil whether they are black or white or yellow. He did not want to hear it. All he could focus on was the fact that black people were superior and whites were the cause of all their problems. He also said that because of his fears he could no longer sleep at night, so he started staying up all night and sleeping during the day when it was light out. We were waking up in the morning to dozens of texts sent at two, three, and four in the morning. We knew he was not sleeping.

His therapist from New Directions tried to come by to speak with him but Dylan would not let him. He "couldn't be trusted." The therapist felt that Dylan's breakdown happened because he quit taking his medications. We were not convinced his lack of meds would be the cause. Amy then called Dylan's friend, Andy, in Miami and asked him to go up to see Dylan and report back to us what he found. Andy took the Tri-Rail all the way to Deerfield and then Dylan wouldn't let him in either. After a lot of coaxing, Dylan finally allowed Andy to come in his apartment. Andy called to say Dylan seemed really confused and "kind of crazy." Then it got scarier when he said he would not let Beautiful Boy in because he didn't trust him. It was at that point that we knew we had a major crisis on our hands. Amy was due to leave the next day for Idaho to attend a conference for legislators about economic development. She called the head of her committee to say that, as bad as she felt about wasting the trip, she could not go. She had to fly to Florida to see Dylan. She booked a flight and was on a 6:00am plane the next morning.

When Amy arrived at Dylan's apartment, he refused to let her in. She pleaded with him until he finally agreed to unlock the doors. She found Dylan to be in a state she had never witnessed before, frantic and delusional. They went straight to the psychiatrist who gave him a shot of Risperdal. He also told Amy that Dylan's behavior was a psychotic episode and was likely the beginning of a new reality for all of us. Amy called me as upset as I have ever heard her.

She drove Dylan to my parent's house in West Palm Beach so Dylan could get some sleep. They had a nice quiet bedroom on the second floor with dark shades. Dylan had hardly slept in days and that will really mess with your head. Add that to whatever mix of medications he was on and it was a recipe for crazy. She was hoping with a long and deep sleep he would come back to his senses. She was committed to staying in Florida as long as it took or bringing him home with her. When Dylan finally went to sleep, he crashed hard and slept for almost eighteen hours. Several times Amy went up to the room to make sure he was still breathing. Meanwhile, I was at home feeling helpless because from 1,500 miles away there was nothing I could do. We considered the possibility of both of us going to Florida but someone had to stay home with the girls. As much as I wanted to be there for Dylan, there was no keeping his mom away. As hard as that was for me, I have to be honest and say that I felt Amy would be able to handle it better. I was feeling overwhelmed by the thought of Dylan being permanently mentally ill. I was worried about Dylan and how that would change his life but I cannot deny that I was also worried about how it would impact the entire family dynamic. Our daily lives had become much more peaceful with Dylan away. The thought of him coming home to live with us concerned me and the thought of him coming home to live with us, as a mentally ill young man, scared the hell out of me. How would that impact the girls? How would it affect our marriage? We had all we could handle with Dylan being Dylan. Dylan being mentally ill, was a whole new level that I was not sure I could manage. I prayed to God asking for strength in the storm that our family may have been heading straight into.

When Dylan finally awoke he was mostly back to his old self. For the next few days he occasionally brought up the black race being superior but had dropped all the Nordic talk and was no longer speaking in choppy, frantic sentences. We were not comfortable yet that it had all passed so Amy stayed in

Florida for a week until she felt Dylan was back to his normal self. However, even as Amy arrived home we still had great concern that this could be simply chapter one in a new phase of our life. We watched every text closely for the next month or two anxiously waiting for relapse. We prayed like we had never prayed before. And we talked about how we would deal, as a couple and as a family, with a mentally ill Dylan. Thankfully, those behaviors never returned. His brief and bizarre behaviors were a perfect storm of being on too many medications (he was taking six or seven different prescriptions), the stress of losing the first job he had held for more than a couple of months and a lack of sleep. Dylan was back to being Dylan, and that was a blessing.

DYLAN'S TAKE: *It is very embarrassing to me that this ever happened. After growing up in Maine, it was the first time I had ever lived in a diverse place like South Florida. I had been taking it all in since moving to Deerfield Beach and I was really soaking up the different cultures. I was spending a lot of time with black people and thinking about race relations. One night, out of curiosity, I Googled something like "black race is superior" just to see what came up. All of a sudden I was reading all this propaganda and really crazy stuff. I even watched an entire documentary about it. The way my mind was at that moment, and because of the perfect storm my dad described, I did not take in what I was reading in a reasonable fashion. Since this experience I have tried really hard to block out these few days. I know I said and did things that were outrageously inappropriate, even for Dylan standards! I really wish it never happened. What an awkward conversation to force on so many people. It was definitely not one of my shining moments!*

Visual Memories

While we were in Florida visiting with the family for Thanksgiving, we took Dylan out for dinner. He told us something during that dinner that, in all the years discussing how Dylan's brain works with him and with others, we had never heard before, and it fascinated us. Dylan described how he remembers so many details of the past. He has an incredible memory and he told us what helps him remember. One of the interesting things about this story is that Dylan didn't realize that what he was telling us was unusual. He told us that he has visual memories, almost like a slideshow. Whenever we mention a certain month and year, he gets visual memories, like photographs, of that month and year, and can remember in great detail what happened during that time.

We told him that that seemed very unusual and neither one of us had the ability to do that. I don't know what it is about his brain that allows him to connect visual images with calendar dates, but we thought it was pretty cool. He can remember in great detail because of this. He's always had a keen grasp of detail, sometimes to the point where it was actually a disadvantage when doing things like reading a book or watching a movie. This is very common for people on the autism spectrum. They've done studies where they would have someone talking and show the person's whole face. The person on the autism spectrum would be able to pull out only a small portion of what the person was saying. However, when they eliminated all the rest of the face except the mouth so that was all the person on the autism spectrum could see, they had no details to focus on and therefore retained a much larger amount of information. Dylan would often read books when he was younger, he wouldn't know the plot of the book but he could remember incredible details that most people wouldn't recall from the chapter of a book or a section of a movie.

I remember one time when we were watching the movie *Footloose*. We were about halfway through the movie and Dylan turned to me and said, "I have absolutely no idea what this movie is about." I asked him what he thought it was about, and instead of giving me any kind of plot, he went into detail about some of the clothes and the haircuts of the characters.

The movie was set in the 1980s, a time that Dylan was always very interested in, so I thought he would enjoy it, but really what he was interested in were the characters' haircuts, clothing and the music of the movie. His comments about the movie had absolutely nothing to do with the actual storyline so he was therefore lost when trying to figure out the plot.

We saw this as a disability, as a disadvantage, to his learning, and maybe it was. But, if the right environment or circumstance were created, that skill could potentially be a benefit and he would be an incredible asset. The problem is, we've never been able to figure out what career path would be able to take advantage of such a skill.

Dylan Decides to Leave Florida

When we were in West Palm Beach, Florida, over the Thanksgiving holiday in 2011 Dylan told us that he was no longer happy in Florida and wanted to give college a try. We were not totally shocked that he wanted to leave Florida. He was not feeling like the New Directions staff had his best interest at heart.

Once you lose Dylan's trust, you have lost him. There is very little chance we were going to convince him that New Directions was interested in anything but our monthly check. Although we were very grateful for all New Directions had done for Dylan, it was hard to argue that they seemed disengaged with him as of late. I do not hold any ill will towards them. Their program is built for young people in college. They were not sure what to do with Dylan. It was not the first time that happened with a program Dylan was in.

Amy had come up with an idea to have New Directions buy some vending machines, which Dylan and some of the other students in the program could place at businesses and then service. It would give the students a source of income, while helping New Direction find work for a difficult-to-place demographic. I have since learned a great deal about the challenges of employment for those with disabilities. The unemployment rate among people with disabilities is staggeringly high. The unemployment rate among those on the autism spectrum runs in the mid to high 70 percent range. It is not much different for those in other disability classifications and that includes our veterans who suffer from both physical and mental disabilities like Post Traumatic Stress Disorder.

Dylan was also tired of the fast-paced life of South Florida. Everything moves faster in South Florida. From the highways to the people, the lifestyle is just faster. We would learn later that there were also disadvantages for Dylan to be in a quiet, slow paced lifestyle. Basically, there is no perfect place for Dylan. Wherever he lives he is challenged by circumstances that you and I handle without a thought.

Dylan's best friend, Andy, was moving back to Minnesota to be an air traffic controller. Andy was a great friend to Dylan. In fact, he has probably been the best friend Dylan has ever had. On the surface you may not have thought Dylan and Andy would be friends. Andy was several years older than Dylan. He was in school and had definite plans for his life. They actually met through a website focused on the "art of seduction." Before Dylan left for Florida he was fascinated by a VH1 show called, *The Pickup Artist*. The star of the program Erik von Markovik, was the self-proclaimed "World's Greatest Pickup Artist." It was like *Survivor* for picking up girls. Each week the nerdy guys on the show would have assignments from Markovik. The guys would do their best to be something they were not in an effort to seduce a woman. At the end of each episode Markovik would decide who got to stay on the show and who had to leave. Dylan watched the show like a classical violinist attends the symphony, watching the programs over and over and trying to gain any insight he could that would help him with girls.

In Dylan's senior year of high school he had basically given up hope for a girlfriend. Between his lack of success and the womanizing, misogynistic brain washing he received by listening to countless hours of Tom Leykis, his attitude was not one his mother and I would approve of. Amy and I both found it very frustrating that our son, who had been raised in a good Christian home with loving parents, would be influenced by a radio show. I especially had a hard time with it and often showed my frustration in anger. Amy was always better at controlling her frustration with him than I was when it came to topics like this. She would be patient and listen to him and then express her thoughts about his opinions. I could not do that. I would shut him down and tell him I did not want to hear anything about his opinions. That was not effective in changing his mind and often alienated Dylan even more from trusting me to speak his mind. I just did not know how to handle it as a man and as a dad.

When Dylan was a baby I read a bunch of books about raising a son to be a man of character and integrity. There is not a single paragraph in any of those books that explained how you handle it when you think you did everything right but your son is a jerk.

It sounds mean, but that is what I thought of him and it absolutely pissed me off. I have always considered myself the exact opposite. I am a hopeless romantic to the point that it sometimes drives my wife crazy. I buy her flowers, send her cards, and sometimes get caught just staring at her for no reason other than because I think she is the most beautiful woman on earth. My daughters often make fun of me saying I am "obsessed" with Amy. I have never thought of myself as obsessed, which has a negative connotation. I just feel like I am the luckiest guy in the world to be madly in love with my wife after thirty years together. I am also the dad to three beautiful, confident and strong daughters. So, given all that, you can imagine how aggravating it was to have a son, my only son, not treating women the same way. And yet, deep down, I knew he was aware of the right way to do things. Once again, since Asperger's is a developmental disability, he did not have the maturity that matched the age on his driver's license. But we were confident that he would get there eventually.

When Dylan moved to Florida and joined the New Direction program we were hoping he would find a couple of guys in the program, other high functioning young people with Asperger's, that he could be friends with. When Dylan told us he had made a really good friend by meeting up with a twenty-six-year-old on a pickup artist chat room we were quite suspicious. It turns out Andy was a great guy who was using that forum to advance his chances to find a girlfriend. He was a super great influence on Dylan. Over time Dylan matured and toned down the Tom Leykis talk. He worked with Andy to use the skills he learned to find a girlfriend. It turns out that behind all the bravado, what Dylan wanted more than anything was a steady and meaningful relationship. Now it was almost two years later and Andy was graduating. He was headed home to Minnesota, leaving Dylan without his best friend, mentor and dating wing man. This had a big influence on his decision to leave Florida.

Dylan did successfully land a girlfriend for a while. Her name was Ashley and he was crazy about her. However, she was younger and her parents had some issues with Dylan so they made it impossible to maintain the relationship. This led to a difficult break up. Dylan had very strong feelings for Ashley. He was so sweet to her, romancing her in the ways that I would wish for my daughters. He liked to brag about how kind and thoughtful he was to her. It was so much nicer to listen to him brag about taking Ashley outside to kiss her in the rain "because all girls love that" versus the constant macho image he was projecting a year earlier. However, that relationship was over and he was very discouraged again that he could ever have a long term girlfriend. He wanted to get as far away from Ashley as possible and Bangor, Maine, seemed the logical option.

Even given all the factors, we were surprised and quite nervous that he was interested in moving to Bangor to attend the New England School of Communication (NESCom) at Husson College. Dylan's love and in-depth knowledge about music made him dream of being a radio program director. The days of starting in a radio station out of high school and working your way from disc jockey position and then program manager were over. Most radio stations these days are corporately owned, with one company owning several radio stations in a town.

Most kids that want to get in the radio business want to be an on-air personality. Dylan considered that option as well but that would just be an added perk for him. We always thought, with his outrageous personality and comedic skills, he would make an amazing "shock jock" but jobs as a "shock jock" are limited. Despite all the potential hurdles, we could not come up with a plan B that would satisfy him.

There is a radical difference between life in southern Florida and life in Bangor, Maine. We talked at great length about his options, but once Dylan gets something in his head it is very difficult to change his mind, regardless of the information or facts he receives. After high school he had deferred his acceptance to NESCom so he could open it back up again. We knew college, even a program like NESCom had, was a long shot. Dylan really struggled in high school and that was despite being in special education classes with significant one-on-one help. There is no way he would get through a four-year college program without a tremendous amount of private tutoring to supplement the classes. We were prepared to do whatever was needed to give him the opportunity for success. We were just not very confident it was going to happen for him.

— 9 —

The Old College Try

"Why Don't You Just Give Him a Job?"

When looking at Dylan's long term job opportunities, we were often overwhelmed by the lack of opportunity that seemed to be available to him. One of my greatest frustrations is that the public school system failed to properly equip him. I know that everyone wants to think and believe that their son or daughter has the necessary skills. I say skills because I don't believe Dylan is lacking intelligence—he's lacking *skills* to go to college.

I had a number of people say to me, "Why don't you just give him a job? Just put him on the payroll, just find something for him to do!" First of all, I don't have much at Volk Packaging that Dylan can do. Working in the factory is too loud and fast-paced for him. Customer service and some of the other office jobs require too much attention to detail and an ability to problem solve. Sales requires a tremendous amount of self-discipline, organizational skill, and an ability to build relationships.

"What would he do?" I would say. "I can't just take company money and let him come in to the office every day and do nothing. Not only is that unfair to the company entity but it's unfair to all the people that work there who work hard every day to earn their income. More than that, what would that be teaching him? What kind of message would that send to him at twenty-one years old? The same message it would send to put him on Social Security Disability Insurance."

Many people have said to us, "Why don't you get him Social Security Disability Insurance? He would certainly qualify for SSDI." We have actually met with an attorney who specializes in social security disability to find out if that was an option. We discovered that it was, and Dylan would probably qualify and most likely be labeled as *permanently disabled*. But is that really the message that we want to send to our son? Is it fraud? No, it would not be fraud; he has a permanent neurological disability that makes it almost impossible for him to earn a decent living and possibly even maintain employment.

All indications at this point were that he could not keep a job. He had never kept any kind of job for more than a few months and he had never in his life had a full-time job for more than a couple of weeks. We didn't even think about it enough to take the paperwork home, because we did not want to send the message to Dylan at twenty-one years old, when we still had hope that there was some career that he could succeed at, that he should just give up, live off the government, accept a life of poverty, making just enough money to get by without working. Plus, Dylan has always liked to work. He doesn't want to sit around all day waiting for his next paycheck from the state to come in. That's not healthy for him. We saw what happened in Bangor when he had nothing to do. His schoolwork wasn't terribly demanding, he was only taking a couple of classes and he felt like he didn't have anything worth working for, so he gave up. We were not going to set him up for a life like that. Autism is a developmental disorder. We knew he was maturing but he was doing so at a slower rate than his peers. We still felt confident that he would reach a point of maturity where he could be a productive member of society. We were not even close to giving up on Dylan's ability to function as a contributor.

I'm sure there are people reading this who have a child on permanent disability. Please understand that I'm not judging you. The one thing, of many, that Amy and I have learned raising a child on the autism spectrum is that we don't know what other people are living through. We don't judge other people's parenting of a child with a disability because every situation is different. Every child's potential is different; every child's reactions to their potential are different. So I hope that if your child is on permanent disability or if you have a company and you found busywork enough to pay your child, that you don't close the book because you feel I'm judging your parenting skills or your parenting decisions. I would never be so bold as to say how another mom and dad should raise a child with a disability. They're all different and just like when Dylan was five and I talked about those folders on the desktop of his brain, as parents we all have folders on how to raise our child. Inside those folders are a million different documents. Whatever document you choose to open will never be criticized by this dad.

Bangor/NESCom

In December 2011, Dylan packed up his apartment in Florida with the help of my parents. I arranged for a truck to pick up everything in Deerfield Beach and bring it back to Volk Packaging, where we would store it until Dylan started at the New England School of Communication in Bangor. We were all anxious about where this next path would lead us, but Dylan was 100 percent sure he wanted to leave Florida, and we really couldn't force him to stay if he wanted to come home and give college a try.

He came home for Christmas vacation, and we went for a day to find an apartment in Bangor. Amy had done some research ahead of time and found six or seven possibilities that might be viable for him. We drove to Bangor and the first place we visited was a small apartment within walking distance to Husson and the New England School of Communication. It was right behind the school. He could walk through a field to get there if he wanted to. We saw several advantages to this. Advantage number one would be if he lost his driver's license, either for speeding, an accident, or for whatever reason he was without a car, he could walk to school. He could also walk to the gym, and at the time he was still working out quite a bit. Husson had a very nice gym, which was in eyesight from his back door. There was also a large field behind this apartment which made it a good spot for his cat. Beautiful Boy was used to being outside and surely did not want to be in an inner-city apartment where he could not explore the outdoors. We were also concerned about him getting hit by a car if we were not at a location where he could go outside safely.

The apartment was two floors and so small his limited furniture didn't even fit. However, it was in the price range we were looking for and the landlord seemed to be flexible and understanding with Dylan. We then drove around Bangor for the rest of the day, looking at basically one unacceptable option after another. Each apartment we looked at was dumpier and more rundown than the one before it. We didn't even get out of the car at some of them because they were in such horrible condition on the outside. They were in downtown Bangor, which would be an awful location for Beautiful Boy, and we could not even imagine spending seven or eight hundred dollars on some of these disgusting looking apartments. Dylan was starting to realize maybe South Florida wasn't so bad. For less money than anything we could get in Bangor, he had a spacious apartment with a big living room in sunny Florida. He was already starting to have second thoughts about his decision to move back to Maine.

We were nervous about losing the apartment near the school after seeing how terrible the other ones were, so we called the landlord and told him we would meet him back there at two o'clock and sign the papers. We didn't want anyone else to scoop up the last apartment in that complex and have us be forced to rent one of the other choices.

Dylan was smoking at the time and the contract for the apartment specifically said "No smoking." So as we read through the contract, we circled that and showed him that it would be very expensive if he smoked in the building because there would be costs involved in repainting and changing the carpets if the apartment reeked of smoke and the landlord couldn't rent it out after he left. Dylan assured us he would smoke outside and not in the apartment. I think that promise lasted about two days.

There were problems almost from the beginning when Dylan moved in. As I mentioned before, his furniture would not fit. The giant leather sectional that Amy had scored at a resale store in Florida became a partial leather sofa that awkwardly fit in a strange-shaped living room. The TV didn't work the way it was supposed to and everything just seemed wrong. But we were too far in to turn back. Dylan was enrolled in three classes at NESCom, plus an introductory class that was called College Prep. It was a one-credit class that basically taught you how to do college. We thought this would be very helpful to Dylan.

One of the biggest concerns we had about him being in Bangor was the lack of support that he had experienced when he was in Florida. He was not in a program anymore. He was basically completely on his own. We had reached out to Amy's Aunt Anna Blake and her cousin Corinne Vaillancourt and asked them if they could keep an eye on Dylan, pop in every once in a while, and maybe Corinne, who was a nursing student, could come by and help Dylan with his meds. They said they would and we really appreciated their willingness to help him, and thankfully Dylan was open to that help. He was nervous himself about being all on his own.

We also tried to find somebody at the school who could be a mentor/big brother to Dylan. We went to the school to see what they could offer in regards to this idea. They told us that they would be open and willing to help out, but after a few weeks in we realized they really didn't have anyone in place to do what we were asking, and we had not made any progress.

The school did find someone who would work with Dylan as a tutor, but not as a mentor, which was really what Dylan needed. He needed someone to be kind of like a "big brother" to him, to look out for him and maybe invite him out—basically a paid friend to get him started in his new life in Bangor. The tutor was a freshman with a girlfriend who was not what Dylan would consider "cool." He was a very nice kid, very bright, and would come to be very helpful to Dylan in getting him through the semester academically, but that's as far as Dylan was interested in his help. The tutor was kind of nerdy and not someone who Dylan wanted to hang out with beyond the academic help.

So instead, I reached out to an old friend and customer of mine, Lisa Tardy. I knew Lisa's son John was a student at Husson University and a baseball player as well. Historically, Dylan has not been friends with many athletes because he's never been into sports. I knew that John could use the money, and from all accounts from Lisa, he seemed like a really nice kid. I asked Lisa if John would be interested in being a mentor/big brother to Dylan. She talked to John and he was up for the task. I told him about Dylan and his obsession with black people, but it didn't seem to bother John and he decided he would give it a try and see how it went.

Dylan and John got together a few times, but unfortunately they just didn't connect. What we were hoping would lead to something more than a paid mentor just didn't happen. Dylan was not very cooperative in the process himself. Over the next three months while Dylan was in Bangor, his emotional and mental state got worse and worse, and his physical condition went with it. Dylan was smoking more and more, and gaining weight. He had stopped going to the gym, and he was sleeping long hours as if trying to sleep his life away—classic depression symptoms. We had seen this pattern before. It quickly grew from concern to fear that we were headed down a very bad road with Dylan, and we had no idea what our next option would be.

Academically, Dylan was doing alright. According to his accounts, he was acing his classes. We did speak with the advisors at the school a couple of times and they did not report the same optimism that Dylan's final grades would be as high as Dylan told us they would be. They said that he had caused some problems in a couple of his classes.

Comedy Dream Still Alive

In April 2012 Dylan came home from NESCom for the Easter weekend. We had been very worried about him because we had heard from both his counselor and from Corinne that he had been shoplifting. I was still working on getting the shoplifting charge in Florida wiped away, so another arrest for the same thing would be very bad on his record. It would virtually eliminate any chance of him ever working in retail. It is one thing to get caught once and say you made a stupid mistake as an immature nineteen-year-old in a new place, but two charges of the same thing almost two years apart is pretty hard to explain away. We started thinking that maybe he was just incapable of living on his own and maybe he needed to be in a residential facility like what they offered at Talisman in North Carolina. Amy did some research and found a place in Utah that is not just for young adults with Asperger's but for kids who are just kind of lost. They called it young people who were having a "failure to launch." My concern with that, besides the battle it would be to get him there and $5,000 a month was that the place was really full of troubled young men with the potential to be bad influences. Dylan tends to be drawn to the worst element around him, usually because he thinks they are the coolest. He wanted to be cool in the worst way.

The weekend home ended up being a tough one for Dylan because on Saturday night, while out for dinner with Mariah and her friends, he became violently sick. We were visiting my uncle and aunt, Doug and Gail, because my cousin and her little girls were in town for Passover. Amy got a call while we were in Cumberland, about twenty minutes away, that they were at the Texas Roadhouse near the Maine Mall and Dylan was throwing up. We drove down to get him where we found him on the walkway to the restaurant projectile vomiting. It was gross. The next twenty-four hours were about the same for him. The strange thing is that one of the times I woke up during the middle of the night to the sound of him puking I actually thought, "This would be a good time to talk with him about his future and shoplifting because he won't have the energy to put up much of a fight." It is kind of sad that I actually was thinking about addressing a serious issue like that with him when he was so sick but I think it points out the impact of twenty years of arguing with him. As it turns out, Amy did have that conversation with him at around 6:00am when I was still trying to get some kind of sleep.

She said to him, "Where do you see yourself in ten years?"

He said, "Honestly, I see myself doing stand-up comedy. It is the only thing I have ever done where I knew I was better than everyone I know."

Amy told him that we had just been to a comedy show a few weeks back at The Gold Room in Portland. It was an annual fundraiser for the Southern Maine Flame softball organization. There were four professional comedians there that night and none of them were any funnier than Dylan. In fact, he was probably funnier and definitely more original than all of them.

After Amy told me what he had said, I sent an email to Bob Marley, Maine's most successful comedian. Bob is often called "Maine's King of Comedy." He was also in my brother's high school class and knew Dylan from the classes Dylan took at The Comedy Connection which was owned by Bob's dad. Much to my pleasant surprise, Bob called me back and we spoke for over forty-five minutes about the comedy business. He had some terrific advice. The big questions were, "Is this what he really wants to do? Is he willing to work for it? Is college something worth pursuing?" They were difficult questions to answer. Stand-up comedy is not something you can make a living at if you do it halfheartedly.

Dylan Comes Home

In May of 2012 it was clear that things at NESCom were not working out. While Dylan was, from the reports he was giving us, getting decent grades, he was struggling to get them in two basic classes and he was really having difficulty socially. We had not yet seen any of his grades but he claimed that they were good. To get those grades, however, we had to have a private tutor and the school had to give him many accommodations. Ironically, the class he was failing was called "Success at College." This was a mandatory, once-a-week class that all freshmen had to take about how to be successful while at college. He was failing it mostly because he simply was not attending class often enough. This leads to the issue of his social failures in Bangor.

The problem someone like Dylan has in a small town like Bangor is that everyone knows everyone. Even though Bangor is the third largest city in Maine, it is still a city of under 30,000 people. When you take into account demographics, the population of young people is small. What Dylan quickly discovered is that people know people, a lot of them. Dylan has a habit of alienating and annoying people or, in some cases, pissing them off so much they do not want anything more to do with him. When he was in Florida and his relationships with a group of people deteriorated to that point he could just move on to a new group of kids and the chances were that group one would never know or have any contact with group two. He could essentially start all over until he made the same mistakes with group two at which point, he could move on to group three and four and so on. However, things were different in Bangor.

For example, one day, while in church, I received a very disturbing text from Amy's aunt, Anna. The text was a snapshot of a Facebook post in which Dylan had told a girl that because she was not responding to his Facebook post he hoped she would die. It was chilling to think our son, who had never shown any violent tendencies, would say such a horrible thing. At the time, Dylan had a very hard time understanding why girls ignored or disregarded his posts online. He did not understand that it is creepy to be approached by some strange guy online, so it is easier to simply ignore his advances than to respond with a rejection. Many times the girl probably thinks she is being nice by just ignoring him instead of hurting his feelings by saying she is not interested. Dylan takes the ignoring as a complete rejection and an insult. He often became extremely agitated when girls ignored him or stopped responding to him online.

It was mid-May, and for us mid-May meant softball was in full season. I was coaching Lilly on the middle school's seventh-grade team as I did with Mariah when she was in seventh and eighth grade. Coaching the middle school is a lot of fun but it is also a lot of work. A middle school coach has to be at the school every day by 1:45pm to get ready for practice at 2:00pm, which means leaving work early for eight weeks. On top of that, I was also coaching Serena's farm league team, so I would often leave the middle school practice or game and head straight to the intermediate school, where I would practice with Serena's team. This of course meant that there was less time for Amy during softball season. One day in May when I had no practices and the kids all had plans I asked Amy if she would be interested in a date night. The plan was to go to dinner and maybe a movie. Of course, I hoped for some romance when we got home, especially with the kids out. However, the evening took a different turn.

Amy was very edgy as we drove to dinner. I sensed something was up but was not sure what it was. I assumed she just had a stressful day and was hoping that a night of a quiet dinner and some romance would relieve her tension. I was not aware of her conversation with Mariah from earlier in the day. As we sat down for dinner at 555, a very nice restaurant on Congress Street in downtown Portland, she was very quiet. After we ordered our food she said, "I need to talk to you and you probably won't be happy with what I am going to say." Before she even continued, I knew where the conversation was going. I was not surprised when she said, "I think Dylan should move back home."

My heart sank, even though I expected almost those exact words. Dylan had made progress in Florida and was not the same person who left in 2010 after stealing Amy's credit card and incurring $2,000 in debts, but I was not eager to have him move back home. Our house without Dylan was peaceful. Everyone got along well and it was a nice, comfortable environment for all of us. I knew that would change if Dylan came home. However, at the same time, I knew she was right. Things were not working out in Bangor at all.

What I didn't know was just how bad things had become for Dylan there.

Mariah had talked to Amy earlier in the day. She and her boyfriend Matt had stopped to see Dylan and take him out to lunch on their way to our camp in Lee, Maine. Mariah reported a very different Dylan from the one who came back from Florida only five months earlier. She said he was huge, had gained a ton of weight, and the apartment was a disaster, reeking of cigarettes, which was clearly forbidden in his lease. She said he had visible open scabs all over his body where he had been picking from anxiety. Her report was of a Dylan in crisis. He may not have been throwing temper tantrums like when he was twelve, but he was a mess, and Mariah knew something had to change. Amy knew it, and now I knew it.

Amy asked me what I thought about Dylan coming back home. I paused for a moment to figure out how to respond. I wanted to say, "No. No way. He's not coming home and destroying our family life again." But I knew that was not an option. I knew Dylan needed to leave Bangor, but I honestly did not think we could fix him at home.

"Amy," I said, "if you feel that we need to bring him home, we'll bring him home. But I think it's going to be a nightmare."

She slowly nodded her head. "Yeah," she said, "it may be. But I don't see how we have any other option. We can't just leave him up there and he has nowhere else to go."

"Yeah…I know," I nodded.

We talked for a little while about what we could do to get Dylan back on track. Amy, I felt, was being unrealistically optimistic. She was talking about getting him connected with church, back in the gym, and working. I may have been overly pessimistic as I sat quietly and listened to her, thinking to myself, "There's no way in hell any of this is going to actually happen." But I didn't have a better plan. There was no plan B.

Amy asked if Dylan could work at Volk Packaging until he found a job. I said, "Yeah, sure. He can make phone calls and do some paperwork for me." I knew there was not a lot of paperwork I had that he was capable of doing and he didn't like making phone calls. But we needed to do something with him. He couldn't just come home and sleep all day. So I agreed. Like with coming home, I didn't have any better options.

We sat through the rest of the dinner, neither one of us with much of an appetite and with heavy hearts as we knew our life was about to change dramatically. Dylan's impact on our family was always significant and having him move back home would be a huge adjustment for all of us.

Amy and I have a wonderful marriage. We have been blessed in so many ways, and the fact that we get along so well after thirty years together is a gift from God. However, if there is one thing that creates conflict and anger between us, it is our beloved son, Dylan. We had talked about it before and knew how it happens but it was still almost impossible to prevent. It usually started with something Dylan did that would make me angry or frustrated. I would lash out at him and speak harshly or even say something unkind. I am not proud of how I sometimes reacted. Dylan could be extremely frustrating and he was quite talented at bringing me to my boiling point. The same thing happened to Amy as well. She, too, has been brought to the point of being verbally and even physically aggressive with Dylan. We have never been abusive but we both have had times, especially when he was in his late teens and breaking every rule we had and sometimes smashing things or walls, that we were forceful with him, both verbally and physically. The biggest problems that occurred between Amy and me in these situations were when our "battle strategies" were in conflict. You may think the word "battle" seems harsh when discussing interactions with my child but if you lived in our home when Dylan was young you would not find that term out of place. My strategy was what I call "Sacrificing for the greater mission" and Amy's was "Leave no man behind." There was often an instant during these mutually hostile interactions when Amy would turn from being the loving and supportive wife battling an out of control son, to the protective mother defending her baby boy. And I never knew when I was going to cross that line that sent her into battle mode. I understood her position and admired her unconditional devotion to her child. I got it. But I didn't like it and I resented her for it. I am not sure if it is because I am a man or because I have a place in my heart that allows me to disconnect, but when these battles occurred I genuinely disliked my son. I did not care about his feelings or his emotions or his self-esteem. He was destroying my family, tearing apart my home life and I saw it as a war that only one of us could win. I was concerned about the damage Dylan was doing to our family unit, including our girls and our marriage and, on this night and many others, our sex life. I am not proud of how I reacted during times of stress with Dylan. My good senses and fatherly instincts were gone. It was essentially a strategy in which I was willing to sacrifice the one, Dylan, for the whole, the family and our marriage. I was willing to sacrifice the son I loved more than just about anything on earth to save my family. There will be many moms who read this and think to themselves, "What a heartless bastard! He is not only saying that he was willing to defeat his son but he is also blaming his wife for their marital tension because she was defending her son with the love of a mother." Yes, that is a true statement. If someone reading this book thinks less of me because I had those feelings, I am sorry. I think many dads will be more likely to connect with my emotions whereas moms will be more likely to relate to Amy's "leave no man behind" mindset. If the ship was going down she was going to hang on to Dylan with everything she had even if it took all of us straight to the ocean floor. As you can imagine, our different thought processes created stress in our marriage. At the time, we did not understand that much of the stress was originating from our different strategies. It was years later, looking back and talking together for hours, that these theories became clear to us. If you are reading this and experiencing a similar tension in your marriage, talk about it openly because understanding where we were each coming from made conflicts with Dylan a lot easier. But on this night, we were not aware of the strategies and Amy was suggesting we bring Dylan home to live with us again. Since he went off to nursery school he has been to schools, crisis units and special programs that deal only with kids on the autism spectrum and many of them conveyed to us the same words, "Dylan is one of the most difficult kids we have ever had here." So, was I excited on our date night when Amy told me she wanted him to move back home? I was anything but excited.

After dinner, we went home, watched some TV, and went to sleep. It was not the night I was hoping for. The next day, we got up and began the plan to bring Dylan home.

— 10 —

Can It Get Much Worse?

Why Didn't She Just Offer to Help Him?

Dylan came home from Bangor and we tried to get him into a routine, but it was really difficult because there was no routine to be had. He didn't have a job; he wasn't in school. There really wasn't much for him to do. I tried to think of what he could do at Volk Packaging, but he didn't really want to work there so he was hoping to get a job somewhere else. Our task was to encourage him to wake up at a decent hour and go look for a job.

At this point, he was obviously depressed and sleeping most of the day. He had no energy, was so overweight and he truly felt like there was nothing to get up for. He was still smoking and we fought with him almost daily about not smoking in the house. He would try to sneak cigarettes in his room by opening the window. Once in a while, he would even smoke downstairs, figuring he could air the house out or spray enough air freshener to cover up the smell by the time the family came home. We are always very busy in the spring with softball, so we're not home a lot.

One of the ways we tried to get him some exercise was by making him take the dogs for a walk. We had three dogs and one of them was a Siberian Husky puppy, so he needed to get out frequently. Dylan had been home for about three weeks one day when I came home from work briefly before leaving for a softball game. That day we had a game almost an hour away and after the game we planned to take both the seventh-grade girls and seventh-grade boys to a fast-food dinner on the way home to celebrate the end of the season. Every year, the middle school allows us coaches to take the team for one dinner after an away game, usually toward the end of the season.

When I stopped home to change before heading over to the middle school Dylan was still sleeping. I woke him up and told him he needed to get outside and get some exercise, so he should take the dogs for a walk. He wasn't very excited about that but I insisted and made him get up and come downstairs with me. I wasn't thinking about the challenge of taking three dogs for a walk and I hooked up the dogs the same way that I had walked them that morning. I told him to take all three for a walk and then I headed off to the game.

We took the bus down to the game. The other team was terrible. There was not a single girl on the team who really knew how to play softball so I played girls at positions they do not normally play to make the game more competitive. That led to one of the longest games of the season from what would have been one of the shortest games of the season. A definite mercy in four innings turned into a two plus hour marathon 19-17 win.

Normally this would not be much of a problem and I didn't think it was a problem that day either. I didn't have my phone with me because I didn't want to be talking on the phone or texting while trying to coach. The game finally ended and when we got on the bus, I turned on my phone. I had several missed calls and a text from Amy to call her immediately with several exclamation points. As the bus picked up the boys team, I called Amy from a very loud bus and asked, "What's going on?"

She was a wreck and told me that Dylan had been arrested and was in the county jail for assault with a deadly weapon. I almost threw up. I couldn't believe what I was hearing, "What do you mean Dylan was arrested for assault?"

Amy was very upset, as upset with me as she was about the situation because I had given Dylan three dogs, including a puppy, to take on a walk. What could I have possibly been thinking to allow or to suggest that Dylan could walk three dogs at once? The fact is, I wasn't thinking. I was just in a hurry to get out the door to the game and to get Dylan some exercise, and it honestly didn't occur to me that it would be a big deal for him to take three dogs at once. I figured he would probably just walk around the neighborhood and then back.

Unfortunately, Dylan took a much longer walk than I expected, leaving our neighborhood to walk on a more major road in town. As he headed down the road, the dogs were getting tangled up in their leashes. The puppy, Cole, who was only three months old at the time and known as kind of a wimpy puppy, kept crying whenever he would get tangled up. It wasn't unusual for him to cry excessively loud at seemingly minor injuries. He was, and still is, a bit of a drama queen. Cole's yelping was making Dylan more and more frustrated, and although I wasn't there, I can imagine that he started to get a little rough with them as he tried to untangle them. Dylan has never been abusive to animals. In fact, he's always been very good with them. However, he was probably very frustrated and jerking them a little harder than normal. It would be frustrating for anyone to have three dogs get tangled up over and over again. For someone with low frustration tolerance to begin with, it was even worse.

A woman drove by and saw Dylan with the dogs. She rolled down her window and yelled at him to stop being so rough with them. Dylan was very frustrated and yelled at her, "This shit ain't easy." But that just made her yell at him some more. Now if she had simply said to him, "You look like you're having a tough time, can I help you out or give you a ride?" he almost definitely would have taken her up on it. Instead, she verbally assaulted him. If there's one thing you have probably learned from reading this book, it's that if someone comes after Dylan verbally, he does not back down.

Dylan kept walking, and this woman, instead of simply driving away or offering to help, followed him at a slow pace all the way back into our neighborhood and to our house, making Dylan more and more anxious and more and more frustrated. He was clearly frustrated by the three dogs. Why wouldn't she just ask him if he needed help? A simple kind word and offer for a ride home would have defused the entire situation. But she antagonized and harassed him for over ten minutes as he walked home. He even walked past our house into the cul-de-sac in an effort to make her just drive away, but she followed him the whole way with her window down, verbally assaulting him and telling him that she was going to call the police for his "abusive" behavior to the dogs. As he usually does when stressed or confronted, he fought back verbally.

Finally, he entered our driveway and walked the dogs back up the driveway at which point, she sat at the end of our driveway and videoed him with her phone. Now, if this happened to a typical twenty-year-old, he would have just gone into the house and ignored her, knowing that once he went into the house and the dogs were back in the yard, she would have nothing left to do but drive away.

However, that's not the way Dylan reacted. He yelled at her from the end of the driveway to go away and she refused, again threatening to call the police for the way that he was treating the dogs. Dylan then went into the garage and grabbed one of the many softball bats that hang above the window facing the back of the yard. He walked down the length of the driveway, holding the bat and telling her to drive away. He finally got to her car after walking the 100 feet of our driveway. The woman had plenty of time to diffuse the situation by just driving away, but she agitated him even more as he approached her.

He said, "I'm gonna count to three and then I'm gonna hit your car with this bat."

Again, at any point, this adult woman could have driven away, but instead, she simply replied, "Bring it on." Who in their right mind, or should I say, who not looking for an opportunity to call the police, says that to an angry 250-pound twenty-one-year-old man with a baseball bat in his hands?

Dylan, within earshot of several neighbors, counted loudly and very slowly to three. "One. Two. Three." Before he even touched her car, instead of hitting the gas pedal and driving away, she used that time to call the police. He then approached the passenger side of her car, and with the bat, knocked off her outside mirror. There was clearly no intent to hurt her, as he went to the passenger side and did not hit the actual body or windshield but instead knocked off a mirror on the outside of the car.

The police arrived and Dylan was still very agitated. It was about this time that Amy pulled into the neighborhood and saw the police car in front of our house. She tried to explain that Dylan has a high functioning form of autism and doesn't always handle situations like another person might. The woman had absolutely no empathy or sympathy for Dylan or for the situation and insisted on pressing charges. The police then handcuffed Dylan, drove him to the county jail and charged him with a felony.

* * *

Not only did I put Dylan in this situation by giving him too many dogs to walk, but when everything went down, I was not even available to be helpful. Amy was furious at me and I don't blame her. But at the time, I put up an argument that it wasn't my fault, which just made Amy even angrier with me because I was refusing to accept any responsibility for putting Dylan in a situation that he could not handle.

There was not much we could do for Dylan that night because he had to go in front of a judge and find out what the bail would be. I called our company attorney. They are the firm that Volk Packaging has been using for labor law, as well as other legal advice for many years. I knew I could trust them to give me a good referral on who I could call to help us with this situation. They recommended that I call Walter McKee from McKee Law Firm. He was actually located in Bangor, but my attorney felt that he was the person that he would call if his son was in trouble and that advice was good enough for me.

We called Walter McKee's office and it didn't take long before Walter called us back and said he would be available to represent Dylan. He would find out when his arraignment was and be in touch with the next steps. It was a long night at home, knowing that Dylan was sitting in the Cumberland County Jail and we couldn't get him out. Amy felt that it was all very avoidable had I not given him three dogs to walk at once. After the girls went to bed, we were alone and Amy was still very upset with me as well as the situation. I was still denying that I had done anything wrong. She finally blew up and was very vocal that all she wanted me to do was admit that I had screwed up. That's not something that I generally do well. It's definitely a character flaw that I'm aware of but am not always able to see in the moment. When I finally did admit that I was mistaken in letting him take all three dogs, that's when the guilt set in. I think that was a big part of my denial as well. I knew that once I admitted that I put him in a bad situation, I then had to take responsibility and absorb the guilt of the situation.

The next morning, we talked to Walter again. He found out that the arraignment would be a couple of days later and they would probably request some kind of bail for Dylan to get out. He would try to get it as low as possible, and he would try to get the charges dropped to, at most, a misdemeanor. We talked to Dylan in jail, as he would call us with collect calls through the Cumberland County Jail system.

For those who are reading this book and have never had to talk to somebody in jail, they don't make it very easy. The inmate cannot just call for free or even collect. Nor can they use a credit card or simple form of payment. The receiver of the call has to sign up for a service in advance through the jail system by going online and registering for a program that allows you to give a credit card at a certain amount and receive calls. The calls are very expensive and you never know when you're going to run out of money. They're really taking advantage of people who are in a dire situation as it is and often don't have the money to pay for these calls. The minimum charge is $32 for thirty minutes of phone time. We called in with our Visa number so they could put the $32 on our credit card. Only then can the inmate call collect, but you burn through that thirty minutes pretty fast. It also takes about twenty-four hours to register, so we were not able to talk to Dylan for the first day or so until the money was in the system.

When we finally talked to him, he felt terrible about what had happened. He knew that he should not have hit her car with a bat, but she got him so frustrated he didn't know what else to do to get her to drive away. She was smart enough to not pull into our driveway, so she was on town property when it occurred. He was in our driveway, so in his mind, he was on our property when it happened.

When we went to the arraignment, it was extremely difficult to see Dylan come into the room, grossly overweight, unshaven for a couple of days, and dressed in an orange jumpsuit. The whole experience was surreal. It was hard to believe this was happening to us, but there was our one-time "boo-berry muttin" eating little boy, standing in court facing felony assault charges.

As I sat there in the courtroom I couldn't help thinking about the song by Casting Crowns. The lyrics talk about how we need to praise God even during the storms of life because he holds our tears in his hands.

I am a big fan of Casting Crowns so I thought about how many times I have heard and sung those words. And yet they were always just words, lyrics to a really good song. I stared at my son and realized that I was in the storm. It was swirling all around me at the Cumberland County Courthouse. I said to myself, "Okay, Derek, for years you have sung that you would praise him in the storm so here is your chance to walk the talk. What are you going to do? How strong is your faith?"

I thought about the old cliché that people love to use during difficult times. They optimistically say, "God will never give you more than you can handle." That statement is both biblically incorrect and utterly ridiculous. As humans we are frequently given more than we handle. When someone is diagnosed with terminal cancer, Alzheimer's, ALS or Ebola I am pretty sure they often feel they have been given more than they can handle. It certainly felt like more than I could handle when I was sitting in the courtroom watching my once handsome son crashing into the rocks right in front of my eyes. Life can be difficult, very difficult. God does give you more than you can handle because that is life in a broken and imperfect world. It is during those times that God wants us to turn to Him to carry the burden. It was time for me to Praise Him in the storm.

Walter told us they would call his name and he would say that he was defending Dylan and Dylan had to plead *not guilty,* and they would give him some kind of bail. The bail was set at $1000 and it had to be paid in cash, so we bailed Dylan out and took him home. Walter felt pretty confident that they would drop the charges to a misdemeanor given that there was clearly no danger to the woman, as he hit the other side of the car.

The next day, the bad situation got worse when a reporter from the local newspaper contacted Amy for a statement about what happened to Dylan. Amy was in the process of running for her second term in the Maine House of Representatives and the reporter felt that this story was something worth printing. He had well-known "left leanings" and Amy, as a Republican representative, was in his crosshairs.

He asked about the incident and Amy said, "I don't understand how this is a story."

The reporter responded, "Well, any time a public figure gets in legal trouble, we consider it newsworthy."

"But my son is not a public figure. He's an adult who's not running for office, so this isn't really a news story other than an opportunity to go after me."

"Well, when Sean Flaherty got in trouble, we covered that story."

Amy was becoming frustrated, "But Sean Flaherty was my opponent. He was a state rep who was running for office. My son is not. Not only that, but he has a developmental disorder, and this is a very personal matter. It's not really newsworthy."

The reporter disagreed and told her he was going to write about it anyway, and asked if she had a comment. Amy simply said, "Okay if you need a comment, my comment is that our nearly twenty-one-year-old son is developmentally disabled. This was a regrettable incident which we are trying to deal with constructively as a family."

Sure enough, he was going to write about Dylan getting in trouble with the law in an effort to make Amy seem like a horrible parent and to create any doubt possible in the minds of voters who had not formed an opinion about her. There was almost no question in our minds what his intent was. Now we had to just hope that it would not get picked up in the other local paper. The first one is a paper that is not delivered to people's homes. It's found at local supermarkets, fast food chains and convenience stores. People have to make an effort to pick it up and read it. The other, however, arrives in every single household's mailbox on Fridays, so if it got in that paper, it would get a lot more attention.

The paper came out that Friday and we actually went around and tried to collect as many as we could, thinking that the story would be less visible. In the grand scheme of things, it was silly for us to think that we could quell the story, especially since it was online and most people read online anyway. Sure enough, our efforts did not make much difference.

A few days later, the other paper came out with the same story. What was most disturbing about the whole situation was that the information that they printed clearly came from the police report. When we called for the police report, we were told that we had to write a letter to receive it, and yet somehow, somebody leaked the police report to this reporter in just a day. He had information that he could have only known from reading the police report, and that was very upsetting.

We didn't know how this was going to impact Amy's campaign, but we figured it probably wasn't going to be good. It was, if nothing else, very embarrassing for us as respected members of the community. Dylan felt very bad about it. He asked Amy, "Am I going to cost you your campaign?"

Amy said, "Yeah, you very well might."

I am sure the story lost her some votes. However, many people read the story and later told Amy, "I think that is terrible what they are doing to your son" or "Why are they going after your son like that?" Even in local politics, people do not feel that children are fair game. Amy would later go on to win her election by a mere twelve votes after a tense re-count. She served her second term in the Maine State House of Representatives earning a tremendous reputation as a strong conservative who could also work across the aisle. She became well known across the state after passing landmark legislation protecting the victims of human trafficking and becoming chair of Maine's first virtual charter school. In November 2014, after the most expensive state senate race in Maine history, Amy was elected to the Maine State Senate to represent the towns of Scarborough, Gorham and Buxton. She was outspent nearly ten to one by special interest groups. We went through many hurdles to win Amy's house and senate seats. In 2010, when Amy decided to run for public office, she said, "I think I can make a difference. If God wants me in Augusta, doors will open. If he doesn't, doors will close." Despite what often seemed like an uphill battle, doors kept opening wider and wider for Amy. God had a plan for her, and it clearly involved changing lives for the better in our state capital.

Dylan felt bad, but still took no responsibility for his actions and defended what he did even though we explained to him over and over again the other ways he could have handled the situation. However, all those other ways really didn't matter at this point. All that mattered was Dylan was in some serious trouble. He had been in trouble before, but this was about as serious as it ever got for us because actual charges were filed. Also concerning was that he was being played up in the newspaper as a very violent person, and if there's one thing we always counted on and took comfort in was that Dylan was rarely violent, and he certainly wasn't violent with animals. The fact that they reported him as a "violent, animal abuser" was very upsetting.

The headline read, "Scarborough man faces criminal mischief charges" with the third sentence making sure to mention Rep. Amy Volk.

The whole situation just kind of sat there all summer long because these things take time. Walter had to work through the system with court dates, and in the meantime, Dylan was out on his own recognizance but with some limits. He had to be living in our house, and he had to have a curfew. He was not allowed to be out after 9:00. This was very challenging because not only was he a twenty-year-old boy who wanted to have a life, but he was trying to get a job and we really needed him to get a job. However, there was almost no job that he could get at that age with his experience that didn't involve being out after nine o'clock.

We tried to monitor him as best we could but, monitoring Dylan is like keeping an outdoor cat inside. There was almost nothing we could do to lock Dylan in the house and prevent him from causing more problems for himself. A few weeks later, that's exactly what he did.

Spiraling Downward and Out of Control

Now that we had Dylan home, we were not sure what we were going to do with him. He was angry and frustrated with his life. He was sleeping most of the time with no interest in going to the gym or doing any kind of physical activity to bring his weight down. He just kept getting bigger and bigger. And now, after being arrested and being told that he had to be home by nine o'clock every night, there was almost no way he could get a job. I could bring him to work with me at Volk Packaging but many of the jobs that he could do were already being done by a couple of other teenagers who had been brought in for the summer. I had to find work for him, which mostly meant making phone calls to potential customers.

Making sales calls over the phone was something he was actually very good at, although he did not find the job enjoyable. It is very discouraging to call prospects all day. It can take 100 to 150 phone calls to get one appointment, therefore it's very tedious and often frustrating work, not something that Dylan tends handle well. However, we had no other options because without being able to be out at night, there was almost no job that he could take at this point in the summer.

It was a Thursday morning in late July 2012. Things had not been going very well at home with Dylan. We were fighting with him almost constantly. He refused to work hard at Volk Packaging, which was very disappointing and embarrassing for me. I would bring him in to work and he would disappear for long periods of time and I would have no idea where he went. I would walk by the office that he was using and it would be empty, and I would walk by minutes later, and it would still be empty. I never knew where he was but I didn't have time to go look for him. Sometimes, I would walk by and the door would be almost totally closed, and I would push the door open a little to find him sleeping on the couch. On the rare occasion that I would walk by and find him awake, he would often be on Facebook or online doing something other than working and I would try to redirect him and tell him that I wasn't going to pay him to sit in the office surfing the web. It got to the point where I started telling Dylan that I would be paying him from now on by the task and not by the hour. I would give him a task of calling a certain number of potential customers or a specific project to do, and then I would estimate how long the project would take and that's what I would pay him. I could not count on him to work hard and stay focused on the task at hand.

It was halfway through the year, so one of the assignments I gave him was to call all the new customers we had picked up in the first six months of the year and ask them how they heard about us so I could do some market research as to what was effective in our efforts to bring in new business. I gave Dylan about 150 names to call and gave him the timeframe I expected the task to take and that's all the time for which he would receive compensation. If he wanted to spend the whole day doing nothing, I was going to pay him the same amount as if he did it in an hour and came to me for a new project. He wasn't very happy with me about this.

Instead of taking this new method of payment and saying to himself, "Okay, now I have to get these tasks done quicker so I get paid more because he'll give me another task," he took it upon himself to put even less effort into it, which I didn't think was possible. Yet, Dylan found a way to do it, sometimes not finishing a single project in an eight-hour day. I eventually even sent an email to all the office employees of Volk Packaging and told them, "I just want you to know that I am paying Dylan by the task and not by the hour. So if you see him wandering around outside on a smoke break that seems to be exceedingly long, sitting at his desk texting, or even taking a nap on the couch, please do not think that I am taking the company's money and paying him for these activities." The people in my office work very hard all day long, they're very loyal, and they deserve the pay that they receive. I felt very uncomfortable having anyone think that I was just giving my son money to take a nap on the couch.

On one Thursday morning, Dylan did not want to go to work with me but I dragged him out of bed, brought him downstairs and told him that he had to come with me and that I had to get going. Amy made a comment to him about being lazy and not wanting to come to work with me. For whatever reason, Dylan often would lash out against Amy for making the same comment that I would make. I don't know if it's because she is a woman and he had some kind of masculinity complex that he felt he could mistreat her or if she was just an easy target because he was so much bigger than she was or if he would lash out at her simply because she was the mom and somewhere in his head, he knew he had never-ending and unconditional love no matter how he treated her. That morning, Dylan started yelling at Amy. I told him to be quiet and just have his breakfast, but as we experienced so many times before, he refused to back down. Amy was not one to back down either. She was having it out with Dylan when he called her the c-word. That was the tipping point for me that threw me over the edge during this heated argument, and I screamed at him, "Dylan, you should be down on your knees every day thanking God for your mother because I can tell you right now if it wasn't for her, I would have thrown you out of this house a long time ago!"

Amy, who had had enough at that point said, "Throw him out!" She didn't have to say it to me twice. I was at the end of my patience with him. I felt that he was completely taking advantage of us and had no motivation to turn his life around.

"Fine, you're out of here," I shouted.

"You can't throw me out of the house," Dylan argued back.

"You wanna fucking bet." I said, "Get out of this house now. Get whatever clothes you need. Get your car, you can take your car, and go. I don't even want to talk or hear from you until at least Monday."

Dylan just kept screaming, "You can't throw me out of the house! You can't throw me out of the house!"

I grabbed him and said sternly, "You have three minutes to go pack whatever you need for the weekend and leave. We're leaving for the weekend, locking the door, and putting the alarm on. Do not come back into this house."

He kept insisting the whole time that he was packing and even after he came downstairs that we couldn't throw him out of the house, and the more he said we couldn't throw him out, the more firm we became in our conviction to do just that. We knew we were taking a risk because Dylan still had his bail conditions in place from the softball bat incident, and he was not allowed to be out of our house after 9:00. But we couldn't think of another meaningful way to get his attention, so we figured it was time to do something drastic. As he continued to scream that we can't throw him out of the house, I escorted him out to his car and told him to drive away. We don't want to hear from him until Monday morning. We were going away that weekend to our last softball tournament of the summer in Concord, New Hampshire, so not having Dylan in the house doing who knows what was actually going to be a relief for the weekend. With that came the added stress of knowing that we were putting his bail conditions in jeopardy.

We still had the GPS tracker on Dylan's car so we could track his whereabouts from wherever we were. That night, as we lay in bed, as angry as we were with him, we still couldn't help but worry what he was up to and what trouble he might get himself into. We texted the device under Dylan's hood and it reported that he was just a few turnpike exits away. We were unfamiliar with anyone he might know in that area so we thought he was likely sleeping in the car. We were hoping that he was sleeping in the car. We were counting on the fact that he did not have any close friends to turn to. His sleeping in his car would have the best impact to him from our punishment. Our objective was for him to realize that he needed us and that he also needed to respect us and the rules of our home. We had already called my parents and told them that they could talk to him but under no circumstances should they let him come there. Dylan still had a good relationship with my parents from his time in Florida, so we thought he might reach out to them hoping that they would invite him to stay there for the weekend. I explained to my parents that not only would that be no punishment at all, but it would actually be a reward for getting thrown out of the house. Dylan would be able to spend the weekend lying on the nice leather couch at Nana and Papa's and watching TV and going on their computer. That was the exact opposite of our goal, so we begged them to not invite him in no matter how much he pleaded. My parents understood what we were going through and they agreed to cooperate. As it turns out, Dylan knew better than to call them and they did not hear from him all weekend. We took this as evidence that he had enough sense left to be embarrassed.

The next morning, we texted the GPS device again and it still reported that he was in the same place, about fifteen minutes north of our home. I went off to work and Amy couldn't resist getting in the car and driving over to peek in to see if he was okay. No matter how angry Amy ever got at Dylan, her incredible love for him was never something that she could tone down, and I was always very impressed with her ability to love him unconditionally. I love my son unconditionally as well but I would be lying if I did not admit that I often let my anger at him get the best of me.

There is a song by a Christian artist, Mark Shultz, who sings about how his mom tells him that no matter what, she's always happy to see him come in the door and always happy to have him home. I felt ashamed that I could not feel the same way about my only son. But there we were in the situation we were in, and as hard as I tried to have that total unconditional love and total acceptance, I just was not able to do it. I threw Dylan out of the house, and the next morning, his mother went to check on him. Amy slowly pulled into the Holiday Inn parking lot, the address that was showing up on the GPS tracker. She parked her car on the front side and walked around to look for Dylan, and there he was sleeping inside the back seat of his Oldsmobile, holding onto the same blanket that we put in his crib before he was even born. Amy felt okay just knowing that he was safe, and she came home.

That night we drove over to Concord, New Hampshire, for Lilly's last softball tournament and, for a couple of days, we tried not to worry about Dylan, while at the same time regularly checking the GPS to see where he was.

All summer we had been going to softball tournaments. I was not managing Lilly's team that year, and the manager of the team created a schedule with tournaments every other weekend, so it was not a particularly grueling softball schedule. We were having a fantastic summer on the field, winning game after game and tournament after tournament. Lilly had stepped up as our number one pitcher on a young U-14 team and was completely dominating almost every team that we played. It was a lot of fun and a great relief to us as a family to have those weekends away from Dylan. Leaving Dylan home alone was challenging but we had a small apartment above the garage that a young couple was renting so they were able to keep an eye on him and make sure that our house did not become party central while we were away for the weekends.

The tournament in Concord was called the Bow-Two. On Saturday, we had lost our first game of the whole summer and tied a game, leaving us with a 1-1-1 pool performance and a sixth seed. As a consequence, we were up early that Sunday morning to face the top teams headed into the bracket play. Sunday is single elimination.

We had a great day despite the rain in the morning. We won the first game against the number three seed. Our number two pitcher came in and won the second game against the number two seed. And then we faced the number one seed. Lilly pitched that game beautifully and we won, bringing us to the championship game which, after several rain delays did not start until after 7:00.

Our number two pitcher started the game because Lilly had already pitched the previous two games. But, after the first inning we had found ourselves in a six-run deficit. The coach called Lilly to come in with the bases loaded and no outs. She got us out of the inning and continued to pitch the rest of the game, allowing only two runs, giving us breathing room to come back and win 14-8 against our friends but our rivals, the New Hampshire Comets. It was a wonderful night, finishing our season with one loss and four championships. I was flying high. We got in the car to head home at almost ten o'clock at night. We had not been on the highway for more than a couple of minutes when we received a phone call that changed our night and killed our mood instantly. It was a collect call from the Cumberland County Jail. Dylan had been arrested for a hit-and-run and violating his bail conditions by being out after 9:00.

Dylan came on the line and said that he had been arrested but he didn't do anything wrong and it wasn't his fault. We told him that we didn't want to hear about it. There was nothing we were going do that night. He could spend the night there, or maybe even longer. All the frustration from Friday morning was back and we had a two-hour ride to think about it. We talked on the ride home and decided that we were not going to bail him out. He could stay there and learn a lesson, and maybe we would have a break and some time to figure out what on Earth we were going to do next.

The next morning, we called Walter McKee, told him what had happened, and asked him to get involved and find out what the charges were. Apparently Dylan had been at a shopping center in South Portland with a bunch of kids, seventeen to twenty-year-olds or so, and according to the police report, one of the girls was saying something that made him angry. He got in his car and she stood in front of the car. Clearly not thinking, as it was a chaotic situation, Dylan let his foot off the gas and accidentally bumped her with the car. She was not hurt in any way but some of the boys that she was with started threatening Dylan and saying that they were going to beat him up, so he took off. When he left, they called the police. The police came to the scene and although she was not hurt, they called Dylan and told him that they had reported a hit-and-run and he needed to come back and answer some questions. When he came back, they arrested him and brought him to jail for violating his bail conditions as well as the hit-and-run. The local media was going to have a field day with this one. Now, our son who had never been violent in his life to any serious degree had been charged with abusing animals, smashing a woman's car with a baseball bat, and intentionally trying to run over a teenager. We knew this was not going to be good for Amy's campaign and, more importantly, not good for Dylan.

Walter called back and told us what the bail was and what would happen if we didn't pay it. Dylan would stay in the Cumberland County Jail until it was paid. We felt he was safe there and it gave us time to figure things out. It also gave us a much needed break from Dylan, and as selfish as that may sound, our family really needed it. Softball season had ended, soccer was starting up in a couple of weeks, and we had an opportunity to go up to our camp in Lee without the worry of Dylan.

While Dylan was in jail, Amy and I had some time to talk as a couple about where this was going. What was our strategy going to be to get Dylan out of this terrible situation that he had led himself into? He was insisting that he did not do anything wrong on that Sunday night, but it was obvious that whatever he was doing had gotten those kids upset enough to call the police on him. We were feeling extremely guilty about kicking him out of the house the previous week. If we had not done that, he might not have been in that situation. However, the more we thought about it, the more we realized that Dylan was making his own bed with the poor decisions he was making. Whether or not we had kicked him out that weekend, we still would have been away for the weekend and he would have been left to his own devices to make good or bad decisions. When that option was presented, Dylan seemed to always make the bad decision. Now he was sitting in jail, we were going to be out another $5,000 or more to defend another case.

When we came home from the lake, we set up a time to go visit him. It was very sobering to visit our son in jail. It was very much like you see on TV and in the movies. He was wearing an orange jumpsuit on the other side of what was once a clear plastic window. We picked up a phone to communicate with him.

Dylan had spent some time in jail writing us a letter. In the letter, he said all the right things. He apologized for all the trouble he had gotten himself into; he thanked us for all we had done for him; and he wrote how committed he was to turning his life around. He even wrote out a list of goals for how he could change his life. We were very pleased to see some remorse with regard to his behaviors. It was the first time in a long stretch that Dylan showed any acceptance of responsibility for the circumstances he found himself in. Maybe, just maybe, he had finally reached bottom, and it was time to start climbing back up again. It had only been a year since Florida, living almost entirely independently, maintaining a job at Boston Market, fit and happy, and now he was sitting in jail grossly overweight, a complete mess emotionally and physically.

Writing down goals and objectives and writing down apologies is a start, but we had come so far down this road that it was not a U-turn. We needed to *see* the changes in him. We needed to *witness* an effort on his behalf to make his life better, to improve his decision making, to break off his friendships with people who just tore him down. We had been manipulated and lied to far too many times for us to believe that this was legitimate emotion and not opportunistic manipulation. Amy and I went into the jail that night determined to keep him there. He needed some very tough love; he needed to know how serious this was. We were not going to just rescue him and bring him home.

We knew Dylan was safe at the Cumberland County Jail, but when we visited him, he gave us some concern about his safety. We knew one of the guards at the jail. His wife and her ex-husband had been friends of ours when the kids were little. Their oldest son is also on the autism spectrum and although our sons went different directions over the years, we stayed friendly. When they got divorced and she remarried, we saw her new husband quite often at school events. Her kids were very active in the theater program, as was Mariah. We talked to Joe when Dylan was arrested. He promised us that he would keep an eye on him and make sure he was safe. What we didn't know was the best place to keep him safe in the jail was to put him with the sex-offenders and homosexuals. Those were the people that were most often targeted for violence. They had their own area of the jail, so they could be protected from the general population. While we knew we needed to keep Dylan there, we were very uncomfortable knowing he was spending all his time with pedophiles. Yet, we held firm and walked out of the jail that night without paying his bail.

Dylan kept asking us what he needed to do to convince us to bail him out. We told him we didn't know. We weren't sure what we were going to do. Dylan has always had a hard time when we say we don't know. He always wants a plan and a direction, a firm yes or no. But what he *really* always wants is a yes. He claims that he just wants a yes or no answer, but if you give him the answer that he's not looking for, he won't let up, so sometimes it was better to just say we didn't know because it wasn't a yes and it wasn't a no.

We spoke to Walter several times over the ensuing few days. He said he would do his best to clear Dylan of the charges or at least plead them down, but he needed more information. On paper, it did not look good. The incident with the bat and now the incident with the car were creating a pattern of violent behavior and they were going to play that up to make Dylan look like a dangerous threat to society. We knew our son. We knew he was flawed in many ways, but being violent, being a danger to society was not one of them. Another week went by, a couple more visits to the jail. My parents also went in to visit him. After two weeks, we decided it was probably time to bail him out. He had a hearing scheduled for a few days later, so we would wait and see how that played out.

At the hearing, the judge agreed to release Dylan but only under certain guidelines. These guidelines were very restricted and made life for both Dylan and us very difficult. He had to live at our house, be home every night by 9:00 and was not allowed to leave our house until 7am. That curfew again made it very difficult for him to find work. Many of the jobs he was looking for were retail and would require working until after nine o'clock. We asked Walt if the judge would consider letting Dylan stay out past 9:00 if it was for work. He said that would be very unlikely, and he didn't feel it was something worth pursuing. Dylan had to find a job that would only require him to be out during the day. He found that very frustrating and gave up looking. We had a 250-pound Dylan, a frustrated Dylan; an angry Dylan; and a bored Dylan. We had a bigger problem than we had when we kicked him out of the house. We were stuck with him and he knew it. He knew if we kicked him out of the house he would be arrested again. That would cost us more money, cause him more problems, so with no fear that we could do anything to him, he became almost impossible to live with.

As the days and weeks went passed, Dylan became more and more angry and more and more hopeless about his future. It was not only hard to watch our son go through this pain but it was very difficult for the whole family to live with him. I tried to bring him to Volk Packaging each day, so he would at least have some place to go and something to do. The days that I was not going to the office, he would sleep almost the entire day. Amy was unable to get him out of bed to get any exercise or to even have a positive interaction with her.

One day, without my knowledge, he took my car, a Ford Expedition XL, and drove it to Subway near my office for lunch. My ATV trailer was hitched to the back of the car, so instead of unhooking it, he drove to Subway with the ATV trailer dragging behind. I don't think he had any idea how to unhook it and knew if he asked me, I probably wouldn't let him use my car. When we got out of work at the end of the day, I went to put some box samples in the trunk of the car, and I saw a sizable dent on the back of the passenger's side of my truck. I said, "Dylan, what the hell is this?"

Without missing a beat, he said, "You can't prove that."

"What?" I said

He repeated, "You can't prove I did that."

I was shocked by his response. It seemed so ludicrous that that would be his defense. It was almost funny. I said, "Well, there was no dent when I left for work this morning. Somebody told me they saw you take my car at lunch because you were having a hard time getting it parked with the trailer the way I had it, and now I have a dent. You're telling me you didn't do it?"

He said, in an almost hostile tone, "I'm not saying I didn't do it. I'm saying you can't prove I did it, so I'm not going to be responsible for paying for it."

I have to be honest and say my first instinct was to punch him in the face for such a disrespectful way to treat me, but of course I didn't. I asked one more time, "You're not going to take any responsibility for this big dent on the side of my truck?"

"Not unless you can prove that I did it, which you can't."

I was speechless. "Just get in the car and let's go home." That is the way most encounters went with Dylan in September of 2012. It was a terrible time for all of us.

DYLAN'S TAKE: *I had forgotten most of this stuff until I read my father's recollections. I remember most of 2012 as a really dark period of time that I never want to slip back to again. It's hard to even remember the level of "Not giving a f---" I had sunk to. To do things like openly sleep on the job at Volk Packaging with my dad two offices down, or calling my mom the C-word and then bullying my parents about kicking me out of the house. Yikes! After this chapter, you the reasonable, level-headed reader would probably feel like "This kid is a major prick" and lose a certain amount of respect for my plight after reading about some of this unthinkable crap I was pulling in 2012. What you need to understand about me, is I'm a man of extremes. When things are going well and I'm in a place where I have goals and I have ventures I'm pursuing, I don't just do kind of well, I pour everything into whatever I am after. Whether it's birds, music, prank phone calls,* *comedy or just being a disaster, I'm a really intense person and whatever direction I go, I go in that direction all the way. In 2012 I was completely directionless, leaving my life in Florida and moving back to Maine was, to this date, the worst decision I've ever made. I had given up on my fitness, fallen back into smoking, and everything had just kind of tumbled to the ground. So just like how when things are good I take it to an extreme, when things are bad like they were then, I took it to an extreme. I completely let go. I let go of years-worth of maturity I had acquired, all the skills and good habits I had gained. I just said screw it. But I didn't just say screw it, not my style...I went really hard the other way. That's the best way I can describe to you how a good man like myself was capable of the train-wreck I caused for my family in 2012. The way I look at it, is that many celebrities have had periods of time where they publicly went off-the-rails through a series of scandals and outrageous behaviors. For Lindsey Lohan, it's pretty much been 2012 for coming up on ten years now, Justin Bieber's definitely going through this phase as I write this, and Britney Spears had 2007. She shaved her head, walked barefoot into a public bathroom, had a disastrous "comeback" performance at the VMA's, and some of you might remember there was even an incident where she was caught on camera attacking a car just like I did! The point is, just like when Britney Spears released "Womanizer" in 2008 (chart-topping comeback hit) I came back from all this, too. And for anyone reading this who might be going through a struggle as well, remember that Britney Spears made it through 2007, I made it through 2012, so you have got a shot, too!*

Pepper Spray Leads to Utah

In October 2012, Amy was in the middle of a highly competitive re-election campaign for the Maine State House of Representatives. She was running against a former Cumberland County District Attorney named Paul Aronson. Although he was an older gentleman with grown children and not very active in the community, he had some name recognition, special-interest money behind him, and most importantly, he had Barack Obama at the top of the ticket in November. The candidate at the top of the ballot often drives the votes below it. In addition to President Obama bringing out the liberal vote, there was also a gay marriage bill on the ballot that would draw people to the polls that were less likely to vote for any Republican.

On October 8, a good friend and customer of mine, Carolyn Brodsky, owner of Sterling Rope, which is right up the street from Volk Packaging, and her partner were kind enough to host a fundraiser for Amy at their house in Scarborough. Often times, these "meet-and-greet" events draw very small crowds, and the candidate is mostly preaching to the choir. The main objective to a neighborhood meet-and-greet is the opportunity to put flyers in everyone's mailbox, letting them know the candidate is open to meet with constituents. It's one more chance to put your name in front of the voters. Carolyn and Julie's event, however, drew a nice crowd. There were close to twenty people at her house for cocktails and hors d'oeuvres. Amy worked the room beautifully and gave a nice speech explaining why she was running for re-election and talking about her accomplishments in the 125th Maine Legislature. She was in the process of taking questions from the guests when my phone rang.

I picked up the phone and heard screaming in the background as Amy's mother on the other end told me that Dylan had sprayed Lilly in the eyes with pepper spray. I told Amy I had to go, and I jumped in the car and flew home. When I arrived at home, Lilly was still screaming in pain from the burning in her eyes. Janet, my mother-in-law, was screaming at Dylan, and Dylan, completely unremorseful, was screaming back. It was a chaotic and terrible scene. I immediately called my neighbor, Ian Bristol, who is a doctor. He jumped in his car and shot right over. I told Dylan to leave the house, but he refused to leave and I had to physically grab him and throw him out the door, telling him this was the final straw. He had lost his right to live in our home. I told him to get out, and I would deal with him later. My primary concern at that moment was taking care of Lilly. Ian looked at her and explained that pepper spray was not permanently damaging; it was pretty much just what it sounded like—taking pepper and putting it in your eyes. He told Lilly she needed to shower and let the water wash out her eyes as much as possible until eventually, the burning would go away. Lilly, still crying, went upstairs to take a shower.

That night, I also had to deal with a completely overwhelmed mother-in-law, who had never witnessed Dylan in his full fury. Amy's mother is not a big woman, and it would be impossible for her to physically control Dylan in any way. She told me that this entire incident was over the volume on the television. Dylan had been watching TV very loudly, as he often did. We were constantly telling Dylan to turn it down. He rarely cared if someone was trying to sleep or do homework. On this particular night, Lilly wasn't feeling well so she was trying to get to sleep early. Our house has all hardwood floors, so the sound of the television tends to echo right up the stairs. Lilly had come down the stairs two or three times, asking Dylan to turn down the TV, each time asking less and demanding more, as her initial polite requests were ignored. When she came down the third or fourth time to insist that he turn down the volume so she could get to sleep, he reached under the pillow where he had pepper spray and sprayed her in the face. We never figured out why Dylan had pepper spray to begin with, and we'll never understand what he was possibly thinking when he used it on his fourteen-year-old sister. No matter what he was thinking, there could be no excuse or even a warped logic to explain his behavior. I knew this was the last time Dylan would be allowed to live in our home. It was the beginning of a new chapter that we would have to deal with, because living with us was over.

Once the situation was calm, Lilly was in the shower, my mother-in-law was settled down, and Ian had gone home, I went outside to deal with Dylan. A month earlier, Amy and I had purchased a small home in South Portland, Maine, about five miles from our house. We bought this home as an investment with the plan that Dylan would live in it until he either decided to move out on his own or would buy the house from us if he was very happy there. We didn't feel that he was ready to live on his own at this point, but we were hoping that by the end of the year we would be able to move him in to our small two-bedroom house in South Portland. It was at a dead-end that led to Casco Bay, so we figured it would be a great spot for him and Beautiful Boy. We even had a chance to talk to the next-door neighbor who had a thirty-six-year-old son on the autism spectrum.

"What a blessing," we thought, "a neighbor who would be understanding and not judgmental if he got to know Dylan."

Yet, after he pepper-sprayed Lilly, I made an executive decision that he was done living in our house. While Amy was still at the fundraiser, I collected some of Dylan's clothes, his toothbrush, and some bedding, and I brought them downstairs and told him to get in the car. He asked where we were going, and I told him he had burnt his last bridge living in our house. This was the final straw. I was going to take him to the other house and he could live there from then on. He then had the audacity to tell me that I was overreacting, which made me even more angry at him.

On top of his insistence that I was making a bigger deal out of this than it was, he also insisted he did nothing wrong, that Lilly deserved it because she yelled at him to turn the TV down. It was the most ridiculous argument I ever had with him, and that's saying something. However, to think that there was any way a twenty-one-year-old that weighed 250 pounds could justify pepper-spraying a fourteen-year-old girl is so outrageous that it is beyond logic. I drove him to the street in South Portland. There was no furniture, nothing in the house except a running toilet, but as far as I was concerned, that was all he needed and all he deserved. I told him to go inside, lay down on the floor and go to sleep. We would deal with getting a mattress and anything else he needed to live there the next day.

Amy and I talked a long time that night about our options. When we were done, we decided we would try to find a roommate for Dylan. So the next day, we started asking around to see if anybody knew a young man looking for an apartment or a room to rent. Some friends of ours said they knew someone who was looking to move to the area and would be a good influence on Dylan. Despite the fact that Dylan had been kicked out of our house, was living in this lovely little home in South Portland rent free, and was being provided for, he was still not happy. He insisted that *he* would have the final say on who would rent the other room. He said it had to be somebody that was "very cool" with a lot of social skills. We told him we would simply be happy to find someone willing to live with him who might be a positive influence. The young man that we found to live in the other room was a very nice guy with good morals but he was not what Dylan would consider "cool" or someone with a lot of "game" with the ladies. Dylan was not very friendly to him from the beginning but we told him that he needed to figure out how to make it work.

Each day, I would head over to the house on my way to work to pick Dylan up. Usually when I would arrive, even after calling him and telling him to get up and be ready, he would be either sleeping or not prepared to leave. Almost daily, I had to drag him out of bed. One afternoon I took him to sign up at a gym right up the street in hopes that he would start using it. All of our efforts were getting us nowhere. Dylan had no motivation and no interest in getting his life back on track.

A few days later, Dylan got a hold of my phone and wrote on my Facebook page, "Dylan killed himself today" and hit post. Luckily, I saw it very quickly and erased it before too many people had read it. When I told Dylan how upsetting this was, he asked me, "Can you give me five things that I have to live for? And don't tell me my family loves me because most families love you. Give me five things in my life that are worth living for."

At that time, that was a very difficult question to answer. He didn't want to hear about sunsets and rainbows. He wanted five concrete things that were going well in his life enough to wake up another morning for. It's horrible to say that that question was extremely hard to answer so I would often just tell him how ridiculous he was and remind him that a lot of the things that weren't going well in his life were simply because of decisions that he made, not because his life was so horrible. If he made better decisions, he could turn a lot of the negative around very quickly. He didn't want to hear that either.

About a week later, he went to the dentist with Amy for a cleaning. When she went in for her appointment she left her phone in her jacket. Before Dylan went in he took Amy's phone, opened up Facebook and wrote, "Dylan killed himself today. We probably should have seen it coming. Your prayers are appreciated." As part of the legislature, Amy had close to one thousand Facebook friends. Her message screen and comment section lit up like a Christmas tree. I was in a meeting and didn't have my phone on me, so I was unaware of what was going on. Amy was in the dentist's chair, also completely unaware that dozens of people were responding to "her" post. The governor's office even put together a press release in response to what they read. Dylan's act was a desperate cry for help. At the time it felt like anger and hostility, but as we look back now we see it very differently. It was deep sadness. Dylan was begging for us to help him and we were not doing it. We were getting mad and frustrated but we were not finding the help he truly needed. The help he was screaming for us to find for him.

When Amy finally came out of the dentist's office and I came out of my meeting, there were fifty-seven comments and dozens of private messages. People in my company who saw the message and were crying. Some of those people have known me since I was very little, and they have known Dylan since he was born. When Amy saw what was happening and confronted Dylan about how serious it is to leave a message like that, his response was, "All those people that are leaving comments are talking about you and how sorry they feel for you. They're not even talking about missing me." Amy tried to explain to Dylan that most of those people didn't know him. They knew her and as far as they knew, he was dead, so when someone is gone, you console the family, especially the mom. He couldn't understand that and kept insisting over and over again that it just proved that nobody cared about him.

As angry as we were and as embarrassing as it was to have to explain to all those people that that was a prank, we were very sad for our son. Our hearts were broken by how he saw himself and the people in his life as uncaring and not concerned with the possibility that he had killed himself.

Amy called me at work and said, "We have to do something. This is just like when he was sixteen and we sent him to boarding school. We have to do something dramatic, and we have to do something now before all these threats become a reality."

We had looked into some programs for young adults, including one in Utah. Amy said, "Maybe it's time we send him to Utah."

I said, "It probably is, but he's not going to go unless we give him an ultimatum. We have to tell him that we're kicking him out of the South Portland house, that he's on his own unless he gets on a plane for Utah."

When I got home from work that night, Amy had all the information and flight schedules. She was ready to click the button to buy a plane ticket. She had already talked to the people in Utah, and they were ready to take him. She said to me, "Are we going to do this? Are we going to call his bluff if he says he's not going?"

I said, "I'm ready to do it if you're ready."

She was ready. She bought the plane ticket before we even talked to Dylan.

The next morning, instead of going to pick Dylan up for work, Amy and I went to his house to present him with his options. As soon as Amy walked in the door, he knew something was up. We sat him down on the couch and said, "Dylan, you may have given up on yourself, but we're not ready to give up on you. So you have two choices. Tomorrow morning, we're going to come get you. We can drive you to the homeless shelter or we can drive you to the airport where you'll get on a plane and fly to Utah to enter a program out there called At the Crossroads.

Dylan said harshly, "There's no way I'm going to another program! I don't need a program. I know what I need to do."

We remained calm, despite the fact that he was clearly getting agitated and his emotions were elevating. We said, "No Dylan, you don't know what you need to do and you don't seem capable of doing it even if you did. You need help. We think these people can help you."

"That's a waste of money. You don't need to be spending all that money for another program."

"Dylan, it's our money. We can do whatever we want with it. If they can turn your life around and save you from this path of self-destruction that you seem to be on, it's worth every penny."

"Well, how long do I have to stay in the program?" he asked.

"As long as it takes."

"Well how long is that?"

"They said that most kids are there six to nine months."

He got quiet for a second, then asked, "Can I bring my cat?"

"No," we sadly responded, "you can't bring Beautiful Boy."

"Well, I'm not going if I can't bring Beautiful Boy!"

"Dylan, we told you your choices. You can't bring Beautiful Boy to the homeless shelter either."

"You're going to kick me out of this house?!"

"Yes," we calmly stated.

"Why? I thought it was going alright."

"What did you think was going alright? Nothing is going alright. It's been nothing but bad for a long time."

"You didn't even give me a chance to live here on my own!"

"No, we didn't," we admitted.

"Well you gotta give me a chance to live here on my own!"

"No, we don't. We don't think that you're ready to live on your own."

"But you didn't even give me a chance!"

"Dylan, we see what's going on with you, and we don't see anything changing unless something dramatic happens in your life. That's going to happen tomorrow morning when you tell us where to drive you."

"Well what's in Utah?"

"There's a program out there—"

"For kids with autism? I don't need another autism program!"

We explained to him that it wasn't just for kids with autism. It was called At the Crossroads because it's for young adults who are at a crossroads in their life, whether they are dealing with a mental disability, an addiction, an anger problem, or any number of things. Regardless, they are all at a place in their life where they have to make a decision about which direction they are going to take.

"You are at that place too, Dylan," we said, "This isn't working, and we aren't going to just sit back and watch you self-destruct."

"When can I send my cat out?" he asked, completely ignoring what we said.

"We don't know."

"Well, you have to give me a timeframe."

"We don't have that."

"Well, you have to give me something! You have to let me know when I'm gonna be able to have my cat."

"We don't know. That's up to you Dylan—how you do in this program and when you're ready to get out of it."

"What does that mean—get out of it?"

"It means that you are able to live on your own."

"Able to live on my own? What does that even mean?"

"It means that we don't have to support you. It's time that you grow up and learn to live truly independently."

"I can't live independently."

"Well, that's what this program is going to teach you."

"I'm fucked."

"Why do you say that?"

"What happens if I don't get through the program?"

"Then you're on your own."

"I'm on my own? What does that mean?"

"It means that you're going to have to get through life somehow. You're gonna have to figure it out."

"So I'm fucked," he repeated.

"Why do you say that, Dylan?"

"Because if I don't get through this program, I'm fucked. And if I do get through this program, you're going to expect me to live on my own, which I can't do, and I'm not going to be able to do in nine months. So basically, I'm fucked either way."

"No Dylan, you're not fucked," I said, starting to get more frustrated with him, "That's the whole point of this program—to get you un-fucked, to get you to the point where you don't feel like you're fucked, where you can live on your own independently."

"But how am I going to do that? They aren't going to get me a college degree or any real skills in six to nine months that are going to let me live on my own."

"Dylan, we're not going to just abandon you if we see that you're doing everything you can to live independently. If you get through this program, and you're doing the best you can, everything you can, including working hard, maintaining a job, and staying out of trouble, we'll help you out. But if you're not even trying, if you're just sitting back and waiting for us to do all the work, we're not going to bail you out. We can't do that anymore. We're not just going to sit back and watch you ruin your life while we don't do anything about it. If you want to give up, you can do that on your own. We can't watch it anymore."

"Well, when can I bring my cat?" he said, again.

"We don't know."

"I need to know when I can bring my cat. I'm not gonna go unless I know when Beautiful Boy can come."

"We don't know that, Dylan. We don't know when you're going to get through this program and be able to live independently in an apartment that's not part of the program. The program's apartment building doesn't allow cats, so you're going to need to be able to move out of their apartment into your own. The guy told us six to nine months, so I would use that as a guide."

We went around and around for quite a while, mostly about the cat and about how unnecessary Dylan felt it was to be in another program. But we were determined to hold firm and call his bluff if he said he was not going. Yet we had already bought his plane ticket. We were counting on him to make the right decision about Utah. He knew he could not make it by himself. He knew his life was a wreck. He may not have been ready to admit it, but he knew it. And he knew that he needed help.

I took him to work that day and we didn't talk about it the rest of the day. We told him we would take him out to dinner wherever he wanted to go, and in the morning, we'd head to Manchester, New Hampshire, where he would get on a plane and fly to Las Vegas where the program would pick him up. This was not an inexpensive program. It was going to be a huge financial burden for us. Even with Mariah in college, it was significantly more than her tuition. But we'd go broke if we had to in order to get our son back—the son that we'd seen glimpses of over the years, the son who was doing so well just a year ago in Florida before he moved back to Maine and spiraled down so far.

That night we went out for dinner. We called the director of the program from the car because Dylan wanted to hear for himself when he could get his cat. The director told him the same thing that we did, which was good. Dylan's friend, Mike Josephs, joined us for dinner, and we actually had a nice time, some good conversations, and some laughs. Mike was a good friend and seemed genuinely sad to see Dylan leaving but was also encouraging him that it was the right decision. Dylan went out with some friends that night and we prayed that he would stay out of trouble. The last thing we needed was for to him to get arrested doing something stupid and mess up the opportunity to get to Utah and have a fresh start.

We were very pleased when Dylan came home relatively early that night. We asked him to call when he got back to his house and we hoped that he was legitimately going to stay in. Amy and I went to bed but neither of us slept much. This was a huge decision and there was no turning back if it was a bad one. Now Dylan would be 2500 miles away. We were putting a lot of trust in the staff of At the Crossroads. The only thing we could do was pray that it was the right decision.

The next day, we went to South Portland early to pick Dylan up and head to the airport. He was scheduled to fly from Manchester to Las Vegas where he would be met by a representative from his new program. He would then be driven to St. George, Utah. We picked Dylan up and brought him back to our house for a little bit to give him a good breakfast and to bring Beautiful Boy home to stay with us. Beautiful Boy wanted to go outside so Dylan let him out. Unfortunately, when it was time to leave for the airport, Beautiful Boy was still exploring the neighborhood and Dylan had to leave without saying one more last goodbye to him.

We were very quiet on the ride to the airport. There wasn't much left to say at this point. Dylan asked very few questions, which was fine since I couldn't answer most of them anyway. I really had no idea what this program was all about or whether they had what it took to help Dylan. Amy and I were just walking by faith that there had to be something better for Dylan, that his life was not supposed to be the way it was. We could do nothing but pray that this choice was the right one.

Manchester is a small airport so I could almost walk him to the gate. I waited in the security line with him until he got to the point where he had to give his ID. I gave him a hug, told him that I loved him and it was going to be alright, and I stepped back as tears rolled down my cheeks. As horrible as it was to have Dylan around, I was still sad to see him go. I wasn't really sure why, because it was a relief when I thought about him not being around, but I was still very upset. I didn't know what the next part of his life would be like, and I worried how bad it could get if this was the wrong choice. I wondered if I would ever see my son again and, despite what he had done to our family, it broke my heart.

One of the security guards, a young African-American woman in her early thirties, saw me standing back from the security line wiping my tears. Unbeknownst to me, she went and talked to Dylan, and then he went through the security clearance and went off to his gate. Before I left, the TSA agent walked over to me and she said, "That's your boy?"

"Yeah," I responded.

"I just went up to him and told him, 'Your dad really loves you.'"

That just made me cry even more, but I thanked her and said, "Yeah I do." I got in my car and thought about heading home, but there were too many tears in my eyes and I wasn't ready to leave. I drove around the back of the airport where the private jets come in and out. I had a clear view of the runway. I sat and watched Dylan's plane. I just stared at it and cried. About a half an hour later, I saw it unhook from the gate and start to back up. The tears started all over again, and when the plane went down the runway and up into the air, I started crying uncontrollably. That's it, he was gone on his way to Utah for the next chapter in his life. If this didn't work, what would happen to my son? Could we handle the real possibility that a failure in Utah meant we had to let Dylan go and live whatever his life would be? I was terrified that I was leaving my son's future in the hands of complete strangers over 2,000 miles away but I knew we could not help him. It was time once again to test our faith and trust that God had a plan for Dylan and the people in St. George, Utah, were part of that plan. As I sat alone in my car behind the Manchester airport with my shoulders shaking and tears pouring down my face, I prayed for my son.

— 11 —

The Transformation

"It is the excitement of becoming—always becoming, trying, probing, falling, resting, and trying again—but always trying and always gaining."
~ Lyndon Johnson

Dylan in Utah

Dylan's arrival in Utah was pretty much as we expected it to be. The people at his program, At The Crossroads, found him to be confrontational, argumentative and generally uninterested in their opinions. He was assigned a young man in his twenties named Magnum Morgan. Magnum had a wife, a couple of kids and lived right across the street from an apartment they set Dylan up in. He was rooming with three other young men in the program, none of whom were on the autism spectrum, but they were dealing with challenging issues of their own.

The first couple of weeks were rocky but in only a few weeks we were pleasantly surprised with the relationship Magnum was creating with Dylan. He seemed extremely capable to us. He understood Dylan remarkably well from just a short period of time. They were connecting at a level that was critical for Dylan to make progress.

As weeks turned into months we got to know Magnum very well from our weekly conversations with him. We did not talk to Dylan much, except through text messages, as he has never really been much for talking on the phone. I generally don't do well talking on the phone with him because I often find I run out of things to ask him. Amy seems to be very good at keeping long conversations going with him over the phone, and it was nice that their relationship was strengthening now that Dylan wasn't battling us every day over one thing or another. We got along great with Dylan when he was in Florida and were starting to rebuild that relationship with him in Utah.

One of the missions of At The Crossroads is that the young people in the program build adult-to-adult relationships with their parents instead of adult-to-child relationships. That means we do not provide him with everything he needs and it is not our responsibility to tell him what to do. We were okay to buy him just what he needed, things like toothpaste and a haircut. When he did complain that he didn't have enough money for food, we told him he needed to learn how to stretch his money better. Dylan was fond of buying things that were unnecessary like flavored water and packaged meats instead of deli meats and drinking out of the faucet. We reminded him that a carton of eggs could provide multiple meals and he should learn how to do basic cooking. With the help of the people in the program, he eventually learned how to manage his finances better. He was making good progress and things were starting to turn around for him.

One night, out of the blue, we received a phone call from Magnum. There had been a misunderstanding in a text conversation between Dylan and Magnum, which led to Dylan being arrested and charged with a bomb threat, a felony. This was the most serious charge Dylan had ever faced. We were devastated to learn of this setback. The next day Dylan called us from jail and we asked him what happened. He told us a few days before, a couple of the guys and Magnum had been talking jokingly about bomb scares. I do not know the exact context of the conversation but I do know it was lighthearted. The previous night before he got arrested, Dylan was using an anonymous online texting website through his computer and sent Magnum a text telling him there had been a bomb placed in the building. Dylan, under the strange misconception that because the number was coming from a 206 area code and Maine is a 207, thought Magnum would know it was him. We don't know how Dylan would come to such a conclusion but that's the way his brain works sometimes. Magnum asked him if it was a real threat and he said yes. Magnum told him he was going to text the police. When Magnum said he was going to "text the police" instead of call the police Dylan thought Magnum knew it was him, and it was just a joke because nobody texts the police. People call the police. This sort of black and white thinking is very typical of people on the spectrum. Because of this response by Magnum, Dylan played it up more talking about a bomb in the building. Magnum had no other choice. So, protecting the safety of the other kids in the program, he called the police.

When the police arrived, Dylan came downstairs and told them it was him all along. He thought that would be the end of it, but the police turned him around and arrested him on charges of calling in a bomb threat. The police asked Magnum if there was any concern that this was real and if they should search the building.

Magnum quickly responded, "No, absolutely not. I'm not concerned at all. This is just a misunderstanding." There was no search of the apartment as it was clearly a misunderstanding.

The police, who have to do their job when they receive a call like this, had no choice but to take Dylan in and let the authorities deal with whether it was a hoax or not—a misunderstanding or just a joke gone badly. Magnum felt terrible for turning Dylan in but we were not angry with him. He had to do what he had to do, given the circumstances. Not knowing that they were dealing with someone on the autism spectrum who often misunderstands social interactions, the police did what they had to do as well. So now Dylan was in jail in Utah, and the bail was $10,000. We told Dylan we were not going to bail him out. The last time he got arrested we told him that was the end of our bailing him out and so we left him there. He stayed in jail for two and a half weeks until a judge released him back to the program.

When we asked Dylan how it was being in jail in Utah for two weeks, he joked that it was a pretty nice jail, not as nice as the one in Cumberland County, but nicer than the one in Florida. We laughed at the strange idea that our son now had enough jail experience that he could make comparisons between various jails. Dylan, who was still fascinated with black people, said, "What kind of place did you send me to that's whiter than Maine? How could you send me to someplace that's so white that they don't even have black people in jail? What kind of place doesn't have black people in jail?" We told Dylan to hang onto that comment, as it would make a great stand-up routine. Sometimes the only thing you can do is laugh at some of these situations.

We hired an attorney, at a cost of several thousand dollars, to defend Dylan. As Dylan's luck would have it, his case came due for him to appear in court on April 16, 2013. When he was assigned that date, we didn't think much about it. However, on April 15 of that same year, just the day before Dylan was to appear in court, two radical brothers bombed the finish line at the Boston Marathon, killing three people, including an eight-year-old boy, and injuring hundreds. Dylan's court date was the next day. With the Boston bombers still on the loose and no idea how anyone would ever catch them, the timing could not have been worse. The plan for the attorney to drop it to a medium class-B misdemeanor, a deal that they had previously verbally agreed to, was now off the table.

The assistant DA in St. George told Dylan's lawyer, "He's very lucky that I can even keep the misdemeanor charge, given what happened yesterday." Dylan was charged with a Class-A misdemeanor and told that if he stayed out of trouble for a year, it would be dropped to a lower class misdemeanor.

Another misdemeanor, and all based on a lack of understanding by the police and the DA in St. George that Dylan's brain just doesn't work the same as theirs does—a misunderstanding by a young man who just took a joke too far because he didn't think through the consequences or understand that Magnum didn't know who was on the other end of the text messages.

Despite the bomb threat charge, Dylan started to make some real progress in Utah. His two primary contacts, Magnum Morgan and Norm Thibault, the psychologist with At the Crossroads, both seemed to enjoy Dylan's company and appreciated his potential. Amy and I enjoyed our Thursday night conversations with Magnum as he told us how Dylan was starting to accept the program and gain more independence. As time went by we heard less and less from Dylan asking us for either things or money. He was truly on the road to gaining independence.

We decided he had not been there long enough when Thanksgiving came, and it would be too risky to have him come to Florida with the family, so he stayed in Utah for Thanksgiving. That was very difficult for us as it was the first time we were not with him for Thanksgiving. When we went around the table before the Thanksgiving dinner saying what we were thankful for, my father talked about how thankful he was to have his family together but then got very teary eyed and emotional when he said, "But the family is not all here together because Dylan's not here." Tears rolled down my cheeks as he spoke. I thought about how much we all wanted Dylan to turn his life around so he could be with us the next year.

Christmas came and we decided that Dylan was not ready to come back to Maine to be with the family. The thought of Dylan being in his apartment all by himself on Christmas was too heart-breaking for us to accept, so we suggested he go to his grandparent's in Florida. We would have him spend a couple of days with Amy's parents celebrating Christmas and going to church with them, and then he would spend a few days with my parents in West Palm Beach. Amy's parents were in Lakeland, so everyone had to agree to meet in the middle for the Dylan exchange. The grandparents all agreed and were really hoping that Dylan would behave himself on his visits. We told them he was making a lot of progress, he'd be happy to be with them, and we felt he would be fine.

Miraculously, everything went well over Christmas break. Dylan had a nice visit with both sets of grandparents. We were very excited when he told us that while in Florida, he decided he was going to quit smoking and start getting back in shape. My father, a year or so earlier, had extremely generously offered Dylan $5,000 if he quit smoking. My father was a former smoker and watched his father, who had smoked his whole life, have a heart attack at fifty-seven and almost die. My grandfather gave up smoking after that heart attack and went on to live another thirty years, eventually dying of esophageal cancer in 1996. My father hates smoking and detested the thought of Dylan smoking, so he offered Dylan $100 dollars a month until he got to $5,000 dollars, with the stipulation that if Dylan started smoking again, he would take out $100 for every month that Dylan smoked.

Dylan said, "How are you going to know if I'm smoking since I'm in Utah and you're in Florida?"

My father told Dylan, "Because I'm going to trust you to tell me."

Dylan, with honesty, responded, "I don't think that's a good idea. Why don't you have me do a urine test every couple of months or something like that?"

"No, Dylan," my father said, "You're a man, and I'm going to trust you as a man and as my grandson to be honest with me, because if you're smoking and you're not telling me, but if you're taking my $100 anyway, then you're stealing from me. And if you can lay your head on your pillow at night knowing that you're stealing money from your grandfather then you're going to have to live with that."

It was the perfect response at this time in Dylan's life, and it echoed exactly what he was hearing every day from Norm, Magnum, and the staff of At the Crossroads. Personal responsibility was a difficult lesson for Dylan.

We were scheduled to see Dylan in April at parent's weekend. We were excited to see him, but nervous at the same time. The program had very specific guidelines about visits from parents. We could take him out for dinner, buy him some toothpaste, or get him a haircut, but under no circumstances were we to buy him clothing, shoes, or groceries. It was not a time to take him shopping for a new wardrobe or even clothes that he may or may not need. Our job was just to visit him and spend time with him. It was very important to not set back the work they had been doing toward self-reliance. We were nervous that Dylan was going to pressure us to buy him things while we were there but that didn't happen.

We had a terrific visit; he didn't ask for anything except some deodorant and soap. When we took him out for dinner, he was appreciative and careful to order something very large so he could bring home some leftovers. He never actually said that, but we thought it was funny that at each meal he ended up with food to take home. Dylan had been working out feverishly since Christmas and was on his way to getting back in shape but he had gone so far in the opposite direction that it was going to take a long time and a tremendous amount of hard work to get himself back in shape. When he saw us in April, the first thing he wanted to know was whether he looked thinner. He did look thinner, but it was not a dramatic change. He asked us repeatedly over the weekend how he looked and we told him that he looked great, he looked healthy, and it was obvious he was working hard to get back into shape.

Amy and I didn't see Dylan again, except in pictures that he would occasionally post on Facebook, until we went back for another parents weekend the following October. At this visit, even though we had seen some pictures of him, we were truly shocked at how great he looked. He had lost a tremendous amount of weight, had built up some muscle, and was running regularly as well as going to the gym. Just like he did in April, he asked us over and over again how we thought he looked. He was still concerned because his stomach had some excess skin, which was bound to happen after he had become so overweight. His skin had stretched out and even when he was in shape in Florida, he had always been challenged to build up his abs. While he was very pleased with the way he looked, he was very frustrated that he could not get his mid-section toned. It was confusing because one minute he would talk about how great he thought he looked and the next he would say how frustrated he was because he didn't look better. We were happy to see him in such good shape physically, but we were concerned emotionally that he was becoming obsessed with his weight loss.

He was pleased again at Thanksgiving when everyone saw him for the first time in two years. The difference now was dramatic. He was happy that everybody gave an appropriately shocked response when they saw him, and we had a nice visit with him over Thanksgiving break.

The next year in St. George had its ups and downs, as it always did with Dylan, but for the most part, he was doing really well. He was staying physically fit, relatively happy, and had even made some friends in the program. I truly believe, and do not feel it is an exaggeration, that Magnum Morgan, Norm Thibault, Jason Ayotte and all the staff from At The Crossroads saved Dylan's life. Just before, and for a while after he moved to Utah, our son was headed down a path of self-destruction that would probably have led to either jail or death. I am convinced that God put At The Crossroads in Dylan's life as a roadblock down that horrible path. I will forever be thankful beyond that which words can express.

My relationship with Dylan was improving tremendously during this time. I spent too many years mad at my son. I always loved him very much but I was angry with him. I knew it was wrong, at the time, but I just couldn't help myself. Dylan got me to say things I never thought I would say to my child, he drained my patience and often squashed my sex life. My son has Asperger's and, due to no fault of his own, I was pissed at him, for years! Time passed, Dylan matured and I grew emotionally. I forgave Dylan for something he never needed forgiveness for. I stopped being angry. It was not easy to get to the point where I could genuinely enjoy and appreciate Dylan. The only boy in my life would teach me everything I would ever need to know about vacuum cleaners, birds and cars and would have me recognizing more gangsta rap music than I ever thought possible (or desirable). One day when Dylan was in Utah he texted Amy and me a cartoon picture of a mouse entering a giant maze. The only words on the text were, "My brain every morning when I wake up." It was a pivotal and emotional moment for me. I had to close the door of my office as I cried as I stared at my phone and tried to imagine a life where everyday tasks felt like a mouse entering a complex and never-ending maze. How could I be angry at him when I should be doing everything I can to help him navigate that maze. He was never intentionally creating an emotional tsunami wherever he went. He was just trying to live in a world that was often too fast-paced and confusing for him to make much sense of. I was learning through the staff of At The Crossroads that I cannot spend my days walking him through the maze. What I can do, however, is try to guide him, teach him and provide encouragement for him to enter that maze every day. Each day he was learning to find a way through it on his own. He may never reach the point where his brain doesn't see the maze but with my help, patience, love, and with no more of my anger he was beginning to gain ground on it. When he called me, from then on, frantic and confused, I started to quietly picture that mouse and remember that while I can't get him to the other side of the maze, I can walk him around the next corner so he is back on track.

* * *

He struggled with dating in St. George because almost everyone in town was

Mormon. As Dylan describes the Mormons, "They are excessively normal, in a good way." They are wonderful people and they were a great influence on Dylan in the program, but they tend to only want to date other members of the Latter Day Saints Church. We tried to get Dylan hooked up with a church in St. George. There was a non-denominational church literally a stone's throw away from his apartment, and we took him to visit it one Sunday morning while we were in Utah. However, the service was long and boring, the music was dull, and we didn't blame him for not wanting to go back. It was disappointing because we really felt strongly that a connection with a church was something that would greatly benefit Dylan. His faith and his walk with Christ were as up and down as his general walk in life. We know how important it is to have a strong relationship with Jesus. We hoped and prayed that Dylan could find that but it didn't seem like St. George was going to be the place to do it. We would send him web links to sermons that we enjoyed and thought might help grow his connection with God. Most of the sermons were preached by Eric Samuelson from The Rock Church in Scarborough, Maine, Miles McPherson, the pastor of The Rock Church in San Diego, or Stephen Furtick, from Elevation Church in Charlotte, North Carolina. The key was only sending him occasional videos, when the message was clear and on point to Dylan's life. He had a difficult time following messages that were abstract or philosophical. They had to be direct, practical and logical. We also had to send them sparingly or he would tune us out and stop watching. Amy and I pray every day that he will discover God's love and someday find a church that fulfills him and allows him to use his talents for others.

DYLAN'S TAKE: *The first few months in Utah I was still the same person I was throughout the year 2012. I didn't really understand how far I had fallen in every way. I resisted most aspects of the program and I pretty much lived for smoking cigs, sleeping most of the day, and eating everything. I think the turning point was when I got booked for that stupid bomb-threat. I spent over a week in jail and when I came out I was surprised that most of the guys in the program were excited to see me. They were quick to tell me how they had been laughing their asses off at my mugshot. I purposely made a really thug-like face at the camera. Apparently they had predicted I would do that when they heard I got arrested! The real turning point came when I started losing weight. When I became dedicated to getting in shape it quickly turned into my whole life. I knew I could be a really good looking guy and, for the first time in my life, I wanted to fully realize all my* *physical potential. I worked out for at least two hours every single day and gave my diet a complete overhaul. From about March of 2013 to that November I went from 230 pounds, the biggest I had ever been in my life, to 150 pounds, the thinnest I had ever been. Of course, most of my life I had been about 170-180, average weight. Luckily for me nobody in St. George knew me before I was fat so everybody was shocked as they watched my transformation take place so rapidly. I'm sure it looked like one of those stories you would see on Oprah. I was working myself to the bone to get in shape that fast but it was pretty sweet to get treated by everybody in the program and all the guys at the gym like a rock star. As I kept looking better and better, things just started really looking up in all facets of my life. I hadn't realized until this point that what had been keeping me in such a deep, deep hole was feeling terrible about how I looked and how I was presenting myself to the world. Once I could see a genuinely good-looking guy in the mirror, it was pretty much the key to going out and being successful in finding work and in social situations. Having positive self-esteem, in whatever way that manifests itself for you, is critical to overall happiness and success.*

They are Beautiful Creatures: Dylan and His Cats

Dylan loves cats. However, he didn't always love cats. In fact, when he was younger, he was more of a dog person. When he was eleven, we even signed him up one summer to go to dog training camp where he would help train future service dogs. But, somewhere around thirteen or fourteen, Dylan became a cat person. Not only that but he became a devoted cat owner. The ironic thing about the timing of Dylan's new-found and long-lasting love for cats was how close it was to the time when the counselor we were working with told us that Dylan was incapable of loving us or anything else. We had a really hard time with that statement because we felt it was grossly inaccurate. We had seen Dylan show love for us. We had seen him show love for his grandparents and his siblings, and probably more than any of those things, we saw him show love for his cat.

His cat at the time was a black, brown and white cat named Marley. Marley was a sweet cat who would sit with Dylan for hours while he would watch TV or be on the computer. As the years went by, Marley became the standard for what Dylan looked for in a cat's personality. And thankfully, he was lucky enough to find it. More than once, in fact.

In early 2005, Marley passed away. It was very sad for the whole family. One day, she just disappeared and we didn't see her until she was discovered a month later under the neighbor's shed.

When Dylan was fourteen, we thought a nice lap dog would be good for him—a little buddy who would hang out with him, always be happy to see him, and be his friend. We purchased a maltipoo, a mix between a maltese and a poodle. We thought he'd be between ten and twenty pounds, just the right size to hang out with Dylan and cuddle with him whenever he needed something to feel close to. He named this dog Winnie even though we told him everyone would assume it was a girl. However, because it was a buff colored maltipoo, he associated it with Winnie the Pooh and named him Winnie. Today, Winnie is more well-known on Twitter as @poorwinnie. Winnie never connected with Dylan. Instead, he bonded with Serena, who was one year old at the time.

Since Winnie wasn't the right fit for Dylan, he thought it would be better to have another cat. We went to the shelter and found a little kitty, whom Dylan named Little Jerry, after the episode on the TV show *Seinfeld* when Jerry Seinfeld's neighbor Kramer gets a rooster and names it Little Jerry. Unfortunately, Little Jerry grew up very quickly and turned out to be quite the feral cat with very little interest in sitting on Dylan's lap for hours or even minutes.

Some time went by and we saw that even with the addition of Winnie and Little Jerry to the family, Dylan yearned for a pet to love and one that would love him back. He insisted that he wanted an older cat, one that would be more settled in its nature, less playful and more sedentary. We started going to the shelters, looking at cat after cat. He would pick up every cat, put them on his lap, and pat them. If they fidgeted at all or seemed anxious in any way, they were rejected as not the right cat for him.

Dylan picked out a cat that he named Stella. *Stella* was a TV show that Dylan loved at the time. It was an obscure show about three guys and their strange adventures through life starring Michael Ian Black. Stella was a very unpredictable cat. She seemed to be what Dylan was looking for at the shelter, but when we brought her home, we discovered that she had a very quick and sometimes aggressive temper. Dylan would pat Stella nice and calmly in his room while looking at a book or watching on the computer and all of a sudden Stella would have a momentary bit of insanity and scratch him or try to bite him.

I became more and more nervous around Stella myself and starting questioning whether we made a bad decision. Dylan was growing attached to Stella, but with Serena only two years old, I was very anxious about what Stella might do.

We were scheduled to go to Florida for Thanksgiving, and we had somebody lined up to come over to keep an eye on the animals. However, the morning of our flight, Stella crossed the line. While Dylan was holding her, she suddenly reached up and bit him in the face, cutting his cheek open. That was too much for me to accept, and I put my foot down and said, "I don't care if everybody in the family hates me. That's the end of Stella in this house. I'm not gonna wait around for Serena to have some little playmate over and then we have to explain why our cat bit a little girl and she has a scar on her face. That's not gonna happen. Stella's gone." While I received some protests at first, everyone knew I was right. We put Stella in a travel box and brought her to the animal shelter on the way to the airport.

One day, a few weeks later, I was looking through a local swap-and-sell magazine called Uncle Henry's. In this issue, there was a cat in Brunswick, about thirty-five minutes away that was described very much in the terms Dylan was seeking. I called the owner and asked some questions about her cat. She described a wonderful cat—caring, affectionate, patient, calm, quiet, but too expensive. She simply could not afford his food and vet bills anymore. Although I felt badly about her situation, her cat seemed like the perfect fit for Dylan. We drove to Brunswick to meet Boomer. Dylan fell in love, bonding instantly with Boomer. There was no question he was coming home with us.

Unfortunately Boomer was eight or nine years old, and for some reason we have never had one of those cats that lives to twenty, although I wouldn't put it past Little Jerry. In 2010, on the way home from visiting Dean College in Franklin, Massachusetts, when Dylan was a senior, we received a phone call from our next-door neighbor. She said Boomer, who Dylan more often referred to as "Favorite Boy," was lying on her lawn in a very strange manner and had not moved in hours. She was pretty sure he was dead. We didn't tell Dylan in the car because we didn't know how he was going to react. "Favorite Boy" had become the love of Dylan's life. When everything else around him seemed to be crashing down, he could always count on his cat loving him unconditionally. Boomer would sit with Dylan for hours while he watched TV or sat at the computer. He never seemed to tire of Dylan's company. That was something that couldn't be said about anybody when it came to Dylan. How many people do you know who will spend endless time with you and never get tired of your company?

The thought of watching Dylan go through the loss of another beloved cat made Amy and me very sad as we drove home from Massachusetts. When we arrived home, I went right over to see Boomer, and, as our neighbor had suspected, he had passed away. I picked him up, brought him home, found a box for him, and then we sat down to tell Dylan. I think he was in shock at first, not really believing what had happened. He just stared blankly at us, and then he asked if he could see him. We took him out to the garage and opened the box to show him his Favorite Boy. He handled it surprisingly well, but we knew he was broken inside.

The love that Dylan has for his cats is special. It's not uncommon for people to have very strong bonds with their pets and everyone gets sad when they lose a beloved cat or dog. I've been through it, and I know how it hurts. But I do believe there was something unique about Dylan and Favorite Boy. Most of us have many acquaintances and a few true friends. Dylan had many acquaintances but really no true friend. Favorite Boy was his only friend so his loss was much like that of an elderly man or woman who is all alone and loses their lap dog. Boomer was often all Dylan had, all he could count on when sometimes he felt as if no one liked him, including his parents.

Favorite Boy never had a harsh word for Dylan; he never didn't want him around and he never thought less of him because of anything he did. Even though his mother and I always loved Dylan unconditionally, Dylan's cats gave him constant unconditional love that he didn't always feel from anyone else, including Amy and me.

Amy and I knew that after we lost Boomer, we would have to get another cat for Dylan. Even though he was looking at colleges and other opportunities, it was very important for him to have a cat in his life. We started going to the shelters again, and just like last time, we looked at cat after cat, usually leaving without any success. He knew what he was looking for and was not willing to settle for less.

After a couple of weeks of visits, Dylan found a cat that he thought would be a good fit and we adopted it. However, after only two days at home, he knew it was not a good fit. We brought the cat back to the shelter and explained to them that although he was a very nice cat and we did not have any major issue with him, he just wasn't what Dylan was looking for. He wanted a cat that if he sat down to watch a movie or wanted to lie in bed until 11am, the cat would stay with him no matter what. However, that personality trait is not typically one people would associate with cats, so we knew it would take a while to find Dylan's new companion.

A few weeks and several visits later, Dylan called me at about 5:00 one evening and said he had found the cat he was looking for. He wanted me to come over to the shelter to fill out the paperwork. The shelter was only about ten minutes away from work, so I wrapped up what I was doing and headed over to the Kennebunk Animal Shelter.

When I went in, I saw Dylan with a couple of his female friends who were kind enough to keep him company on his many visits to different animal shelters. He had a nice full grown, brown cat on his lap, and he said, "He is a gorgeous creature. I'm going to name him He Who Is Gorgeous."

I laughed and told him that probably wasn't the best name for a cat. When we would open the front door and call to him, it would be very awkward to yell, "He Who Is Gorgeous! He Who Is Gorgeous! Come here, He Who Is Gorgeous!" Dylan laughed and I think it made him want to name the cat He Who is Gorgeous even more. Thankfully, Dylan's friends persuaded him against it until he agreed that it might not be the best name for his new friend. He went with Beautiful Boy instead.

Beautiful Boy was somewhere around seven or eight years old, but he was definitely full-grown and mature. With that, he was settled and calm and seemed to be able to sit with Dylan as long as he wanted him to. As soon as we got Beautiful Boy home, we were convinced Dylan made the right choice. There was never a question that he and that cat were meant for each other.

When it was determined that Dylan was not going to attend college in New England and instead go to Florida and join the New Directions program, Beautiful Boy went along for the ride. It was of great comfort to us and to Dylan to know that he had his faithful companion with him while he was all alone down in Florida. Even though my parents were only forty-five minutes away, it eased our minds to know that at the end of a challenging day, he could lie down with his beloved cat and relax. And he did that. Dylan would sometimes sit for long periods of time and just gently pat Beautiful Boy and the cat never complained or tried to move.

When we visited Dylan in November for Thanksgiving and saw Beautiful Boy up on the roof, we became very concerned. We could not see how he could get down but when we said that to Dylan, he just laughed and said he always finds a way down. Then he looked up at the cat and yelled, "My baby!!" or "That boy!!" Sometimes Dylan would just randomly yell one of those phrases when seeing Beautiful Boy.

When he was living at our home later, after returning from Florida, we would be lying in bed just about asleep and all of a sudden we would hear, "My baby!!" Dylan would come across Beautiful Boy somewhere in the house and yell at the top of his lungs. He couldn't contain his love for that cat. And although it was sometimes jarring to be awoken out of near-sleep with a loud

"That boy!!" we usually would smile, and his sisters always got a kick out of it. Dylan would ask us over and over again, "Don't you think that Beautiful Boy is more attractive than the average cat?" And then he would jokingly talk about how manly it was to have a cat. It was fun to see him laugh at his own expense, knowing the image of men with cats. But he really didn't care and never held back.

When everything came tumbling down for Dylan and we insisted that he join the At the Crossroads program in Utah, we also had to tell him that he could not take Beautiful Boy. We had talked to the director of the program who, in turn, had told Dylan that in time we could send him his cat. He would have to earn that by moving to an apartment off campus. He told Dylan it would be six to nine months. Dylan was more upset about the idea of spending six to nine months without Beautiful Boy than anything else about going to Utah. He kept saying to us, "I'm never gonna see him again. How could you take me away from my cat? He's gonna die, and I'm never gonna see him again."

Beautiful Boy did have some health problems but nothing serious. Amy and I told Dylan that we loved Beautiful Boy and we knew how important he was, but it was more important that Dylan join this program and have a chance to turn his life around. Yet all he could focus on was being alone in Utah without the love of his life. Even on the ride to the airport when we were sending him off, he said again that he was never going to be able to see Beautiful Boy again. I assured him we would do everything we could to keep him healthy and safe, and we would send him out as soon as Dylan was ready.

A week after Dylan left for Utah, Amy was in the kitchen. Cole, our Siberian husky puppy, was in the woods barking in a very strange way that she had never heard before. Amy went out in the woods to see what Cole was so worked up about and discovered Beautiful Boy lying on the ground with his tongue sticking out, barely alive. She picked him up and rushed him to the animal hospital, telling the veterinarian to do anything she could do to save him. Beautiful Boy had had a heart attack and the vet said his chances of survival were not great. Even if he were to live, it appeared he had lost the use of his back legs and may never get them back. The thought of putting Beautiful Boy down only a week after Dylan left is still heartbreaking today. I told her to do anything she could to keep him alive, it didn't matter what it would cost. I went and visited Beautiful Boy that night and brought a picture of Dylan to put in the baby incubator with him. I prayed over him and cried like a baby. I was not crying about Dylan losing this cat. I was crying and praying for my son's broken heart and crushed spirit. I thought of one my favorite Bible verses, Psalm 34:18, which says, "The Lord is close to the broken-hearted and saves those who are crushed in spirit." I had been drawn to this verse many times over the years and it always comforted me.

The next morning, the veterinarian called us a little before eight o'clock to tell us that Beautiful Boy had had another heart attack and she had to recommend that we let him go. We told her we would be right over as soon as we put Serena on the bus in order to say goodbye but she said there wasn't time for that. He was clearly in pain and she needed to do it immediately. We told her okay, and then cried like babies. How were we going to tell Dylan that only a week after he left, Beautiful Boy was gone?

We talked to the people in the program and told them that we felt it was best to not tell Dylan right away. Even though we didn't like lying to him, it would have crushed him so soon after he left when he was still unsettled in Utah. They agreed and asked if they could have three or four weeks to try to build a relationship with Dylan, so that when we told him, he could feel like he had someone to talk to. I said, "We can't buy you much more time than that. I took one picture of Beautiful Boy last night right before he had the heart attack that I can send Dylan, but if he starts asking me to send him pictures, I won't be able to do it, and we'll have to tell him."

Three weeks went by, and Dylan didn't ask for any pictures—then four weeks, then five. And one day, Magnum, his colleague at the program, went into Dylan's apartment to see him. His bedroom was covered in pictures of Beautiful Boy. Dylan looked right up at Magnum and said, "My cat is dead."

Magnum said, "Why do you say that?"

"Because I haven't asked about him, and my parents haven't mentioned anything about him in three weeks, and I don't dare to ask because I know he's dead or else they would have talked about him."

Magnum called us immediately after he left and told us what Dylan had said, so we called soon after that to tell him the truth. He had already prepared himself mentally, but it was still hard to hear. We were glad that he had time to form a relationship with Magnum so he could have someone to talk to.

Dylan stayed in the program for almost two years without a cat but he never stopped talking about getting one. As soon as the opportunity arises, we have no doubt that he will have a cat to love again.

DYLAN'S TAKE: *My father does a great job in this chapter talking about how much my cats mean to me. It is always fun to be into something many people have mixed feelings about, such as cats. Most people will tell you they like dogs better but I just found cats to be beyond cute, to the point of just extreme beauty. And I always tend to gravitate towards things that are the opposite of what everybody else in the room likes. It doesn't matter whether it's a movie or a music artist or even just a person, if everybody is talking badly about it, I start looking at it in a better light. I also tend to be interested in several things at once. I put all my passion into one topic. People often talk about how they like cats but it's usually followed by, "I just love all animals." That is where I am different. I just politely respond, "Oh, that's nice, I just love cats." It is true, and usually makes people laugh. Being a guy who is an unabashed cat-lover has a few perks. I can't tell you how many girls it has helped me make progress with because they have cats and they think it's cute that I love them so much.*

Dylan's Employment History

"Nothing in the world can take the place of persistence. Talent will not; nothing in the world is more common than unsuccessful men with talent. Genius will not; unrewarded genius is a proverb. Education will not; the world is full of educated derelicts. Persistence and determination alone are omnipotent." ~Calvin Coolidge

There is an episode of *Seinfeld* when Jerry tries to rent a car but the lady tells him they are out of cars. He asks her how they can be out of cars if he had a reservation since the purpose of the reservation is to hold the car. She replies to Jerry and Elaine that she understands how a reservation works. He quips, "I don't think you do. If you did, I'd have a car. You see, you know how to take the reservation. You just don't know how to HOLD the reservation. And that's really the most important part of the reservation, the holding." That is a terrific analogy for Dylan's employment history. He is fantastic at getting the job, he just doesn't know how to HOLD the job. When Dylan was in Utah with At The Crossroads they were so impressed with his ability to get jobs they asked him to teach job search seminars for the other students. Keeping the job, however, was not part of the class. We were never able to see one of his lectures but the staff at ATC said he was a great instructor. Dylan enjoys helping others so we were not surprised when we heard how seriously he took the preparation for the seminars. The following is a listing of some of Dylan's jobs and the length of time he maintained them.

Job/Employer	Location	Length of employment
Jim's Pizza	Maine	3 months
McDonald's	Mane	3 weeks
Dunkin' Donuts	Maine	2 weeks
T-Mobile	Maine	1 week or less
Chili's	Maine	3 months
Selling Time Shares	Florida	2 months
Selling Golf ads	Florida	2 months
Selling Septic Cleaning	Florida	1 month
Selling used cars	Florida	1 week or less
Waffle restaurant	Florida	1 day
Selling spy software	Florida	1 week or less
Boston Market	Florida	6 months
Bloomingdale's	Florida	3 days
Burlington Coat Factory	Florida	1 week or less
Marshall's	Florida	6 weeks
Volk Packaging	Maine	Off and on for 7 years
Selling Internet Packages	Utah	2 weeks
Staple's	Utah	6 weeks
Applebee's	Utah	3 weeks
Jimmy John's	Utah	8 months
Taxi Service	Utah	2 months
Pizza delivery	Utah	3 months
Town Car Service	Utah	3 months
Restaurant deliveries	Texas	2 weeks
Jimmy John's	Texas	Current as of April 2015

Gettit Vending

We had watched over the years as Dylan went from job to job, never able to hold a position for very long before something he did or didn't do would cause him to lose it. Amy and I had talked for many years about the idea of essentially "buying" Dylan a job. We wondered what we could invest in that would allow him to be his own boss; what business we could start or buy so that Dylan could not get fired. When he was younger and loved electronics, I thought about buying a RadioShack or maybe opening my own small electronics store for Dylan to manage. When he became super interested in music, we kicked around the idea of opening a record store. The more we thought about that, however, the more we realized that was not a viable option, as online music was taking over and record stores were dying.

At one point I even looked into buying a radio station. I woke up in the middle of the night with the idea that I could buy a radio station and make Dylan the program director and star DJ. He could run the station, pick out the music. I lay in bed for close to an hour, thinking about this idea of mine and just how fantastic it was. Before going to work I jumped on Google and typed in "radio stations for sale." A website popped right up, giving me a list of radio stations around the country that were currently on the market. My dream became an unpleasant reality when I realized how expensive it would be to buy a radio station.

Even today, with a mini radio career of my own, I still wonder whether that would have been a good long term investment and whether Dylan could have been successful and happy running a radio station.

As the years went by, ideas came and went. Dylan had been in Utah for about a year when Amy and I came up with the idea to buy a small vending machine business. We visited St. George and noticed how fit everyone seemed to be. In this heavily Mormon population, there was hardly any drinking or smoking, and the gyms seemed to be very popular. Our idea was to invest in the new fad of healthy vending machines. Instead of selling soda and junk food, these vending machines sell healthy options, such as Vitamin Water, fruit bars, and low-fat popcorn. It seemed like a terrific idea if we could just get Dylan to buy into it. I did some research and found a company based right in Salt Lake City called Healthy You. Unlike some of the other vending machine companies that required the purchase of a franchise, Healthy You allowed you to simply buy the machines. There was no commitment beyond that. The overall investment, depending on how many machines were purchased, would be between six and eight thousand dollars per machine, with some additional costs for added features.

After several discussions with Dylan about the viability of such a business, we finally got him to buy into the idea that this might be a nice source of income for him. If the machines were successful, we could invest in more of them. Dylan was a natural salesman and I felt confident he would be able to place these very attractive and high-tech machines. After some additional analysis and many conversations with the people who ran Healthy You vending machines, we went ahead and purchased five of their machines. Dylan chose to name his business "Gettit Vending." His tagline on his business card said, "Junk food is so 70's." We were excited that he was showing enough interest to come up with a name and slogan, so we didn't argue, even though those would not have been our first choices.

In November 2013, we bought the machines and I flew to Salt Lake City to meet Dylan for a three-day training program for Healthy You. I enjoyed my time in Salt Lake with him and was very impressed by the company and their machines. The technology seemed incredible. They looked better than any vending machine I had ever seen and I was convinced we had made a good decision. Dylan was even starting to get excited about his new business. There were times during the training when I looked at Dylan and could tell that he was overwhelmed by what the trainers were telling us. The machines were incredibly sophisticated but with that sophistication came complexity. Dylan does not do well with complexity. Several times during the training I leaned over and whispered, "Don't worry, I'll help you with that" or "Don't get stressed, we don't have to do that if it is too much for you."

I knew that if the training became too confusing and intimidating he would check out and our business was doomed. I assured him repeatedly that we were in this together and I wouldn't let it get to be too much for him to handle.

What I enjoyed most about starting this business was that I was starting a business with Dylan. It gave me an excuse to talk to him on a regular basis; it gave me an opportunity to impart some of my business experience to him; and it was something very positive that he and I were doing together. In general, we do not have much in common. We don't hunt or fish or go to ballgames together. One thing we do both like is working out so whenever we are together we always take time to hit the gym. I knew that there was no chance Dylan and I would ever work together at Volk Packaging. This was my shot to be in business with him. I saw it as an opportunity to do some male bonding with my son with whom I often felt disconnected. When he was in Florida I signed us both up for a week long sales training conference at Nova Southeast University in Ft. Lauderdale. Many of the jobs he was getting at the time had some element of sales so I figured the training would not hurt him and it was a good excuse to spend time with him. I often feel as if I missed out on many opportunities to bond with Dylan during his formative years because his behavior was so challenging.

Unfortunately, as time passed, despite Dylan's extraordinary effort and success in getting all five machines placed, the money that they brought in was disappointing. It would take a very long time to see a return on our investment. A couple of the locations were doing alright, but some of them brought in almost nothing. When it came right down to it, even people in fit, alcohol and tobacco-free St. George, Utah, enjoyed junk food. With very little money coming in to the machines and Dylan securing other employment that paid the bills, he quickly lost interest in servicing the vending machines. They sat idle, unfilled, bringing in very little money for months until Gettit Vending went out of business. I eventually sold the machines for a fraction of what I had paid for them less than a year earlier.

DYLAN'S TAKE: *This nine-month long endeavor was the product of such good intentions, parents who care going way out of their way to help me be successful. And I worked very hard at going out every day taking care of all the aspects of getting this business to where it could be a success. There were so many problems; the sales of these health-oriented snack foods were pitiful, places where the machines could really do well turned out to be almost impossible to get into, and on top of all that the machines while flashy and modern-looking, were built very shoddily, so anywhere I did manage to hustle my way into would call me almost daily to complain that the machines were malfunctioning—again. The company that supplied the machines was not much help. What really could they do when the reality was that these things were just constructed so poorly that they had endless issues? When this whole ordeal just crashed and burned and they lost an ungodly amount of money, I really didn't understand what my parents or I did to deserve such a financial mess to happen to us. The answer, of course, was nothing. The experience helped me mature. Unfortunately, it also reinforced my view of the world as a negative place where good will and hard work is not always rewarded. Hopefully someday I will have experiences that change that perception. Maybe this book will help.*

Dylan and Beautiful Boy

Our Vegas "Mini-Hangover"

In July 2014 Amy was invited to attend a charter school conference in Las Vegas. Amy had joined the board of Maine Connections Academy's virtual charter school the previous year and later was named president of the board. Maine Connections Academy was Maine's first virtual charter school so there was a lot for Amy to learn. The conference happened to fall during the first week in July when we would be celebrating our twenty-fifth wedding anniversary. It seemed like a great idea for me to join Amy on the trip to Las Vegas. We could visit Dylan while out there and also celebrate our anniversary. The week before we had been in Maryland with Lilly's softball team. We put Lilly and Serena on a plane home and we flew west. Dylan came out to see us the next day. We hung around the pool, grabbed some dinner and took in a comedy show. After the show, Amy and I were exhausted. On the walk back to the hotel Dylan became very upset with us because we were not being "encouraging and supportive" of his plan to move to Las Vegas. Although Dylan had lived in both Florida and Utah, he had never lived without a good support network. We told him the truth. We were extremely concerned about moving from very safe and Mormon heavy St. George, Utah, to fast and crazy Las Vegas. They don't call it Sin City for nothing. Even without a disability and tendency to become quickly overwhelmed, Las Vegas seemed like a bad idea for any twenty-three-year-old boy who was not clearly mature enough to handle it. I became visibly frustrated by this conversation. I tried to remember that one of the key goals of At The Crossroads is to build an "adult-to-adult" relationship with your child.

I said, "Dylan, you want us to have an adult-to-adult relationship but then all you want us to do is to tell you what you want to hear. That is not what adults who care about each other do." His anger at us was not that we were telling him our opinion. His problem was the opinion itself. He felt very strongly that we "had nothing to worry about" and "there is no way" he would not be successful in Las Vegas. The emotion that came from Dylan was anger but the fact is that he was hurt. He was hurt that his parents didn't have more confidence in his ability to make it on his own. We apologized but said we could not tell him everything would be great when that is not how we felt. Dylan was feeling like, at twenty-three, it was time to start get his comedy career going and Las Vegas was the only place that could happen. He did admit that he was not ready for Los Angeles and was not interested in moving to New York City. To him, Las Vegas seemed like the only option for him to "begin his life."

After attending a comedy show at The Laugh Factory it was almost 11:00pm. Amy and I were ready for bed. We went back to the room and Dylan put on a movie. I did some work on my laptop and Amy fell asleep before the opening scene. When the movie ended Dylan was still not ready for bed but we turned the lights off and went to sleep.

At 4:45am, Amy woke up to adjust the air conditioner when she noticed that Dylan was not in his bed. Amy texted him with no response and started to worry as any mom would after discovering her twenty-three-year-old son vanished from a hotel room in Las Vegas. Finally, at about 6:00 she received a text. Dylan was stranded in another part of the city. He had left his car at a convenience store/palm reader and had driven a drunk guy in a gold Jaguar to Larry Flynt's strip club. Later, they left the club. This part of the story doesn't make sense, but we will probably never hear the whole story. We will have to wait for the pictures like at the end of the movie, *The Hangover*. At some point during the night Dylan decided to leave his wallet and car keys in the front seat of his new drunk, Jag-driving friend's car. Then the guy left abruptly without telling Dylan. He had lost his money, driver's license, credit card and his car keys. We had not rented a car so we told him to taxi back to the hotel and we would figure out what to do. Dylan came back about twenty-five minutes later. He said the guy that drove the Jaguar was scheduled that morning for knee surgery at 9:00am. All we had to do, according to Dylan, would be to figure out where in the city of Las Vegas he was having knee surgery and then wait for him to come out so we could get his stuff back. Dylan said the guy pointed out where his surgery was on the way to the strip club so we would probably be able to find it. What Dylan did not seem to comprehend was that, given he was having surgery on his knee, there was a high possibility someone would give his buddy a ride to the doctor or hospital. If that were the case his gold Jaguar would be sitting in his driveway and we would have no way to find him. Dylan did not even know his name. First we rented a car and then we went to see where his car was to make sure it would not be towed. Sure enough, there was a big sticker on the window of Dylan's new convertible Toyota Solara that said, VIOLATION, TOW. That was a problem. Luckily there was a phone number. Amy called to explain the situation and she told them we were trying to locate his keys. Thankfully, the lady she spoke with was very understanding.

We drove around for about thirty minutes before Dylan received a call from Mr. Jaguar. Dylan's "wallet" was actually a bank bag that he had written his name and number on. His buddy had done the right thing and called him. He said he was just about to go into surgery when he remembered seeing Dylan's stuff on the floor of his car and he brought it with him to the surgery. We said, "Where are you? We'll come to you."

In the continuation of this bizarre series of events, he said, "Don't worry about it. There is a guy here at the hospital that is heading over to the other hospital they own. He is going to be driving right by my condo. I always keep my front door open so I'll have him drop off Dylan's stuff. It'll be on the table just inside my door." He gave his address in Henderson, about fifteen minutes outside the city, and we headed straight there. We drove out to his condo, where his Jaguar sat in his driveway, and retrieved all of Dylan's missing belongings.

Once again, God let Dylan get himself in a difficult situation but it was just enough of a mess to teach him a valuable lesson. We cannot even count the times this has happened in Dylan's life. Amy and I truly believe God has a plan for Dylan's life and these mini disasters are all part of that process. Dylan does not learn anything because someone tells him. He has to experience life's lessons. Some of these lessons have been very scary and potentially life-changing and some have been quick little life instructions.

In Dylan's senior year of high school he was convinced he could start his own taxi service at school. He thought a good name for his budding taxi business would be taken from the world of rap, "Ride or Die." And even better, the photo he had me take of him for the posters which he planned to put up around school had him holding up his fingers like a gun. I explained to him, as patiently as I could, that not only would the school not allow him to put up posters but they would have a major problem with him holding up his fingers like a gun. Did he listen to my advice? Of course not. He had to hang up the posters at school to find out that I was right in my prediction of how the school would react. All the lecturing from me would not make any impact on his decision to act. He had to experience it himself.

Dylan was upset with himself for what happened in Las Vegas but it taught him a lesson. It also convinced him that maybe Amy and I were not wrong when we expressed our concerns about his moving to Las Vegas. The next night at dinner we discussed what his options were if Las Vegas was off the table. He wanted to stay out West, be someplace where it was warm most of the year and also where he could work on his comedy career. Los Angeles was not an option because it was too big and fast paced. Out of the blue Amy suggested Austin, Texas. I jumped on Google and found that there were comedy open mic nights almost every night in Austin. There was also the very large University of Texas. The opportunities for Dylan to perform comedy in Austin appeared even better than in Las Vegas. Dylan had an apartment in St. George until the end of the summer or early fall. We decided that he would stay in St. George until after Amy's state senate race was over. At that point, win or lose, she would be happy to get away for a week or so to help Dylan get settled in Austin. On November 5, after a late night awaiting the exciting election results that sent Amy to the Maine senate, she boarded a plane for Austin, Texas to help Dylan start a new chapter in his life.

People frequently ask me about Dylan. It is always a blessing to us how many people care about him even though they barely know him. When told Dylan had moved to Austin, Texas, they would inevitably ask, "Why Austin?" We would tell them how we decided on Austin. They were always shocked when they heard that he was willing to move there despite not knowing a single person. He moved to Austin all alone and without the support of any program or services. They often used the words "brave," "daring" or even "courageous" when responding to Amy and me about Dylan's next move. Dylan is incredibly brave but we do not always see him that way because he has been very brave so many times before. Even though it was not always his choice to take some of the steps he has taken on this long and bumpy road, it does not change the fact that he has handled it with courage that very few kids, neurotypical or on the spectrum, would display. From age sixteen, when he went to Southeast Journeys in North Carolina, to moving to New Directions in Florida and to At the Crossroads in Utah, he has shown that he is incredibly brave and resilient. And through it all, the trials and tribulations, the fights and struggles, the highs and the dark lows, we are quite proud of our boy.

Dylan's Impact

Dylan has had a huge impact on the way Amy and I see people, especially those with disabilities. I don't think we were insensitive to people with disabilities prior to knowing Dylan, but we have changed as people because of our life with him. Our hearts have a special place for those with disabilities and their families.

I have a weekly radio show on WLOB 1310AM in Portland called "The Derek Volk Show." I have used that voice to talk about people with disabilities, focusing on disabilities in the workplace because the show has a business theme to it. In February of 2012, I did an entire hour called "Asperger's in the Workplace" and I have since become an active member of the Business Leadership Network through the Maine Chamber of Commerce. The BLN works with employers in an effort to promote the hiring of those with disabilities. At my company, we have several people with disabilities employed, including a woman who is deaf, a man who is legally blind, and a young woman with Asperger's and a middle aged man who suspects he has always had undiagnosed Asperger's. We don't treat them any differently. They have the same opportunities for advancement, although occasionally minor accommodations need to be made. We have no issue with making those accommodations to help them thrive in our business environment. They are all good workers, and we are very happy that they chose Volk Packaging as their place of employment. We're lucky to have them.

Amy's decisions when it comes to voting on legislation in the Maine state house have also been influenced because of our experiences raising Dylan. Amy was the lead house sponsor on a virtual charter school bill, which led to her position as chair of the board of Maine Connections Academy, Maine's first and only virtual charter school. When she speaks to various groups or has to do interviews as a legislator, she often describes some of our experiences with Dylan in the public school. Although Dylan will never personally benefit from Maine Connections Academy, there are hundreds and eventually thousands of families (many with children on the autism spectrum) who will benefit from Amy's work in the legislature and in the creation of Maine Connections Academy.

Mariah, Lilly, and Serena have also been influenced by Dylan, and that has impacted how they view and treat classmates with various disabilities. We didn't realize the impact that Dylan was having on his sisters until Mariah was in sixth grade. We attended her teacher conference in November. Her teacher told us, with great emotion, how amazing it was to watch Mariah interact with the boy in their class who had some kind of cognitive disability. Her teacher was so moved telling us about how Mariah showed this boy respect and dignity that her eyes welled up with tears. Amy and I always tried to raise our children with the understanding that everybody deserves respect, no matter what their physical or mental challenges are, but we had never heard how they were actually doing it until Mariah's teacher started crying during a teacher conference because she was so impressed with our twelve-year-old daughter.

There have been many times since that day that we have seen firsthand or heard from others about our wonderful daughters and how caring and kind they are. Every time I hear it, I tell people that Dylan deserves the credit.

People often credit us as parents, and we appreciate it and it feels good, but I have no idea if my daughters would be the same caring, compassionate, and kind-hearted people they are if they did not have a brother who struggles so much. I would like to think Amy and I would have raised our daughters the same with or without Dylan; I'd like to think that we would have taught them to love like Jesus, which includes loving the weird, the awkward, and the downtrodden. However, outside influences can often have more impact on how middle school girls behave than parents can, so I cannot in all honestly (because I'll never know) say whether my girls would be the same with or without Dylan in their life. Mariah set the bar very high, and Lilly has followed in her footsteps. She has been complimented many times, whether because of sitting with a neighborhood autistic boy on the bus or befriending and even going to the mall, the movies, and inviting to church a girl in her class who suffers from Fetal Alcohol Syndrome and has other cognitive issues. I was very proud of all three of my girls on a trip we took to California. After several airline issues caused our flight to get postponed until the next morning, the entire plane full of passengers had to take shuttles to local Chicago hotels. When the small shuttle bus filled up quickly leaving a family including a young girl with Cerebral Palsy standing outside in the cold, my girls did not hesitate to take action. The three of them marched on to the bus loudly but politely insisting that four people give up their seats. Several kind people got off the bus at their urging. The family was very appreciative to not have to wait for the next shuttle.

I hope Serena, who has been aware of Dylan in all his challenges for her whole life but has actually spent very little time living with him, shows the same attitude towards outsiders and those who are different as Mariah and Lilly have shown. Dylan went to boarding school in North Carolina when Serena was very little, came back for senior year, moved to Florida, came back briefly, and then moved to Utah. Serena loves her brother very much, but she hasn't had the same experiences living with him as her older sisters. I hope and pray that Dylan's life and challenges reach into Serena's heart like they have the rest of our family, and I hope this book helps her learn more about her brother.

Conclusion—The Chase Continues

When I sat down and began writing a book about Dylan and with Dylan's help, I was not sure what I would accomplish or if he would even be agreeable to the idea. Dylan has always been very private about his disability, so the idea of publishing and then promoting a book about his challenges seemed like a stretch to me. I was well into the book before I even mentioned it to him. When I finally told him what I had begun I was very concerned he would say, "Absolutely not, there is no way that you can tell everyone about my disability." If he had said that, all my work on *Chasing the Rabbit* would have been in vain. I could never, and would never, have proceeded without Dylan's permission and active participation. After all, it is his story as much as it is mine. I was ecstatic when Dylan was not only supportive of the idea but expressed a genuine excitement about the project. I told him right from the beginning that there would be some parts of the book he would not like, some recollections and perceptions of events and situations that he would disagree with. He understood and, although we have had some heated discussions about certain chapters, he has been supportive and helpful beyond my expectation or imagination.

One of the first questions Dylan asked was, "What is the purpose of the book?" Many people have asked me that same question. My initial objective was to let parents know that they are not alone, others have been down the road they are walking. I also noticed through the years that the bookstore shelves were full of books by professionals and by moms but the dad's perspective seemed absent from the conversations. I felt it was time that a dad expressed the challenges, heartbreaks and also the joys of raising a son with a disability. Unlike what we all see these days on TV, most fathers are not bumbling idiots who have very little to do with the competent raising of their children. The majority of dads I know are active, caring and critically important in the lives of their children. This is especially true of children with disabilities. I believe *Chasing the Rabbit* can help give the relationship between dads and sons with a disability a long overdue and unheard voice in the public forum. We would love to hear your voice. Please send us your thoughts or comments at dsvolk@volkboxes.com or follow:

ChasingTheRabbitBook on Facebook or Twitter.

* * *

Dylan's story is far from over. *Chasing The Rabbit* is only the beginning of what could easily be a series of books. In fact, I most certainly could have added about ten pages from the time of the move to Austin to the day the first draft was sent to the editor. However, we felt the move to Austin was a good event with which to conclude the book. For a long time I hesitated to write a book about our experiences raising Dylan. I always convinced myself to procrastinate, thinking that I should "wait until I knew there was a happy ending."

Although Dylan's story is on-going, we are confident in the knowledge that there will be a happy ending. Amy and I put great faith in the words of Jeremiah 29:11, "For I know the plans I have for you," declares the Lord, "plans to prosper you and not to harm you, plans to give you hope and a future."

Dylan's challenges do not just end with the writing of a book, any specific event, program, counselor or new med. He will probably spend the rest of his life chasing the rabbit. I know we will spend the rest of ours giving him whatever fuel we can provide for the chase and praying that God, whom we know loves him dearly, continues to watch over our son. And when he gets knocked down, there is no doubt in my mind that he will get right back up and start running again. He will show that quiet courage saying, "I will try again tomorrow."

Thank you for reading our book and God bless all the families who have been touched in some way by reading it.

About the Authors

Derek Volk

Derek Volk is a Maine businessman, supporter of autism awareness, volunteer, philanthropist, softball coach, and he can now add book author to the list. He is currently the president and co-owner of Volk Packaging Corporation, a third generation, family owned, corrugated box manufacturer in Biddeford, Maine. Derek actively participates on the Maine Business Leadership Network (BLN), a national organization that focuses on connecting employers with potential employees who have disabilities. His own company currently employs those who are deaf, blind, and on the autism spectrum.

A speech communications major at the University of Maine at Orono, Derek has always been comfortable speaking to an audience. Since 2012, Derek has hosted a Saturday morning radio talk show on WLOB 1310AM in Portland, Maine. His show can be heard online at www.derekvolkshow.com and through podcasts available on iTunes and Stitcher.

Derek has been happily married to his high school sweetheart, Amy Volk, since 1989. State Senator Amy Volk is currently serving her third term in the Maine Legislature. Amy and Derek are the proud parents of four children. Their son, Dylan, is the inspiration behind *Chasing the Rabbit*. They also have three daughters, Mariah, Lilly, and Serena. Mariah is credited for her efforts typing the book, which was originally dictated by Derek into a digital recorder. She learned a lot about her big brother in the process.

Chasing the Rabbit is Derek's first experience as an author. Initially, he began to pen a business book, but his life passions prompted him to put down the business outline and start work documenting his life with Dylan instead.

Dylan Volk

After years of what his parents called "the diagnosis of the month club," Dylan was diagnosed with Asperger's Syndrome at the age of eight. Life has always been challenging for Dylan. When he was little, he struggled with how to learn the rules and follow directions that often did not make sense to him. As he got older, he was challenged, especially socially, by a world that often seemed to go too fast for him to keep up. Even today, Dylan works hard to figure out what he needs to do in order to get through each day as a young adult in a very fast-paced society.

Dylan graduated from Scarborough High School in 2010. Dylan is currently pursuing his goal of earning a living making people laugh. He currently lives in Austin, Texas, where he can be seen around town performing stand-up at open-mic nights. He has also produced a series of satirical videos for his YouTube channel. You can watch them by searching Dielawn Comedy. Dylan hopes his work helping his father write *Chasing the Rabbit: A Dad's Life Raising a Son on the Autism Spectrum* will help families as they navigate through the difficulties of living life on the spectrum. He also hopes to share his story at high schools in an effort to help kids on the spectrum as well as those students living with them.

Acknowledgments

I would like to begin by thanking God for whom all things are possible. I have never heard God's voice audibly but when I sat down to write a business book and heard a voice in my head as clear as day I knew who was talking to me. The voice said, "This is not the book you are supposed to be writing. You are supposed to be writing a book about Dylan." I immediately started typing and found it was so easy to recall my life raising him. I wrote almost the entire book from memory. It is a story that is hard to forget.

My first acknowledgment after God goes to the person I love most here on earth, my wife, Amy. This story would have been so different had it not been for the amazing love we share together. It has been a very long journey but I cannot imagine taking it with anyone else by my side. She has been a wonderful wife and an incredible mother. Even though a paragraph at the end of this book does not begin to do her justice, she knows what she means to me so I'll leave it at that.

My daughter, Mariah, deserves a special thank you. Not only has she been by Dylan's side supporting him, laughing at all his jokes, spending time with him watching countless episodes of *The Office* and keeping an eye out for him when no one else was, she was extremely helpful to me in my efforts to make this book a reality. I have a full-time job, a radio show and many activities outside of those endeavors, so sitting down to type a book was a task that seemed impossible. Mariah was extremely generous with her time and also so passionate about the book's completion that she allowed me to dictate the book on a small microphone and email it to her to type. This book would never have been completed otherwise.

Lilly and Serena, my other daughters, deserve a thank you. They have always been caring sisters to Dylan. They were very patient with me while I added writing a book to my list of things taking up my time. Lilly also helped in the typing when I was filling the recorder so fast it was hard for Mariah to keep up with me.

Some other people require recognition. Thank you to my parents, Ken and Diane Volk, and in-laws, David and Janet Murchison, who were never anything less than encouraging and supportive even during the times when I felt like a horrible father. Thank you to my fantastic co-workers who endlessly understood when I had to run out of work to address a "Dylan issue" or on those many days I was not on my A game because my mind was at home. I want to thank my uncle and partner at Volk Packaging, Douglas Volk, as well as Greg Milligan, Mike Rousselle, Doug Hellstrom, Atoka Dumont, and my Sales Team. Thank you to my editor, David Salter, and my friends and advisors, John Brubaker and Kim Orso. Thank you to the teachers and staff at the different programs who tried their best with Dylan, especially At the Crossroads.

The biggest thank you goes to Dylan himself. This book was almost completed before I even mentioned its existence to Dylan. It would be still sitting in a folder on my desktop if he had said, as I feared he would, "Forget it! You are not going to tell people about everything I went through. No way!" He has been beyond supportive from the start and then contributed some of the most important parts of the book with his "Dylan's Take" segments. He has shown tremendous courage by letting a difficult story be told in order to help others.

And lastly, thank you, the reader, for buying our book. We hope it helps you with your journey and we look forward to your feedback.

Book Group Discussion Guide

Chapter 1
- Did you know anything about autism before starting this book?
- How do you think you would have reacted if your spouse told you your first child "wasn't quite right?"

Chapter 2
- Have you ever had a moment when you had "empty folders" in your brain? How did you react?
- What would you have done if a camp director had called your child a "monster" at age 5?

Chapter 3
- Have you ever known a child, or adult, with a "special interest" that went beyond that of a typical hobby or pastime?
- What did you feel as Derek described their experiences going from doctor to doctor?
- Describe how you think you and your family would react to being on the "Diagnosis of the Month Club" as Derek calls it?

Chapter 4
- Which of the doctors or "specialists" you read about made you the most frustrated? Why?
- There is a lot of talk about "over diagnosis" of autism. Do you think professionals are better at diagnosing autism today than when Dylan was young? Is it too quickly diagnosed?
- Describe how shocked you were by the number of medications Dylan has been on with so few positive results.
- Based on what you read, how do you think the medications helped or hurt Dylan?

Chapter 5
- What do you think of Derek's analogy about "mourning" for the son he thought he would have?
- Were you surprised when Derek wrote that he did not want another boy? Describe how you think you or your spouse would feel in that same situation?
- Derek's frustration with the school system was obvious in this chapter.

How do you think schools have changed since Dylan was in middle school (2004)?

- How do you think your local school system is handling children with disabilities?
- How did you feel as Derek described leaving Dylan at Spring Harbor that night?

Chapter 6

- How do you think you would have reacted if your child talked about having no hope that his life would get better?
- Do you think boarding school was the right decision for Derek and Amy to make at the time? What options would you have considered?
- What would you have done when it appeared Dylan was going to get expelled from the school in NH?

Chapter 7

- How would you have handled Dylan's friends stealing from your home?
- Would you be stressed out if your child was bringing home hitchhikers and runaways?
- Dylan started running into legal trouble during this chapter. Do you think law enforcement officials need more training about autism spectrum disorder?
- If you could provide law enforcement officials with only one bit of information about autism spectrum disorder, what would it be?

Chapter 8

- Derek talks very emotionally about Dylan's high school graduation. Who do you know that may have a similar emotional feeling during their child's graduation? Have you ever thought about what that must feel like for the parent of a child with a disability?
- After the positive feelings you may have felt about Dylan during his graduation, how did you feel about him after he stole Amy's credit card?
- People often confuse autism with mental illness (ie. Schizophrenia, Bi-Polar, etc.) but they are not the same. Autism is a neurological disorder not a disease or an illness. Do you know anyone with a child that has a mental illness? How did Derek's story about Dylan possibly having mental illness make you feel?

Chapter 9

- Derek writes about people suggesting he should "just give Dylan a job." How do you feel about his reluctance to do that?
- Do you think that government should play a bigger role in aiding people with autism through job training and healthcare? Why or why not?
- Many states have passed ABLE laws to help families on the spectrum save for future needs. Are you familiar with this law? What do you think of it?
- What do you think of Derek's "battle strategies" analogy? Can you relate to either strategy of "Sacrificing for the greater mission" or "Leave no man behind" when it comes to raising a child like Dylan?

Chapter 10

- What do you think Derek and Amy could have done differently to avoid Dylan spiraling down so badly?
- What would you do if one of your children pepper sprayed another one of your children?

Chapter 11

- Derek writes about the impact Dylan has had on his other children. How do you think your children would adjust to having a sibling with a disability?
- Why do you think Dylan's cats mean so much to him?
- The unemployment rate for people with autism is close to 80%. Do you know anyone with a disability that is having a hard time getting and keeping a job? What do you think could be done to help Dylan succeed in the workplace?
- Did Gettit Vending seem like a good try or a terrible idea when you started reading about it?
- After reading so many chapters about Dylan doing poorly, were you relieved and/or surprised to read that he turned his life around and is doing very well? Why?

Further Book Discussion Topics

- Many people do not finish books they start. What made you continue turning the pages?
- If you knew about autism before starting the book, did the book enhance your knowledge? In what ways did it change any preconceived notions?

- Do you or anyone you know closely have a child with autism? How does having read the book give you more understanding of the difficulties raising a child with autism or any type of disability?

- What do you think of Derek's honesty in the book? Was he too hard on himself? How did it make you feel to read his inner thoughts about Dylan?

- What did you think of *Dylan's Takes*? How do you think they added to the book? Which *Dylan's Take* was most interesting to you? Why?

- Do you know a father raising a child with autism? How would it be helpful for him to read *Chasing the Rabbit*?

- How do your strategies raising your children differ from how you might raise a child like Dylan?

- What are your impressions about the marriage of Derek and Amy? How do you think your marriage would fare if faced with raising Dylan?

- How do you think your greater family (parents, siblings, etc.) would have responded if Dylan were in your family? Would they have been helpful and understanding or pulled away?

- For Derek and Amy, their faith has been a source of great support. Do you think your faith would be strengthened or weakened under the same circumstances as you read in *Chasing the Rabbit*?

- Discuss how your feelings for/against or about Derek, Amy and Dylan change throughout the book.

- How will reading this book change your initial reactions when you see a little boy or girl out of control in a supermarket or restaurant? Will you be more empathetic to the parents?

- Would you read a sequel to *Chasing the Rabbit*? Why or why not? If yes, please contact us.

Thank you for your interest in our story. If you would like Derek to be a part of your book group discussion please contact him at dsvolk@volkboxes. com or through the *Chasing the Rabbit* Facebook page at www.facebook.com/ chasingtherabbitbook. If you have discussion questions that would be beneficial to other readers please send them to us for future publication.

If you enjoyed *Chasing the Rabbit* we would appreciate your feedback via a review on Amazon. Word of mouth is our best advertising so please tell your friends about it through social media and in person.

Thank you.